BETWEEN GOVERNING AND GOVERNANCE

This book explains the emergence and functioning of three forms of governance structures within the context of the European integration and constitutionalisation process: comitology, (regulatory) agencies and the Open Method of Co-ordination. The point of departure is the insight that the intergovernmental/supranational distinction, which most theories of European integration and constitutionalisation rely on, has lost its strength. A new paradigm of EU research is therefore needed.

Against this background it is suggested that the distinction between governing and governance provides a more appropriate basis for analysing the phenomenon of integration and constitutionalisation in Europe. The distinction between governing and governance allows for an understanding of the EU as a hybrid consisting of a governing dimension, characterised by legal and organisational hierarchy, and a governance dimension, which operates within a network form characterised by legal and organisational heterarchy. The function of governance structures is to ensure the embeddedness of the governing dimension in the wider society. Instead of representing contradictory developments, the two dimensions are therefore mutually constitutive in the sense that more governing implies more governance and vice versa. These theoretical insights are illustrated through two detailed case studies which respectively reconstruct the operational mode of the Open Method of Coordination within EU Research & Development Policy and the regulatory system for the EU chemicals market (REACH).

The book is inter-disciplinary in nature and incorporates insights from law, political science and sociology.

Hart Monographs in Transnational and International Law: Volume 4

Hart Monographs in Transnational and International Law

Series Editor: Craig Scott, Professor of Law, Osgoode Hall Law School of York University, Toronto

The objective of this series is to publish high-quality scholarship in public international law and private international law, as well as work that adopts 'transnational law' as its thematic, theoretical or doctrinal focus. The series strives to be a leading venue for work of the following sort:

* critical reappraisals of foundational concepts and core doctrinal principles of both public and private international law, and their operation in practice, including insights drawn from general legal theory;

* analysis and development of conceptions of 'transnational law', including in relation to the role of unofficial law and informal processes in transnational regulation and in relation to theories and studies of 'governance' in transnational spheres; and

* empirical studies of the emergence, evolution and transformation of international and/or transnational legal orders, including accounts and explanations of how law is constructed within different communities of interpretation and practice.

The series will also be home to monographs that explore the interactions between the ever-integrating fields of public and private international law. Of special interest are explorations of the extent to which these interactions are structured by higher-order principles and policies, on the one hand, and by politics and the exercise of various forms of power, on the other hand.

The series is open to work not only by law scholars but also by scholars from cognate disciplines.

Titles in this series

Volume 1: Terrorism and the State: Rethinking the Rules of State Responsibility
Tal Becker

Volume 2: Transnational Law and Local Struggles: Mining, Communities and the World Bank
David Szablowski

Volume 3: The Institutional Veil in Public and International Law: International Organisations and the Law of Treaties
Catherine Brölmann

Volume: 4 Between Governing and Governance: On the Emergence, Function and Form of Europe's Post-National Constellation
Poul F Kjaer

Between Governing and Governance

On the Emergence, Function and Form of Europe's Post-National Constellation

Poul F Kjaer

·HART·
PUBLISHING

OXFORD AND PORTLAND, OREGON
2010

Published in North America (US and Canada)
by Hart Publishing
c/o International Specialized Book Services
920 NE 58th Avenue, Suite 300
Portland, OR 97213–3786
USA
Tel: +1 503 287 3093 or toll-free: (1) 800 944 6190
Fax: +1 503 280 8832
E-mail: orders@isbs.com
Website: www.isbs.com

Hart Publishing 16c Worcester Place, Oxford, OX1 2JW
Telephone: +44 (0)1865 517530 Fax: +44 (0)1865 510710
E-mail: mail@hartpub.co.uk
Website: http://www.hartpub.co.uk

British Library Cataloguing in Publication Data
Data Available

ISBN: 978-1-84946-026-2

Typeset by Columns Design Ltd, Reading
Printed and bound in Great Britain by
TJ International Ltd, Padstow, Cornwall

Acknowledgements

This book is the result of work carried out during my time at the European University Institute (EUI) in Florence. The Institute provided an optimal intellectual environment and a great platform for communication with scholars throughout the world. My time at the EUI was supplemented by highly beneficial research stays at the London School of Economics and Political Science, Goethe University Frankfurt and the Centre for European Law and Politics at the University of Bremen. I also greatly benefited from my involvement in the European research project 'Reconstituting Democracy in Europe' (RECON), administered by the University of Oslo. I received generous financial support from the Danish Ministry of Science, Technology and Innovation and the European University Institute.

I would especially like to thank the following for important input and assistance: Andreas Abegg, Marc Amstutz, Niels Åkerstrøm Andersen, Marlies Becker, Susana Borrás, Claire O'Brien, Marina Brilman, Damian Chalmers, Hugh Collins, Marise Cremona, Mark Dawson, Erik Oddvar Eriksen, Andreas Fischer-Lescano, John Erik Fossum, Gorm Harste, Richard Hart, Jennifer Hendry, Vaios Karavas, Karl-Heinz Ladeur, Laura Marin, Aldo Mascareño, Rainer Nickel, Rebecca Adler-Nissen, Niklas Olsen, Giovanni Sartor, Christoph Schmidt, Craig Scott, Gregory Shaffer, Alexander Somek, Rudolf Stichweh, Gunther Teubner, Henning Trüper, Rachel Turner, Neil Walker, Rudolf Wiethölter, Marlene Wind and Jonathan Zeitlin. But especially I would like to thank Christian Joerges, who followed the work with great enthusiasm, curiosity and tolerance. Without his continued support and encouragement the outcome of the process would have been very different.

Poul F Kjaer
Frankfurt am Main, July 2009

Contents

Abbreviations

APEC	Asia-Pacific Economic Cooperation
ASEAN	Association of Southeast Asian Nations
AU	African Union
BEPG	Broad Economic Policy Guidelines
CAN (Comunidad Andina)	Andean Community
CAP	Common Agricultural Policy
CdT	Translation Centre for the Bodies of the European Union
CEES	Central and Eastern European Countries
CFI	Court of First Instance
CFP	Common Fisheries Policy
CFSP	Common Foreign and Security Policy
CfRA	Committee for Risk Assessment
CfSEA	Committee for Socio-Economic Analysis
CIS	Classical Institutional Structure
CM	Community Method
Commission	Commission of the European Communities
CoR	Committee of the Regions
COST	Co-operation in the field of Scientific and Technical Research
Council	Council of the European Union
CREST	Committee on Science and Technical Research
CT	Constitutional Treaty
DDP	Directly-Deliberative Polyarchy
EAR	European Agency for Reconstruction
EASHW	European Agency for Safety and Health at Work
EURATOM	European Atomic Energy Community
EC	European Community
ECA	European Chemicals Agency
ECB	European Central Bank
ECJ	European Court of Justice
ECSC	European Coal and Steel Community
EDC	European Defence Community
EEA	European Economic Area
EEC	European Economic Community
EES	European Employment Strategy
EESC	European Economic and Social Committee
EFSA	European Food Safety Authority

EMBO	European Molecular Biology Organization
EMCODA	European Monitoring Centre for Drugs and Drugs Addiction
EMEA	European Medicines Agency
EMU	European Monetary Union
EP	European Parliament
ERC	European Research Council
ESCB	European System of Central Banks
ESDP	European Security and Defence Policy
ETF	European Training Foundation
EU	European Union
FP	Framework Programme(s)
FRA	European Union Agency for Fundamental Rights
GS	Governance Structures
IB	Institutional Balance
ICANN	Internet Corporation for Assigned Names and Numbers
IGC	Intergovernmental Conference(s)
IM	Internal Market
IMF	International Monetary Fund
LRT	Lisbon Reform Treaty
MEP	Member(s) of the European Parliament
Mercosur (Mercado Común del Sur)	Southern Common Market
MS	Member State(s)
MSC	Member State Committee
NAFTA	North American Free Trade Agreement
NMG	New Modes of Governance
NPM	New Public Management
OECD	Organisation for Economic Co-operation and Development
OLAF (Office européen de Lutte Anti-Fraude)	European Anti-Fraud Office
OMC	Open Method of Coordination
PJCC	Police and Judicial Cooperation in Criminal Matters
PPP	Public Private Partnerships
QMV	Qualified Majority Voting
R & D	Research & Development
REACH	Registration, Evaluation, Authorization and Restriction of Chemicals
SEA	Single European Act

SICA (Sistema de la Integración Centroamericana)	Central American Integration System
SGP	Stability and Growth Pact
SIEF	Substance Information Exchange Forum
SME	Small and Medium Sized Enterprises
SPORT	Strategic Partnership on REACH Testing
UK	United Kingdom

Table of Cases and Legislative Instruments

European Court of Justice and Court of First Instance

Table of Legislative Instruments

Treaties

Regulations

Directives

Decisions

Documents, Reports and Communications

1

Towards a Paradigm of Governance

1.1 INTRODUCTION

IN 1972 LUHMANN POINTED out that in the future the democratic state of law might only be remembered as an aberration in the evolution of mankind which had merely gained dominance for a short period of time.[1] A quarter of a century later, Habermas, speaking as an intellectual, raised the question as to whether democracy would survive globalisation.[2] The issue of the future viability of democracy and the rule of law had arrived in the broader public arena, thereby indicating that real challenges had emerged.

In the context of the European process of integration the 'turn to governance' in the 1990s and the official adoption of 'governance semantics' in 2001[3] indicated what was at stake, since it implied de facto abandoning the attempt to create an 'ever closer Union', to be achieved by gradual replacement of the European nation states with a European state built on the nation-state model. But if statehood is no longer the objective this automatically raises questions concerning the extent to which democracy and the rule of law can be safeguarded within the context of the integration process, or what alternatives there might be.

While these questions provide an overall framework, this study probes deeper and investigates why governance structures (GS) have emerged within the context of the European processes of integration and constitutionalisation and how the relationship between governing and governance

[1] N Luhmann, *Rechtssoziologie* (Opladen, Westdeutscher Verlag [1972], 1983) 339. See also A Fischer-Lescano, 'Themis Sapiens. Comments on Inger-Johanne Sand' in C Joerges, I-J Sand and G Teubner (eds), *Transnational Governance and Constitutionalism* (Oxford, Hart Publishing, 2004) 71.

[2] J Habermas, 'Die postnationale Konstellation und die Zukunft der Demokratie' in J Habermas: *Die postnationale Konstellation. Politische Essays* (Frankfurt am Main, Suhrkamp Verlag, 1998).

[3] Commission of the European Communities: COM (2001) 428 final: European Governance. A White Paper.

in the European Union (EU)[4] can be conceptualised, thereby clarifying the structural conditions of democracy and the rule of law in Europe's post-national setting.

The analysis starts with the observation that research into European integration and constitutionalisation is currently in a transitional phase. Classic integration paradigms, such as the dual intergovernmental/supranational paradigm, have lost their strength, but at the same time the decade-long debate on governance has not led to formulation of a new paradigm. This is not surprising since no clear and positive definition of governance has yet been produced, nor has a general theory of governance yet been developed. One characteristic, which most variants of governance research seem to have in common, is their focus on heterarchical, as opposed to hierarchical, legal and organisational structures. At the same time few, if any, participants in the governance debate have claimed that legal and organisational hierarchy has completely disappeared. This indicates a need for further theoretical study to produce a general theoretical conceptualisation of the relationship between, on the one hand, legal hierarchy and heterarchy and, on the other hand, the relationship between organisational hierarchy and networks. This relationship can also be seen to be based on a distinction between governing and governance—a distinction which has increasingly become the most central and basic distinction (*Leitdistinktion*) of the EU. Hence, the ultimate aim should be to replace the supranational/intergovernmental paradigm with one based on the governing/governance distinction.

The rise of the governance phenomenon is not confined to the context of the European processes of integration and constitutionalisation; similar developments can be observed at the local, nation-state and global levels. The EU can, however, be considered an 'avant-garde structure',[5] and this provides a suitable starting point for the development of a general theory of governance. Consequently, the scope of this study is limited to an examination of the EU context. Furthermore, a *preliminary* identification of the object of study can easily be provided within the EU context, since the term governance can be said to refer to regulatory structures which have emerged outside the Classical Institutional Structure (CIS) consisting of the triangle formed by the Council of the European Union (the Council), the Commission of the European Communities (the Commission) and the European Parliament (EP). The Open Method of Coordination (OMC),

[4] Unless otherwise indicated, the term 'European Union' (EU) will refer to the EU as well as its predecessors in the form of the European Communities (EC), the European Economic Community (EEC), the European Coal and Steel Community (ECSC) and the European Atomic Energy Community (Euratom).

[5] K-H Ladeur, 'Towards a Legal Theory of Supranationality – The Viability of the Network Concept' (1997) 3 (1) *European Law Journal* 33–35.

Comitology and (Regulatory) Agencies are the most important structures here. Accordingly, an examination of the logic guiding the emergence and function of these three bodies will be at the centre of this discussion.

1.2 THE DEMISE OF METHODOLOGICAL NATIONALISM

All existing approaches to studying the phenomenon of European integration and constitutionalisation are based more or less directly on the tension between the intergovernmental and supranational dimensions. These two dimensions have also been conceptualised as representing respectively politics and law.[6] Accordingly, this tension can be traced back to the asymmetry which evolved between the legal and the political dimensions of the EU system from the 1960s onwards, as the legal dimension underwent a greater degree of hierarchisation and maturation than the political dimension. Within the legal dimension direct effect,[7] supremacy[8] and pre-emption[9] emerged as constitutional principles through the jurisprudence practices of the European Court of Justice (ECJ)[10] whereas the 'non-hierarchical', and therefore apparently intergovernmental, Council remained the dominant political body of the system.[11]

Over the last two decades this asymmetry has been somewhat reduced, however, due to new institutional developments within the political dimension, such as the extension of majority voting, the expansion of the competencies of the EP through co-decision and the transformation of the European Council into the de facto leading political body of the system. This development has, moreover, been supported by a continued expansion of the number of EU policy areas, thus undermining earlier notions of the EU as a mere economic government (*Gouvernement économique*) based upon an ordo-liberal economic constitution (*Wirtschaftsverfassung*).[12]

[6] JHH Weiler, 'The Community system: the dual character of supranationalism' (1981) *1st Yearbook of European Law* 267.

[7] Case 26/62 *Van Gend en Loos v Nederlandse Administratie der Belastingen* ECR 1. 1963.

[8] Case 6/64 *Costa v ENEL*. ECR 585. 1964.

[9] ERTA Case 22/70 *Commission v Council*. ECR 273. 1971.

[10] For an overview the establishment of the EC legal order see B de Witte, 'Direct Effect, Supremacy, and the Nature of the Legal Order', in P Craig and G de Burca (eds), *The Evolution of EU Law* (Oxford, Oxford University Press, 1999).

[11] Although the activities of the Council remain horizontal in nature, its internal complexity, with several hundred working parties in operation, have reached a level of complexity where the institution has developed a life of its own and no longer can be considered a mere intergovernmental phenomenon. See also G Schäfer, 'Linking Member States and European Administrations – The Role of Committees and Comitology' in M Andenas and A Türk (eds), *Delegated Legislation and the Role of Committees in the EC* (The Hague, Kluwer, 2000) 14.

[12] C Joerges, 'The Market without the State? The 'Economic Constitution' of the European Community and the Rebirth of Regulatory Politics' (1997) 1 (19) *European*

Today both dimensions have achieved a sustainable degree of 'semi-hierarchisation' in that a certain level of hierarchy has been established; in neither case, however, has the final and decisive step been achieved as the ECJ still does not possess competence-competence (*Kompetenz-Kompetenz*) and the Member States (MS) remain the Masters of the Treaty.

Moreover, and more importantly, theories based on the intergovernmental/supranational distinction have been challenged by an understanding of the European structure as a phenomenon in its own right. Hence, the EU cannot be adequately interpreted by simply applying concepts that were developed within the context of the European state-building processes in early modernity.[13] This view profoundly undermines the basis of the classical approaches since their central reasoning may then be dismissed by arguing that they belong to the category of 'old-European semantics' (*alteuropäische Semantik*), and not only possess limited analytical strength but also represent a structural barrier in attempting to adequately describe a contemporary phenomenon such as the EU. The state-centred world perspective of existing approaches reflects the attempt to apply nation-state concepts to the EU. This merely means that the two perspectives represent two sides of the same coin. While intergovernmentalism focuses on the MS as the basis of the EU, the regulatory idea underlying supranationalism, in its traditional federalist variant, is the construction of a European State. Consequently, the intrinsically modern concept of state is the essential point of departure for both dimensions. One can therefore claim that both perspectives are essentially Hegelian, in that they subscribe to the world view which found its highest form of expression in Hegel's Philosophy of Right (*Rechtsphilosophie*).[14] Consequently, the concept of state within these two schools differs only marginally. In its pure form intergovernmentalism starts with the assumption that states can be conceived of as territorially based and hierarchically organised units based on the central distinction between state and society (*Staat und Gesellschaft*). The latest version of intergovernmentalism, known as liberal intergovernmentalism, however, plays down the assumption that

Integration online Papers (EIoP); C Joerges, 'States Without a Market? Comments on the German Constitutional Court's Maastricht-Judgement and a Plea for Interdisciplinary Discourses' (1997) 1 (20) *European Integration online Papers (EIoP)*.

[13] Eg M Zürn: 'Politik in der postnationalen Konstellation. Über das Elend des methodologischen Nationalismus' in C Landfried (Hrsg.): *Politik in einer entgrenzten Welt. Beiträge zum 21. Kongreß der Deutschen Vereinigung für Politische Wissenschaft* (Köln, Verlag Wissenschaft und Politik, 2001).

[14] GWF Hegel, *Grundlinien der Philosophie des Rechts oder Naturrecht und Staatswissenschaft im Grundrisse, Werke Band 7* (Frankfurt am Main, Suhrkamp Verlag, [1821] 1970). For the challenge of overcoming Hegel see, eg, S Barnett (ed), *Hegel After Derrida* (London, Routledge, 1998).

states are unitary actors.[15] This means that intergovernmentalism is rather similar to neo-functionalism, which has provided a theoretical underpinning of the supranationalist federalist vision, insofar as neo-functionalism assumes the existence of pluralist states consisting of a multiplicity of actors, while remaining intrinsically bound to the concept of state, since its vision is that of building a European state.

But the critique goes beyond mere conceptual problems. Intergovernmentalism has never been capable of explaining the dynamics of European integration. Instead this intergovernmental perspective is based simply on the assumption that the MS are firmly in control because they remain the Masters of the Treaty. Intergovernmentalists thus appear to represent the most naive branch of EU studies, as they seem to have total faith in the ability of the MS to effectively control the internal dynamics of the integration and constitutionalisation processes via the signing of a treaty. Not surprisingly, intergovernmentalism therefore remains an area dominated by political scientists since legal scholars seem to have a more realistic understanding of the kind of constraints which can be imposed through the signing of a treaty.[16] Consequently, intergovernmentalism is not capable of explaining qualitative changes such as the rise of the EP, just as it cannot adequately grasp the unexpected rise and independent importance of phenomena such as GS. Nor can it adequately describe the shift away from integration and towards constitutionalisation and the establishment of a legal hierarchy within the EU.

On the other hand, existing variants of supranationalism have never really qualified as genuine theories. Weiler's descriptions of legal supranationalism are precise but do not provide an adequate explanation of how this development was possible.[17] Moreover, classical federalism is a mere normative vision. Neo-functionalism, acting as the theoretical underpinning of federalism, has the advantage that it is aimed at establishing a macro-perspective on the dynamics of European integration and, in contrast to intergovernmentalism, it also highlights the fact that integration for the sake of integration has been an essential element of the EU's development. Its core idea about functional spillover also appears to have a certain

[15] PC Schmitter, 'Neo-Neofunctionalism' in A Wiener and T Diez (eds), *European Integration Theory* (Oxford, Oxford University Press, 2004) 46, note 2.

[16] A Morawcsik, *The Choice for Europe. Social Purpose and State Power from Messina to Maastricht* (Ithaca, Cornell University Press, 1998). For the latest attempt to validate this approach see T Gehring, *Die Europäische Union als komplexe internationale Organisation: wie durch Kommunikation und Entscheidung soziale Ordnung entsteht* (Baden-Baden, Nomos Verlag, 2002).

[17] JHH Weiler, 'The Transformation of Europe' (1991) 100 *Yale Law Journal* 2402; JHH Weiler, *The Constitution of Europe. 'Do the New Clothes Have an Emperor?' and Other Essays on European Integration* (Cambridge, Cambridge University Press, 1999).

strength when observing the EU's long-term development.[18] Neo-functionalism, however, cannot adequately explain why functional spillover initiated through technocratic structures should necessarily lead to political spillover and thus the creation of a European state. Nor why such a state, as this theory assumes, should necessarily be a democratic state. The normative end-goal of neo-functionalism—the establishment of a democratic European state—implies, moreover, that it cannot be considered to be a descriptive theory, although it claims to be precisely that, since it breaks the most fundamental rules of science by deciding the result of the findings prior to beginning the scientific investigation. It is a teleological-based ideology, which simply states that European integration will lead to the establishment of a state because the normative end-goal should be the establishment of a state. A descriptive theory should, however, be capable of explaining all phases of the integration process, as well processes of disintegration, and not only those which are supportive of a specific normative objective.[19] As that is not the case with neo-functionalism, it has been fashionable only in specific periods, such as the 1950s and 1960s and again in the 1980s,[20] when developments pointed in the direction of rapidly increased integration, but not in other periods, such as the 1970s or the 1990s, where the future development of the EU was less clear.[21]

Yet another and probably the most fundamental reason for the failure of earlier theories is that over the last decades the EU has experienced a massive increase in the expansion of GS such as Comitology, agencies and the OMC,[22] which operate outside the CIS. Although often referred to as New Modes of Governance (NMG), these structures are obviously not new

[18] M Albert, 'Governance and democracy in European systems: on systems theory and European integration' (2002) 28 *Review of International Studies* 293–94.

[19] This is also explicitly recognised by Schmitter. See PC Schmitter, 'Neo-Neofunctionalism' in A Wiener and T Diez (eds), *European Integration Theory* (Oxford, Oxford University Press, 2004) 45.

[20] EB Haas, The *Uniting of Europe: Political, Social and Economic Forces 1950–1957* (Palo Alto, Stanford University Press, 1958); LN Lindberg, *The Political Dynamics of European Economic Integration* (Palo Alto, Stanford University Press, 1963); J Tranholm-Mikkelsen, 'Neo-functionalism: Obstinate or Obsolete? A Reappraisal in the Light of the New Dynamism of the EC' (1991) 1 *Millennium Journal of International Studies* 1–20.

[21] For an overview of the various theories regarding European integration, constitutionalisation and governance see P Craig, 'The Nature of the Community: Integration, Democracy and Legitimacy' in P Craig and G de Burca (eds), *The Evolution of EU Law* (Oxford, Oxford University Press, 1999).

[22] To these three main forms one could also add mutual recognition, the partnership concept, originally developed within the context of Community structural founding, the so-called social dialogue as developed under the framework of the Maastricht Treaty, and the concept of Environmental Policy Integration. See J Scott and DM Trubek, 'Mind the Gap: Law and New Approaches to Governance in the European Union' (2002) 8 (1) *European Law Journal* 1.

since Comitology has existed since the early 1960s,[23] and the first agencies were established in the 1970s[24] just as the essential features of the OMC became established elements of the EU system long before the OMC itself was made a formal policy tool at the Lisbon summit in March 2000. What is new is the recognition that these structures are not just transitional phenomena but rather that they are here to stay. Moreover, they have increasingly become recognised as essential features of the EU and are therefore no longer conceived of as simply minor appendages of the institutional triangle. A common feature of GS is their heterarchical nature, which tends to undermine traditional nation-state views that consider Kelsian-style legal hierarchy and Weberian-style organisational hierarchy to be the only important elements of the EU construct. The increased recognition that GS have become permanent structures and essential features of the EU system therefore undermines the plausibility of eventually achieving a Hegelian unity of society through the state at European level. Instead, GS are 'misfits' which cannot be adequately understood within the framework of previous theories.[25] It is against this background that the question of the distinction between hierarchy and heterarchy or governing and governance, and whether this might represent a new basic distinction for the EU system, becomes relevant.

1.3 DISCIPLINARY OBSTACLES

The increased recognition that the EU, as an object of study, must be conceived of as a phenomenon *sui generis* and not just as an extension of the nation-state universe indicates that the concepts previously applied have become increasingly problematic. The underlying assumptions of these concepts are borrowed from academic disciplines such as law and political science, which essentially remain related to the universe of the nation state.[26] Consequently the structures of existing academic disciplines act as barriers that effectively prevent the development of concepts

[23] E Vos, 'The Rise of Committees' (1997) 3 (3) *European Law Journal*, 210. C Vos, 'EU Committees: the Evolution of Unforeseen Institutional Actors in European Product Regulation' in C Joerges and E Vos (eds), *EU Committees: Social Regulation, Law and Politics* (Oxford, Hart Publishing, 1999).

[24] As we will return to in Ch 3, the European Centre for the Development of Vocational Training (CEDEFOP) and the European Foundation for the Improvement of Living and Working Conditions (EUROFOUND) were both established in 1975. In addition, the High Authority of the ECSC can be regarded as the role model on which later supranational agencies have been built.

[25] R Dehousse, 'Misfits: EU Law and the Transformation of European Governance' (2002) 2 *Jean Monnet Working Papers*.

[26] Essentially *sui generis* simply means that the EU is not comparable with any other existing structure. On the problematic nature of the *sui generis* concept see also H Abromeit,

adequate for describing the EU. The combination of conceptual inconsistencies and the inadequate interpretative power of existing theories added to the systematic sabotage of conceptual evolution by the nation-state disciplines of law and political science, has triggered the emergence of a hybrid sub-discipline in the form of 'European studies' (*Europawissenschaft*).[27] This sub-discipline has adopted the concept of governance as its foundation. The concept of governance can be traced as far back as the 1930s when the foundations of what is now called corporate governance were developed within the academic discipline of business administration.[28] In 1992 the concept was introduced within the discipline of international relations[29] whereafter it was rapidly incorporated into a multitude of different debates and applied to a wide range of divergent objectives within law and social science. It was deployed both as an ideological concept supporting the case of the minimal state, and as a tool for achieving 'good governance' in developing countries and in the international system; equally it was incorporated into the so-called new public management (NPM) literature and attempts to describe political-administrative structures as socio-cybernetic systems or as self-organising networks.[30] However it is only within EU research that the 'turn to governance' has increasingly been considered as representing a fundamental break with the nation-state universe. But the governance concept has still not matured enough to achieve the kind of 'closure' necessary for a paradigm to emerge. After more than a decade of European governance studies no general theory has yet been developed and the concept too remains imprecise. Instead only very general descriptions of the EU as a system of 'multi-level governance' have been formulated,[31] and these have then been combined with a large number of partial concepts of governance relating to different aspects of the European structures.[32] In governance

'Jenseits des "sui generis"', in C Landfried (Hrsg.), *Politik in einer entgrenzten Welt. Beiträge zum 21. Kongreß der Deutschen Vereinigung für Politische Wissenschaft* (Köln, Verlag Wissenschaft und Politik, 2001).

[27] For an overview of the sub-discipline, its constitution and objectives see GF Schuppert, I Pernice and U Haltern (Hrsg.), *Europawissenschaft* (Baden-Baden, Nomos Verlag, 2005).

[28] A Benz, 'Einleitung: Governance – Modebegriff oder nützliches sozialwissenschaftliches Konzept?', in A Benz (Hrsg.), *Governance – Regieren in Komplexen Regelsystemen. Eine Einführung* (Wiesbaden, VS Verlag Für Sozialwissenschaften, 2004) 15.

[29] JN Rosenau, 'Governance, order, and change in world politics' in JN Rosenau and EO Czempiel (eds), *Governance without Government: Order and Change in World Politics* (Cambridge, Cambridge University Press, 1992).

[30] RAW Rhodes, 'The New Governance: Governing without Government' (1996) 44 (4) *Political Studies*, 652. For an extensive overview of the use of the governance concept see also GF Schuppert (Hrsg.), *Governance-Forschung. Vergewisserung über stand und Entwicklungslinien* (Baden-Baden, Nomos Verlag, 2005).

[31] B Kohler-Koch, 'European governance and system integration' (2005) 1 *European Governance Papers (EUROGOV)*.

[32] For Comitology see, eg, C Joerges, 'Die Europäische "Komitologie": Kafkaeske Bürokratie oder Beispiel "deliberativen Regierens"' in C Joerges and J Falke (Hrsg.), *Das*

research which departs from a political science perspective this partiality is moreover evident in the unhelpful division between a focus on politics,[33] polity[34] or policy.[35] Moreover, governance theories do not actually aim at explaining how integration or constitutionalisation come about in the first place, but merely focus on how the system works when already operating. Consequently, governance studies have so far been characterised by an inability to explain the overall logic of the European system. Instead it is simply described as some sort of governance system, while few or no attempts are being made to explain the logic which has led to the existence of this universe or what its structural basis might be. Hence, the emerging governance paradigm has only succeeded in provoking a crisis for the old paradigm but has not been able to provide a positive alternative.[36]

A notable exception to this critique is the attempt to combine governance research with insights from various forms of new-institutionalism and especially from the variant labelled historical institutionalism.[37] Historical institutionalism changes the perspective on EU integration. Instead of emphasising exogenous demand it focuses on the internal dynamics of the political and legal institutions and processes. Accordingly, advocates of historical institutionalism argue that institutions have an evolutionary history, and that they therefore possess an autonomous memory; consequently they also produce their own narratives, providing a platform for the continued development of a 'sense of direction', which can be transformed into concrete policy programmes. Thus, historical institutionalism emphasises

Ausschußwesen der Europäischen Union. Praxis der Risikoregulierung im Binnenmarkt und ihre rechtliche Verfassung (Baden-Baden, Nomos Verlag, 2000). For regulatory agencies see, eg, G Majone, 'The Regulatory State and its Legitimacy Problems' (1998) 56 *IfHS Working Paper*. For the OMC see, eg, J Zeitlin and P Pochet (eds), *The Open Method of Coordination in Action: the European employment and social inclusion strategies* (Bruxelles, Presses Interuniversitaires Européennes, 2005).

[33] B Kohler-Koch, 'The Evolution and Transformation of European Governance' in B Kohler-Koch and R Eiing (eds), *The Transformation of Governance in the European Union* (London, Routledge, 1999).

[34] R Mayntz, 'Governance als fortenwickelte Steuerungstheorie?' in GF Schuppert (Hrsg), *Governance-Forschung. Vergewisserung über stand und Entwicklungslinien* (Baden-Baden, Nomos Verlag, 2005).

[35] A Héritier, *New Modes of Governance in Europe: Policy-Making without Legislating?* in A Héritier (ed), *Common Goods: Reinventing European and International Governance* (Lanham, Rowman and Littlefield, 2002).

[36] Renate Mayntz therefore concludes that governance research so far has only provided a gradual shift (*Akzentverschiebung*) and not a paradigmatic shift when compared with the kind of steering theories which dominated the nation-state scene in the 1970s and 1980s. See R Mayntz, 'Governance als fortenwickelte Steuerungstheorie?' in GF Schuppert (Hrsg.), *Governance-Forschung. Vergewisserung über stand und Entwicklungslinien* (Baden-Baden, Nomos Verlag, 2005).

[37] Eg AS Sweet and W Sandholtz, 'Integration, Supranational Governance, and the Institutionalization of the European Polity' in AS Sweet and W Sandholtz (eds), *European Integration and Supranational Governance* (Oxford, Oxford University Press, 1998).

that the high level of autonomy of EU institutions and its internal dynamic are central elements in the drive towards increased competence transfer.[38]

The current transitional state of governance research is not untypical. In constructing the ultimate paradigm of modernity Hegel introduced his concept of spirit (*Geist*) as a universal concept. This concept provided a necessary space within which he could introduce his distinctions and his particular form of logic, allowing him to differentiate the concept of spirit later on, thereby developing a number of more concrete and partial concepts which were better suited to his study of emerging modern society and his attempt to establish the notion that modern society is based on identity.[39] Luhmann repeated this exercise when he introduced the concept of meaning (*Sinn*) as the basic concept of sociology, through his Husserl-inspired conceptualisation of social systems as meaning producing systems.[40] He thereby created a universe within which he could afterwards introduce his distinctions and his particular logic in order to conceive of modern society as based on difference.[41] Common to both, however, is that their universal concepts were 'empty' concepts containing everything and therefore nothing; this simply provided them with a point of departure to reach their objectives of describing how modern society is possible. For both scholars the next logical step was to conduct a large number of partial studies of different aspects of modern society which could then serve as a basis on which their ultimate objectives concerning the development of general theories of society could be realised.

In line with these examples, governance research has gone through the first two out of three steps of paradigm construction. A general concept of governance has been introduced which delineates a new universe but remains essentially an empty concept. This has been followed by the development of a multitude of partial 'sub-concepts', and a massive amount of empirical study has also been undertaken. The decisive step towards a general theory has not yet been made, however. This also explains the resilience of the old intergovernmental/supranationalist paradigm, since, as Kuhn notes; 'once it has achieved the status of paradigm, a scientific theory is declared invalid only if an alternate candidate is available to take its place'.[42]

[38] Eg KA Armstrong and SJ Bulmer, *The Governance of the Single European Market* (Manchester, Manchester University Press, 1998); D Chalmers, 'Accounting for Europe' (1999) 19 *Oxford Journal of Legal Studies* 517.

[39] J Habermas, *Der philosophische Diskurs der Moderne: Zwölf Vorlesungen* (Frankfurt am Main, Suhrkamp Verlag, 1985) 13.

[40] N Luhmann, 'Sinn als Grundbegriff der Soziologie' in J Habermas and N Luhmann, *Theorie der Gesellschaft oder Sozialtechnologie* (Frankfurt am Main, Suhrkamp Verlag, 1971).

[41] N Luhmann, *Soziale Systeme. Grundriß einer allgemeinen Theorie* (Frankfurt am Main, Suhrkamp Verlag, 1984) 18.

[42] TS Kuhn, *The Structure of Scientific Revolutions* (Chicago, Chicago University Press, [1962] 1996) 77.

1.4 THE NEED FOR THEORY

The reason why a new paradigm has not materialised is the lack of a general theory, just as governance research, although often describing itself as groundbreaking, remains far too close to the disciplines from which it has emerged. Consequently, and despite the perceived break with the old paradigm, a large amount of governance literature is still embedded in nation-state semantics. In a recent contribution summing up the state of play of the debate on governance, for example, one can read that 'the common focus of most, if not all, contributions to the governance debate is on "the role of the state in society"'.[43] But the central problem is precisely that the EU is not a state or at least not a state in the nation-state sense, just as continued reliance on the state/society distinction illustrates a firm, though un-reflective, devotion to a Hegelian world view insofar as the state/society distinction is the basis for Hegel's attempt to describe the possibility of an identity-based world. This illustrates very well that the bulk of the existing work on European integration has not taken sufficient notice of the shift within social theory away from an emphasis on identity and towards a focus on difference.[44]

At the level of normative theory, basic debate has also been aimed at accommodating nation-state norms to the new European reality. The main focus has been on how to diminish the perceived legitimacy problem of the EU which is said to have developed due to an ever-increasing imbalance between the legislative and executive branches at EU level and the 'by-passing' of the institutional triangle through structures such as Comitology and the OMC. Moreover, complexity and transparency issues have been raised because of the EU's Byzantine institutional structure, while some observers perceive leftovers from the earlier economic constitution as creating a bias in favour of liberalist policies. Furthermore, to this list of institutional problems one can add the more fundamental 'no-demos' problem.[45]

The theory of deliberative supranationalism as developed by Joerges and Neyer is, however, of special relevance here since it is one of few attempts aimed at developing normative concepts that go further than merely applying nation-state concepts to the EU. But the real reason why this

[43] O Treib, H Bähr and G Falkner, 'Modes of Governance: A Note Towards Conceptual Clarification' (2005) 2 *European Governance Papers (EUROGOV)* 6, quoting J Pierre, *Introduction* in J Pierre (ed), *Debating Governance. Authority, Steering and Democracy* (Oxford, Oxford University Press, 2000).

[44] For a notable exception see C Landfried, *Das politische Europa. Differenz als Potential der Europäischen Union, 2 überarbeitete und erweiterte Auflage* (Baden-Baden, Nomos Verlag, 2005).

[45] JHH Weiler, 'Does Europe Need a Constitution? Reflections on Demos, Telos and the German Maastricht Decision' (1995) 1 *European Law Journal* 219.

theory is illustrative at this stage is that, although groundbreaking, it also highlights the need for further theoretical development, since Joerges and Neyer depart from the assumption that Comitology is an institutional response to the tensions between the intergovernmentalist and supranational elements of the EU.[46] This, however, turns the theory of deliberative supranationalism into a mere parasite attached to the dual intergovernmental/supranational paradigm. In addition, Joerges and Neyer are thereby building on top of a theoretical construct, which in its intentions and objectives is directly opposed to the argument they put forward concerning the possibility of legitimacy through deliberation outside the realm of hierarchical institutions. So even though the theory of deliberative supranationalism represents an important step in the direction of developing a normative theory suitable for the post-national European constellation, one must, paraphrasing Marx's ambition to turn Hegel upside down in order for him to stand on his feet,[47] state that the theory of deliberative supranationalism seems to be missing its legs. Accordingly, the theory needs to be underpinned by a general *descriptive* theory of European governance, which is complementary to but still distinctly different from the normative theory of deliberative supranationalism.[48] This theory must be capable of describing the evolution of integration, the logic guiding the shift from integration to constitutionalisation, as well as the rise of GS such as Comitology, and lastly how the relations between governing and governance structures are being stabilised. Only with an adequate descriptive basis of this kind can a viable normative theory, suitable for a structure based upon a balance between hierarchy and heterarchy such as the EU, achieve validity.[49]

[46] C Joerges and J Neyer, 'From Intergovernmental Bargaining to Deliberative Political Processes: The Constitutionalisation of Comitology' (1997) 3 (3) European Law Journal 273.

[47] K Marx and F Engels, 'Ludwig Feuerbach und der Ausgang der Klassischen Deutschen Philosophie' in *Marx & Engels. Werke, Band 21* (Berlin, Dietz Verlag, [1888] 1975) 293.

[48] For a detailed account of theoretical foundations of such a descriptive theory see P Kjaer, 'Systems in Context. On the Outcome of the Habermas/Luhmann Debate' (2006) *Ancilla Iuris* 66.

[49] With Weiler's distinction between the international, the supranational and the infranational dimensions of the EU in mind, deliberative supranationalism will have to be considered as a partial theory since it only focuses on the infranational dimension. On the other hand, deliberative supranationalism can be seen as complementing Habermas' extensive work on the international and supranational dimensions. For Weiler's perspective see JHH Weiler, 'European Democracy and its Critique' in J Hayward (ed), *The Crisis of Representation in Europe* (London, Frank Cass, 1995) 24.

2

The Context of Governance

2.1 INTRODUCTION

WHAT IS THE societal context within which the EU as such and GS in particular have emerged? In this chapter it will be argued that the processes of globalisation have created the structural conditions within which the emergence of the EU became possible. The process of integration can thus be understood as a symptom of far more profound societal changes by which stratificatory and territorial forms of social differentiation increasingly have been replaced with functionally differentiated structures. After a relatively slow start the integration process has, moreover, developed its own dynamics (*Eigendynamik*), thereby reducing the ability of the MS to control the process.

Establishing a conceptual link between the processes of globalisation and European integration implies that the EU can be understood as a political and legal structure which not only reflects the structural realities of globalisation, but also protects the democratic heritage of the nation-state era by transmitting the basic features of the nation-state to the European level.[1] However, underlying this vision is a somewhat defensive view that considers the EU to be simply an unfortunate but necessary substitute for nation-state democracy and thus a purely negative reaction to the increased asymmetries between the level of globalisation of the political and the legal system compared to other functional systems. The EU is, however, also a transformative structure which itself contributes to increased globalisation. It must therefore be understood as a transitional hybrid, operating in between the nation states and an increasingly globalised world, which—at the same time—produces and stabilises globalisation. From such a 'post-nostalgic' perspective the integration process can therefore be understood as an emancipative phenomenon which potentially leads to increases in

[1] J Habermas, 'Die Postnationale Konstellation und die Zukunft der Demokratie' in *Die postnationale Konstellation. Politische Essays* (Frankfurt am Main, Suhrkamp Verlag, 1998); J Habermas, 'Why Europe Needs A Constitution' (2001) 11 *New Left Review* 5.

meaning (*Sinn*) production as it enables functional systems to liberate themselves from their embeddedness in national settings.[2]

2.2 A POST-HEGELIAN PERSPECTIVE

The notion of transferring the basic structures of the nation states to the European level is a perspective reflecting idealist theories dating from the late 18th and the early 19th centuries, and which is guided by a desire to consider modern society as an organic entity. Hence, a central concern of classical idealist social theory was the question of how society could remain integrated and achieve rationality in the context of increased functional differentiation. Hegel, the classical modernist par excellence, argued for a containment of the functionally differentiated society within the form of the modern territorially delineated nation state, and a limitation of the adverse effects of functional differentiation, especially the problem of social exclusion, through a stratified corporatist system aimed at stabilising the relationship between the social classes. Hegel understood this stratified system as an explicitly modern phenomenon insofar as it reflected the class structure of the emerging industrial society rather than feudal forms of stratification.[3] Present-day systems theory[4] questions the theoretical premises of this model and has instead opted for a radicalisation of the insight originally produced by Hegel concerning the primacy of functional differentiation. Hence, in contrast to the Hegelian approach, modern systems theory conceptualises territorial and stratificatory forms of differentiation as specific forms of internal differentiation (*Binnendifferenzierung*) which develop within functional systems and do not therefore possess an independent character.[5] In practice, modern systems theory thereby argues that it is impossible to consider the modern functionally differentiated society as an organic entity. Moreover, this perspective implies that only one legal system and only one political system exist as the various national legal and political systems can be considered subsystems, delineated on the basis of territorial forms of differentiation, within globally operating functional systems. This radicalisation represents an advance in theoretical reasoning as it makes it possible to emphasise that

[2] See also PF Kjaer, The Societal Function of European Integration in the Context of World Society', (2007) 13 (1/2) *Soziale Systeme. Zeitschrift für Soziologische Theorie* 367.

[3] GWF Hegel, *Grundlinien der Philosophie des Rechts. Oder Naturrecht und Staatswissenschaft im Grundrisse* (Frankfurt am Main, Suhrkamp Verlag, [1821] 1976).

[4] For an overview of the evolution of systems theory see G Kneer and A Nassehi, *Niklas Luhmanns Theorie sozialer Systeme* (München, Wilhelm Fink Verlag, 1994). For the system theoretical approach to law see J Clam, *Droit et société chez Niklas Luhmann* (Paris, Presses Universitaires de France, 1997).

[5] N Luhmann, *Die Gesellschaft der Gesellschaft* (Frankfurt am Main, Suhrkamp Verlag, 1997) 595.

the EU itself consists of a legal and a political subsystem. These subsystems overlap with the legal and the political subsystems in the MS form but nonetheless remain separate and autonomous.

2.3 THE EU IN WORLD SOCIETY

The emergence of the EU is often considered to be a reflection of the catastrophes of the past.[6] These catastrophes undoubtedly created an environment within which it was possible for the integration phenomenon to emerge, just as instrumentalisation of the past and its deployment in the service of European integration indeed is an essential characteristic of the EU. However, the emergence of a complex social phenomenon such as the EU cannot be explained on the basis of mere memory. Instead, the central constituent is the constitution of distinctions. Not only is cognition dependent on the ability to differentiate between this or that but the sheer constitution of a social phenomenon is also based upon a continual redefining and maintenance of boundaries. The processes that constitute suitable conditions for the emergence and continued evolution of the EU should therefore lie in the EU's relationship to its environment, rather than in the memory of earlier historical events.[7]

As the social world consists of communication, its boundaries can be considered to be established according to a code of communication/non-communication. Consequently, only one society exists and that is the world society.[8] But in this form the concept of a world society is only an analytical concept, which is as empty as Hegel's concept of the world spirit (*Weltgeist*), since it merely states that in principle all communications can relate to all other communications. However, as an empirical phenomenon, the world society has also been in the making since the great discoveries of the late 15th century. But as Schmitt has pointed out, the concept of one world originally meant a European world, insofar as it only related to the European area (*Raum*) and the region's global expansion through colonialism.[9] From the late 19th century onwards this area increasingly broke down due to the rise of the United States and Japan as equal players in the colonial game, followed by a progressive recognition of Turkey, China, the Soviet Union, as well as the former colonies as equal members of the state

[6] Eg J Habermas, 'Aus Katastrophen Lernen? Ein Zeitdiagnostischer Rückblick auf das kurze 20. Jahrhundert' in *Die postnationale Konstellation. Politische Essays* (Frankfurt am Main, Suhrkamp Verlag, 1998).

[7] N Luhmann, 'Europa als Problem der Weltgesellschaft' (1994) 2 *Berliner Debatte* 3.

[8] N Luhmann, 'Die Weltgesellschaft' in *Soziologische Aufklärung Band 2* (Opladen, Westdeutscher Verlag, 1975); N Luhmann, *Die Gesellschaft der Gesellschaft* (Frankfurt am Main, Suhrkamp Verlag, 1997) 145 *ff.*

[9] C Schmitt, *Der Nomos der Erde. Im Völkerrecht des Jus Publicum Europaeum* (Berlin, Duncker & Humblot, 1950).

community.[10] The 20th century can therefore be characterised as a protracted transitional period within which the world was increasingly transformed from a European to a global entity.

But behind the legal and political developments reconstructed by Schmitt looms a more fundamental transformation in the form of a change in the structures of social differentiation. Social differentiation can be understood as a specific social construct which generates unity through difference. Segmentary differentiation, familiar from archaic societies, emphasises the sameness of different societies. Differentiation between centre and periphery (eg through clan structures) implies the formation of society through the difference of one part towards the rest. Stratified (eg feudal) society is based upon hierarchically ordered differences aimed at highlighting dissimilarity. In contrast to these earlier forms, functional differentiation is characterised by differences between similar social systems or spheres. Each system or sphere is on an equal footing with the other social systems or spheres, since each monopolises the reproduction of a specific function (eg law, economy, science or politics) which is necessary for the other systems or spheres to operate and thus for society as a whole to function; at the same time they maintain their distinctness due to the specific societal function that they monopolise.[11]

From this perspective modernity can be understood as a societal movement which is characterised by increasing reliance on functional differentiation compared to other forms of social differentiation. In early modernity, moreover, this societal movement was supplemented by the emergence of a new kind of territorial differentiation in the form of the modern states as well as new forms of stratification through the new social class structure which emerged within the context of the industrial society. In spite of these developments functional differentiation has increasingly become the most significant form of social differentiation worldwide. This is reflected in qualitative changes in the level of cross-border interdependence such as the expansion of the international division of labour within the economy, the development of globalised financial markets, increased awareness of cross-border environmental problems, increased global sharing of scientific knowledge, and the intensity of global media coverage. The functional systems of law and politics are characterised by higher levels of territorial structural couplings than the functional systems of the economy, environment,[12] science and the mass media; they have therefore faced

[10] *Ibid*, 200. See also R Stichweh, *Die Weltgesellschaft. Soziologische Analysen* (Frankfurt am Main, Suhrkamp Verlag, 2000) 7.

[11] N Luhmann, *Die Gesellschaft der Gesellschaft* (Frankfurt am Main, Suhrkamp Verlag, 1997) 595 *ff*.

[12] The environment is not a functional system in the strict sense but merely an 'imaginary system'. See N Luhmann, *Ökologische Kommunikation: Kann die moderne Gesellschaft sich auf ökologische Gefährdungen einstellen?* (Opladen, Westdeutscher Verlag, 1986).

increased pressure to 'keep up', since their ability to fulfil societal functions—such as the reproduction of law and collective decision making—has increasingly been undermined due to the widening asymmetry between degrees of (de-)territorialisation of the legal and political systems compared to other functional systems. This has resulted in continued erosion of the problem-solving capacity (*Problemlösungsfähigkeit*) of the nation states.[13]

This development was first felt within the European context, due to the combination of a high level of functional differentiation and societal complexity but also, in contrast to the United States, for example, because of the relatively small territorial basis which the different nationally organised subsystems are structurally coupled to in Europe.[14] Accordingly, it was in Europe that societal pressure for an increased fusion of nationally delineated legal and political subsystems was and is greatest, thereby creating a structural setting within which it was possible for the EU to evolve into a post-national 'avant-garde structure'.[15] Although this development has taken on a global scale with the development of regional configurations such as APEC, ASEAN, AU, CAN, MERCOSUR, NAFTA and SICA, Europe is still the region where this development has achieved the greatest degree of maturity.[16]

The emergence of an entire range of regionally, and therefore territorially, differentiated structures covering almost the entire globe has, moreover, been complemented by the simultaneous emergence and continued expansion of truly global structures, consisting of a vast conglomerate of functionally delineated organisations such as the WTO, WHO, the World Bank and the IMF, courts such as the International Court of Justice and the International Criminal Court, private legal regimes such as the Lex Mercatoria, private governance regimes such as ICANN and an increased number of globally active private actors in the form of multinational companies and NGOs.[17] The emerging post-national constellation therefore consists of two, although not always clearly distinguishable, layers. The first is based on regional configurations with relatively strong territorial features while the second is truly global and almost exclusively based on functional differentiation.

[13] M Zürn and S Liebfried, 'Reconfiguring the national constellation' in M Zürn and S Liebfried (eds), *Transformations of the State?* (Cambridge, Cambridge University Press, 2005).

[14] TM Andersen and TT Herbertsson (2003) 817 'Measuring Globalization', *IZA Discussion Papers*.

[15] As illustrated by Norbert Elias such configuration processes were also the central element of the transformations which led to the construction of the modern territorial states. See N Elias, *Über den Prozeß der Zivilisation, Band 2* (Frankfurt am Main, Suhrkamp Verlag, [1938] 1976).

[16] Eg P Ziltener, 'Gibt es einen regionalen Integrationsprozess in Ostasien?' (2003) 2 *MPIFG Discussion Papers*.

[17] See, eg, G Teubner (ed), *Global Law without a State* (Aldershot, Dartmouth, 1997).

Accordingly, the EU and the other regional configurations around the world can be described as transitional hybrids that act as stabilisers between nation-state constellations, which have become increasingly weakened, and a world society, which has not (yet) achieved the kind of substance and condensation that would be necessary if the world as such should follow the route that Europe has taken in the past 50 years.[18]

The transitional function of the EU means that it is leading the way for a process which, *in principle*, can become truly global. The ultimate borders of the EU are therefore identical with the boundaries of the world. Expansion is limited only by the level of globalisation and the borders of Europe therefore remain a contingent phenomenon. Any attempt to achieve a 'final' definition of the borders of Europe, as is often demanded in relation to the debate on potential Turkish membership, is therefore futile. Already with the enlargements in 1973 and 1981 the EU moved beyond the Carolingian 'core-Europe'. As ever more national 'societies', consisting of configurations of nationally and therefore territorially delineated functional subsystems, achieve a level of complexity and a degree of cross-border interdependency which undermine the viability of those national constellations, the functional demand for enlargement will continue to exist. Moreover, as the Norwegian rejection of membership and the Swiss rejection of the European Economic Area (EEA) agreement illustrate, there is no real alternative to increased integration for highly complex national configurations in geographical proximity to the EU. Norway voted against membership in 1972 and the consequence was a free-trade agreement, which entered into force in 1973. The second negative vote in 1994 was only sustainable because Norway had already become a de facto EU member through the EEA, which entered into force the same year as the referendum was held and contained the provision to transpose the vast majority of the *acquis communautaire* into Norwegian law. Accordingly, Norway's integration into the EU has never been more rapid than when its citizens voted no. In the Swiss case, rejection of the EEA in 1992 has simply meant that the main elements of the EEA (as well as the Schengen agreement) have been introduced piecemeal through a long range of bilateral agreements.[19] Thus Switzerland too has experienced the highest level of integration in the period following rejection.

[18] Hence, and particularly in relation to the WTO, which has an immense impact on the EU's ability to conduct market regulation, one would therefore have to conceive of the multi-level regime as a four-layer, and not as the three-layer regime which is more frequent in EU literature as a focus on the local, national and European levels would have to be complemented with the global level. Ideally it would therefore be necessary to systematically incorporate the interaction between global regimes and the EU. Including this dimension, however, goes beyond the scope of this study.

[19] A free-trade agreement between the EU and Switzerland has been in place since 1972. In 1999 the EC and Switzerland concluded seven bilateral agreements on the free movement of

In the case of Turkey, the provisions for membership negotiations state that Turkey should not only negotiate the conditions for implementation of the *acquis communautaire* but also emphasise that it should be implemented prior to membership.[20] Moreover, in order to achieve this, Turkey has been offered substantial financial and technical aid during the pre-accession period. Should its ongoing societal transformation be successful, the Austrian and French voters will therefore not be able to decide whether Turkey should become a member, as was originally promised by their governments. Instead they will only be able to 'decide' if Turkey should become a de jure member, as the reason for holding the referenda in the first place will be that de facto Turkey already has become integrated into the EU. Consequently, a vote against Turkish membership is unlikely to be politically viable in the long term as it would represent a merely symbolic rejection of a reality that already exists. A rejection by the Austrian and French voters will therefore have to be circumvented one way or another. Thus although the pledge that the decision should be made by the 'peoples of Europe' will probably be able to slow down the continued enlargement process, it is doubtful that they will be able to prevent it. Instead, the basis for enlargement is provided by both the level of interdependence between the still emerging EU configuration and surrounding national configurations, and continued pressure on the legal and political systems to develop adequate problem-solving structures given the context of increased societal interdependence. Consequently, the only viable choice for the EU is to actively Europeanise its surroundings.

As expansion increases the complexity of decision making it is not surprising that a close link exists between the continued enlargement process and increased competence transfers. The Merger Treaty of 1965, the Treaty of Luxembourg of 1970, the Treaty of Brussels of 1975 and the Act of 1976 concerning the direct election of the EP can be seen as part of the prolonged preparations and reactions to the 1973 enlargement. The Single European Act (SEA) evolved parallel to the negotiation and implementation of Portuguese and Spanish membership, the Maastricht Treaty was a direct response to the enlargement which took place with the

persons, public procurement, land and air transport, agriculture, research and mutual recognition of conformity assessment which entered into force on 1 June 2002. Since 2003 nine further bilateral agreements have been negotiated. These agreements concern taxation of savings, participation in the Schengen and Dublin agreements, judicial and administrative co-operation against fraud, trade in processed agricultural products, participation in the European Environment Agency, statistical co-operation, participation in the media programme, preparations for participation in future programmes in the fields of education, youth and training, and avoidance of double taxation of retired EU officials. More than 100 technical agreements are also in place. See also: http://ec.europa.eu/external_relations/switzerland/index_en.htm (accessed 1 July 2009).

[20] Council Decision 2006/EC/35 on the principles, priorities and conditions contained in the Accession Partnership with Turkey.

unification of Germany, the Amsterdam Treaty followed immediately after the enlargement with Austria, Finland and Sweden, and the Nice Treaty was directly linked to the 2004 enlargement. The Lisbon Reform Treaty (LRT) is closely linked to the objective of increasing the efficiency of EU 27 and to the prospect of further enlargements. The EU therefore resembles an 'expanding universe' where widening and deepening go hand in hand.

Hence any attempt to grasp the impressive dynamics of the European integration process must be based on the insight that the process has been conditioned by a structural environment which has allowed the EU to ride on a wave of far more fundamental societal transformations. These transformations take the form of expansions in interdependence due to increased functional differentiation compared to territorial and stratificatory differentiation. The majority of the integration initiatives launched over the years have therefore only been possible because they have strengthened societal developments which were already evolving.[21] Consequently, the idea that the MS are firmly in control of the integration process is to a large extent an illusion, since they are only capable of slowing down the pace of the integration process, rather than effectively bringing it to a halt. In policy areas where a high level of societal pressure for increased integration exists, the refusal of MS to transfer competencies to EU institutions rarely means that the competencies in question are retained. Instead, more or less informal GS emerge as a substitute for a formal handover of competences.[22] Within such areas the MS are therefore forced into a constructive and less ambitious role aimed at influencing priorities and the choice of regulatory tools, rather than actually exercising control. From being unquestioned sovereigns, the European states have increasingly become Schmittian partisans, acting more and more like private actors in an increasingly post-sovereign world.[23] But the actors are only capable of 'irritating' the ongoing transformation processes while their chances of winning an open battle steadily diminish.[24]

[21] A good example is the liberalisation of air transport, where the Commission initiatives in the mid 1980s only became meaningful due to the pressure created by vast increases in intra-community traffic from the 1970s onwards. These increases emerged due to technological and economic changes rather than changes in political preferences. See D O'Reilly and AS Sweet, 'The liberalization and reregulation of air transport' (1998) 5 (3) *Journal of European Public Policy* 447; H Kassim, 'Air transport' in H Kassim and M Anand (eds), *The European Union and National Industrial Policy* (Oxford, Routledge, 1996).

[22] For the relationship between formal and informal governance see T Christiansen and S Piattoni (eds), Informal Governance in the European Union (Cheltenham, Edward Elgar, 2004).

[23] C Schmitt, *Theorie des Partisanen. Zwischenbemerkung zum Begriff des Politischen* (Berlin, Duncker & Humblot, 1963).

[24] Hence, the EU cannot be understood as a 'dependent variable' which is merely a reflection of MS preferences. For this view see A Moravcsik, *The Choice for Europe: Social Purpose and State Power from Messina to Maastricht* (London, Cornell University Press, 1999).

2.4 THE EVOLUTION OF INTEGRATION

Within the context of the overall societal transformations outlined above, Intergovernmental Conferences (IGC) have emerged as the EU's internal form of evolution; it is within these structures that societal demands for integration are condensed and politicised.[25] The frequency of IGC therefore provides an indication of the EU's evolutionary speed. The rise of the EU was characterised by a slow but promising start with the launch of the ECSC in 1952, followed by the Treaty of Rome in 1957. In contrast to the widely held view that the EU was brought to an almost complete standstill after the 1965 empty chair crisis[26] and the outbreak of 'Euro-sclerosis' in the 1970s, the number of IGC indicates a different situation. The Merger Treaty of 1965, the Treaty of Luxembourg of 1970, the Treaty of Brussels of 1975 and the Act of 1976 all represented steps towards increased integration with significant long-term consequences. One of the crucial implications was the gradual introduction of independent sources of financial resources following the Treaty of Luxembourg which considerably increased the autonomy of the Community. Another landmark change was the expansion of the budgetary powers of the EP, which was granted the last word on non-compulsory expenditures in 1970 and the ability to reject the budget as a whole in 1975, thereby providing the EP with instruments that have permitted the gradual expansion of its competencies ever since.[27]

The developments of the 1970s can therefore be seen as a protracted series of step-by-step preparations, paving the way for a change of gear in the integration process which occurred with the launch of the SEA in the mid-1980s. But the SEA not only increased the level of temporality but also produced qualitative changes insofar as the internal complexity (*Eigenkomplexität*) of the evolution process increased dramatically. The introduction of the SEA must therefore be considered the crucial moment when Pandora's Box was opened and the EU finally 'took off', as it enabled the integration process to achieve a level of dynamism and autonomy which made the move towards integration relatively self-sustainable. This self-sustainability was further underpinned by the Treaty of Maastricht. Although the ground for economic and monetary union (EMU) had been prepared since the early 1970s the actual move towards the EMU was

[25] We adopt here the distinction between medium and form developed by Fritz Heider. See F Heider, 'Ding und Medium' (1926) I *Symposium* 109.

[26] JM Palayret, H Wallace and P Winand (eds), Visions, Votes and Vetoes: Reassessing the Luxembourg Compromise 40 Years On (Brussels, Peter Lang, 2006).

[27] That the EU expanded its operations considerably in this period is also indicated by the fact that the number of Council meetings increased every year during the 1970s. For an assessment see J Golub, 'In the Shadow of the Vote? Decision-making Efficiency in the European Community 1974–1995' (1997) *MPIfG Working Papers* 3.

triggered by external events in the form of the fall of the Berlin Wall and German unification. As a response to the fear that Europe would return to the past with rivalry between the great powers,[28] the successful implementation of the Maastricht policy programme effectively burned the bridges to Europe's past as it ensured that the 'turn to integration' could no longer be rolled back. Consequently, in post-Maastricht Europe, integration—in one form or another—has become the only viable option, thereby creating a structural setting within which the robustness of the integration process has expanded massively. It is therefore not surprising that the dual paradigm, with its nation-state foundations, broke down precisely when the EU achieved a high level of self-sustainability,[29] just as the tentative emergence of a paradigm of governance, which assumes that the EU is some sort of *sui generis* structure, emerged in the wake of Maastricht.

The increase in self-sustainability is also emphasised by the fact that since the IGC which led to the SEA, the EU has developed an operational form enabling it to proceed directly from one IGC to another.[30] The IGC leading to the SEA was related to a policy programme (*Zweckprogram*) to be implemented by 1993, while the Maastricht IGC was launched before this programme was completed. This was also the case with the IGC leading to the Treaty of Amsterdam, which was initiated before the policy programme launched with the Treaty of Maastricht was finalised. In the same way, the outcomes of both the IGC leading to Amsterdam and to Nice contained provisions about future IGC to be initiated immediately after the completion of the ongoing IGC. Although no immediate successor was planned for the Convention on the Future of Europe and even though the question of the *finalité* of the integration process was one of the main arguments for launching the Convention in the first place,[31] it remains unlikely that the evolutionary process would have been brought to a standstill if the Constitutional Treaty (CT) had entered into force. Some indication of the continued dynamic was already evident with the de facto

[28] JJ Mearsheimer, 'Back to the Future: Instability in Europe After the Cold War' (1990) 15 (4) *International Security* 5.

[29] JHH Weiler, 'The Transformation of Europe' (1991) 100 Yale Law Journal 2402–53.

[30] The ability to go from IGC to IGC uninterruptedly indicates that the integration process has increasingly gained systemic features since a system can be understood as 'a linking of actually performed operations' (my translation, PFK). See N Luhmann, *Das Recht der Gesellschaft* (Frankfurt am Main, Suhrkamp Verlag, 1993) 40 *f*. This is a view also presented by Maurizio Bach: 'The supranational institutional order, established through intergovernmental treaties, is increasingly liberating itself from the nation state contexts. It is consolidating itself as an institutionally differentiated transnational regime with a strong technocratic component, on the basis of system-specific rationality criteria which generate and implement legal and procedural norms' (my translation, PFK), See M Bach, 'Transnationale Integration und institutionelle Differenzierung' (1993) 14 (2) *Zeitschrift für Rechtssoziologie*, 223, 227.

[31] J Fischer, *Vom Staatenverbund zur Föderation – Gedanken über die Finalität der europäischen Integration*, speech at the *Humboldt-Universität zu Berlin*, 12 May 2000. Available at www.europa-digital.de/aktuell/dossier/fischer/rede1205.shtml.

expansion of the competencies of the EP during the approval process of the Barroso Commission in 2004. Even before the CT was signed, the EP de facto asserted the power to veto individual members of the new Commission and thereby rendered an essential provision of the CT outdated. On substantial issues, for example in relation to energy policy, budget reforms and the Security and Defence Policy (ESDP), external developments and functional demands are, moreover, likely to make the provisions which have been transferred from the CT to the LRT an insufficient basis for EU decisions in the near future. Presentation of the LRT as a mere temporary solution also prepares the way for future treaty reforms, aimed at implementing the few remaining elements of the CT, as well as new integrative initiatives. The implosion of Europe's constitutional moment is therefore likely to indicate a continuation of the incremental integration process rather than to halt it. Consequently, the EU will probably continue to proceed from one IGC to another for the foreseeable future.

More generally, scope for further evolution is also indicated by the fact that the EU has not so far achieved a level of internal differentiation which enables it to distinguish between the development and implementation of specific policy programmes—such as the establishment of the Customs Union, the Common Agricultural Policy (CAP), the Internal Market (IM), the EMU or the realisation of the eastern enlargement—and the evolution of its basic constitutional structures. Hence, the EU is characterised by an amalgamation of polity and policy. It thus distinguishes itself from the political system at the nation-state level where somewhat clearer distinctions between polity and policy have emerged.

Had it been implemented, the CT would probably have led to an increased differentiation between polity and policy as it was intended to formalise the use of constitutional language thereby introducing a distinction between basic structures and policy programmes. After the failure of the CT, such a change is unlikely to come about any time soon. One important element which has been transferred from the CT to the LRT is, however, the possibility of moving from unanimity to majority voting without an IGC, thereby increasing the possibility of launching new policy programmes without major treaty reforms. Hence, under the surface, a tendency towards increased differentiation of constitutional structures and policy programmes continues to develop. This is also underlined by the Lisbon Agenda, which is the first major policy programme to be initiated that is not directly linked to a treaty reform. On the other hand, the relative failure of the Lisbon Agenda might be traced back to the lack of a treaty reform capable of providing the necessary institutional basis for the Lisbon objectives. All in all, this presents a 'mixed picture' where the differentiation between basic structures and policy programmes is likely to increase but is still minor compared to the level which can be identified at the nation-state level.

2.5 THE AUTONOMY OF THE EU

The EU, as an entity relying on territorial differentiation at a regional level, is structurally coupled to the territory of the 27 MS. This does not mean that the EU is identical to the MS. Although structurally coupled to the same territory, the EU and the MS constitute parallel universes. For example, the legal orders of the EU and the MS remain distinct since EC directives harmonise MS legal orders without replacing them.[32] Instead EU legal acts are transplants which are incorporated into national legal universes where they are then observed, evaluated and used on the basis of the criteria inherent in the respective national legal orders.[33] *In principle*, the MS therefore belong to the environment of the EU to the same extent as non-Member States or any other social phenomenon operating outside the corpus of EU law.

On the other hand, the EU strives to replace nation-state constellations with common EU constellations through the progressive creation of common areas characterised by common structures and norms. From the Brussels perspective the measure of success is therefore not only the degree of competence transfer that has taken place, but is equally represented by the extent of 'real' integration based on specific reference points such as the levelling of car prices[34] and convergence of equality between the sexes throughout the EU, among other issues.[35] In practice, meaning components in the form of EU political decisions and legislative acts are therefore not just mere transplants nor is the consequence of integration a direct move towards the abolition of the MS. Instead, the EU and the MS are Eigenstructures (*Eigenstrukturen*),[36] in the sense that the EU is a distinct structure emerging immanently from within the MS universes in the same way as the modern nation states emerged immanently from within the old feudal order.[37]

In most cases the emergence of the modern nation states did not lead to an eradication of the old feudal order. Instead the feudal order was merely

[32] M Amstutz, 'In Between Worlds: *Marleasing* and the Emergence of Interlegality in Legal Reasoning', (2006) 12 (6) *European Law Journal* 766.

[33] P Legrand, 'The Impossibility of Legal Transplants' (1994) 4 *Maastricht Journal of Comparative Law* 111.

[34] Commission of the European Communities, COMP/E2, July 2007: Car Prices Within the European Union at 01/05/2007.

[35] Commission of the European Communities, COM(2007)49 final: Report from the Commission to the Council, the European Parliament, the European Economic and Social Committee and the Committee of the Regions on equality between women and men – 2007.

[36] R Stichweh, 'Strukturbildung in der Weltgesellschaft – Die Eigenstrukturen der Weltgesellschaft und die Regionalkulturen der Welt' in T Schwinn (Hrsg), *Die Vielfalt und Einheit der Moderne. Kultur- und strukturvergleichende Analysen* (Wiesbaden, Verlag für Sozialwissenschaften, 2006).

[37] E Kantorowicz, *The King's Two Bodies. A Study in Mediaeval Political Theology* (Princeton, Princeton University Press, [1957] 1997).

emptied of its societal functions and was therefore increasingly marginalised. However, albeit in a purely ritualised form without substantial content, the feudal order continues to exist, for example in the form, of constitutional monarchies and closed nobility networks. The EU does the same: the British Parliament, the French *Assemblée nationale* and the German *Bundestag* will continue to exist, but through the integration process they are increasingly being drained of their societal functions and hence are experiencing increased marginalisation.[38]

The notion that the EU is a distinct social phenomenon and is not identical to the sum of the MS implies that it is an autonomous structure. Autonomy is an expression of functional equivalence.[39] Functional equivalence implies that in a complex social world any cause can be achieved by a multiple number of different effects just as any effect can lead to a different number of causes.[40] As already indicated, and we will return to this in more detail, the EU must, for example, be conceived of as a structure which both produces globalisation and acts as a stabiliser of the transformations brought about by the globalisation processes. Accordingly, it is impossible to establish clear causality by claiming that the EU is either creating or reacting to globalisation. Instead the EU both creates and reacts at the same time.[41]

The EU's level of autonomy has, moreover, increased over time because the rise in its internal complexity implies greater variation and therefore a larger number of potential operations or strategies from which it can choose. However, like all social phenomena the EU's autonomy is paradoxical in nature in that it is based on a mutual increase between the levels of autonomy and interdependence. At the same time as the internal complexity increases, so does the level of interdependence through external constraints. This creates ongoing tension between autonomy and interdependence.[42] More concretely, interdependence is the result of structural

[38] Eg according to Majone only 20–25 per cent of French legislation is produced by the French parliament in complete autonomy without interference from the EU. See G Majone, 'Dilemmas of European Integration. The Ambiguities and Pitfalls of Integration by Stealth' (Oxford, Oxford University Press, 2005) 145. However, it should be mentioned that such a purely quantitative measure does not say anything about the relative importance or the actual societal impact of the EU-influenced legislation.

[39] N Luhmann, 'Die Funktionsbegriff in der Verwaltungswissenschaft' (1958) 49, *Verwaltungsarchiv. Zeitschrift für Verwaltungslehre, Verwaltungsrecht und Verwaltungspolitik* 97.

[40] D Baecker, 'Why Systems?' (2001) 18 (1) *Theory, Culture & Society* 59; P Kjaer, 'Systems in Context: On the Outcome of the Habermas/Luhmann Debate' (2006) *Ancilla Iuris* 66–7.

[41] Luhmann's definition of autonomy as the absence of causality is identical to Kant's concept of freedom. See N Luhmann, *Zweckbegriff und Systemrationalität. Über die Funktion von Zwecken in Sozialen Systemen* (Frankfurt am Main, Suhrkamp Verlag, 1968) 250.

[42] This paradoxical relationship between autonomy and interdependence is the key insight of modern sociology and its studies of functional differentiation and division of labour. For

couplings which enable a distinct social structure to rely on another social structure in order to reproduce specific elements that are necessary for it to operate and which the structure in question cannot produce itself. The price paid for such couplings is, however, a restriction of autonomy in so far as structural couplings tend to limit the choice of operations which may be selected within the framework of a given social structure. Typical examples of this mechanism are taxation, enabling the political system to 'borrow' components from the economic system, and public spending through which the political system re-introduces the borrowed components to the economic system. In this perspective, central banks also act as structural couplings between the financial market and the political system, while law and economy are coupled via the safeguarding of property through law, in the same way that legally binding contracts regulate the transfers of property within the economic system. Constitutions—as we will see later—serve as structural couplings between law and politics.[43]

The EU's political system is, however, characterised by an extremely high level of asymmetric structural couplings with the political system in the MS form.[44] Three main couplings to the political system can be identified: first, the Council, which is the spearhead of the MS and thus of the political system in the nation-state form within the EU; this structure also operates on the basis of a specific logic of integration. As we will see later, this logic is different from the kind of logic that guides nation-state politics. Consequently, the Council is an 'indecisive' structure exercising a dual role. A second coupling is the IGC where the MS continue to act as the Masters of the Treaties. As already indicated, the IGC are to a large extent reactive rather than proactive structures insofar as the societal forces which carry the integration process forward tend to make increased integration an imperative requirement or even a mere formalisation of already existing structures. On the other hand, they do obviously give the MS immense influence over the development of the integration process. Thirdly, the continued transfer of financial resources from the MS to the EU which, in

the classical works see E Durkheim, *De la division du travail social* (Paris, Presses universitaires de France, [1893] 1973); G Simmel, 'Über sociale Differenzierung. Sociologische und psychologische Untersuchungen' in G Simmel, *Aufsätze 1887–1890* (Frankfurt am Main, Suhrkamp Verlag, [1890] 1989); T Parsons, *The System of Modern Societies* (Englewood Cliffs, Prentice-Hall, 1971).

43 N Luhmann, *Die Gesellschaft der Gesellschaft* (Frankfurt am Main, Suhrkamp Verlag, 1997) 776 *ff*.

44 Whereas the political system in the nation-state form is mainly coupled to the economic system through taxation and public spending the EU's primary coupling to the economic system is through trade associations and other forms of lobbying networks. The explanation is that the EU's main function is regulatory and not distributive. For a general investigation of structural couplings through trade associations (*Verbände*) see A Brodocz, 'Strukturelle Kopplung durch Verbände' (1996) 2 *Soziale Systeme. Zeitschrift für Systemtheorie* 361.

spite of the introduction of the EU's 'own resources', still provide some 75 per cent of the EU's financial means.[45]

As a consequence of structural couplings to the political system in the nation-state form, the EU has been faced with extreme limitations to its evolution. However, the EU is also engaged in structural couplings with the legal and administrative subsystems of the political and legal systems in their nation-state forms, in order to compensate for the EU's failing ability to ensure implementation and compliance. From the perspective of the EU, these couplings have been far more 'constructive' or 'balanced'. The ECJ has, for example, been able to establish substantial mutually beneficial 'partnerships' with lower-level nation-state courts, through their right to refer cases to the ECJ.[46] Additionally, and as we will return to in the following chapter, the rise of GS can be seen as a specific way of circumventing the limitations of the political system in its nation-state form through the creation of structural couplings to national administrations and to private actors. This has led to the Europeanisation of nation-state administrations which tends to undermine the attempt by political leaderships to curb the evolution of the EU. The price paid, however, is that the EU's evolution has been forced along a different path from that originally imagined by the EU's chief ideologists, Monnet, Haas and Hallstein, because the 'turn to governance' implies abandoning the federal vision. Hence, a mixed picture appears regarding the question of the EU's autonomy as the EU must, on the one hand, be understood as a distinct and autonomous social phenomenon, and on the other as a structure which only enjoys a limited level of operational freedom due to MS constraints.

2.6 THE TRANSFORMATIVE FUNCTION OF THE EU

The desire to free itself from the constraints of the MS and to increase its autonomy helps explain the character of EU policies. Throughout its existence the EU has consistently, and with much success, implemented a policy programme oriented towards systematically undermining national configurations through 'negative integration'. As already indicated, the national configurations can be understood as dense webs of overlapping

[45] In spite of this high level of asymmetry the couplings are still reciprocal in that the political system in the nation state form depends on the EU as well. Milward's basic idea of the 'rescue' of the nation state through the EU, in the sense that the transformation of the nation states into welfare states was to a great extent conditioned by the economic growth provided through integration, highlights this very well. See AS Milward, *The European Rescue of the Nation-State* (Oxford, Routledge, 2000).

[46] B de Witte, 'Direct Effect, Supremacy, and the Nature of the Legal Order' in P Craig and G de Burca (eds), *The Evolution of EU Law* (Oxford, Oxford University Press, 1999) 193 *ff*.

internal forms of territorial differentiation in the shape of, for example, national political, legal, economic, educational and scientific systems which are structurally coupled with each other in a multitude of ways. This therefore creates a context where the different systems develop strong limitations to each other's autonomy. Within such contexts the political system has traditionally enjoyed the role of a *primus inter pares* vis-à-vis other systems, thereby establishing the basis for an understanding of society as 'state-centred'. In examining the nature of its policy programme the EU must therefore be seen as a transformative structure, which has itself played a central role in increasingly diminishing the relevance of territorial forms of internal differentiation in the nation-state form, and not just as a reaction to this development.

But the EU is not simply guided by 'self-interest'. It emerged at a time when functional systems (in particular—but not only—the economic system) had exhausted the possibility of continued expansion within the structural limitations imposed by their continued need to rely on territorial forms of internal differentiation in the form of nation-state subsystems. Territorial forms of internal differentiation emerged as a stabilising element in early modernity, but over time they have increasingly become obstacles to further evolution as the price paid for such stabilisation is a considerable limitation to the range of operations that such subsystems may select. This restriction arises from the high level of structural couplings they are engaged in vis-à-vis other subsystems within the same national configuration. Thus, the EU seems to have emerged as a result of a broad societal demand for a 'support structure' capable of supporting the movement towards emancipating functional systems from the restrictions imposed by national contexts.

Hence, the success of the EU is closely linked to its ability to build alliances with societal structures that fall outside the realms of the state and seek to escape the constraints of national configurations. It is not surprising, therefore, that the de-regulatory policies of the EU have emerged in close 'partnership' with structures reproduced within other systems. European business interests have, for example, recognised from the beginning of the integration process that Europeanisation is a useful tool through which reliance on national configurations as a framework for economic operations can be reduced. Hence, and bearing in mind that modernity can be defined as the primacy of functional differentiation over other forms of social differentiation,[47] the contribution that the EU creates towards society as a whole is a radicalisation of modernity. The EU thus

[47] N Luhmann, *Die Gesellschaft der Gesellschaft* (Frankfurt am Main, Suhrkamp Verlag, 1997) 744 *f.*

provides a possibility for functional systems to increase their autonomy by decreasing their reliance on territorial forms of internal differentiation in the nation-state form.

2.7 THE RESTABILISING FUNCTION OF THE EU

In most cases, however, the moves towards negative integration have been followed almost immediately by steps towards 'positive integration' through the emergence of new political and legal forms which develop 'on top' of the already existing national political and legal structures. This produces new forms of European-wide territorial differentiation within the political and legal systems. This development not only illustrates that functional systems are always embedded systems and that a move towards dis-embedment always implies re-embedment,[48] but also that European integration only leads to a *relative* decrease in reliance on territorial forms of internal differentiation. The move towards positive integration within the political and legal systems means that the integration process merely provides other systems with the opportunity to replace the structural couplings with their national political and legal systems with couplings to the political and legal structures of the EU. This kind of substitution will probably contribute to a reconfiguration of the forms of internal differentiation within other systems. It is of course debatable how strong the pull towards internal reconfiguration of other systems is, and it is equally doubtful that the current strength of the pull can be maintained in an increasingly globalised world. To date, however, the pull seems to have been reasonably strong since it is now possible to observe the emergence of a dense network of Europe-wide structural couplings. These constitute a European configuration in its own right, which in many instances acts as an alternative to the network of structural couplings which have traditionally constituted the various national configurations.[49]

The switch from national to European couplings must be considered as a purely internal process which is guided by the incentive of non-political and non-legal systems to achieve a *relative* decrease in their internal reliance on forms of internal territorial differentiation. Such a relative decrease is possible because the form of positive regulation pursued by the

[48] P Kjaer, 'Systems in Context: On the Outcome of the Habermas/Luhmann debate' (2006) *Ancilla Iuris* 66. For the economic system see also K Polanyi, *The Great Transformation: The Political and Economic Origins of Our Time* (Boston, Beacon Press, [1944] 2001).

[49] Apart from the dense Brussels-based lobbying networks which act as structural couplings between the economic system and the political system of the EU, the increased density of European research networks—which, as we will return to in Ch 6, have emerged as a result of the EU's R & D policy— serve as a good illustration of this development.

dominated by a sectoral approach in the sense that it is only oriented towards a small section (most notably the economic section) of society when compared with the almost all-encompassing regulation of society pursued by the political system when the nation-state era was at its height. Hence, the EU often provides more specialised and 'tailor-made' forms of regulation which frequently provide more suitable points of reference for economic communication flows than, for example, national forms of regulation. Secondly, the EU's regulatory measures do not emerge from the kind of corporatist exercises which were, and partly still are, a dominant feature of the welfare regimes of the European nation states. Hence, whereas stratification, at least on the level of self-description, has played a substantial role in the political system within the context of the nation state, and thus also for the development by political systems of regulatory reference points for the economic system, this element is almost absent in relation to EU decision making.[50] Thirdly, the EU provides an opportunity to achieve 'economies of scale' in relation to structural couplings, in that reference to 27 different forms of regulatory measures can ideally be reduced to a single point of reference. European political and legal integration therefore potentially reduces the cognitive resources needed in order to ensure compatibility between, for example, economic operations and the regulatory reference points produced within the political and legal systems. Fourthly, the territorial form of differentiation in the EU is far less profound than the national equivalents. This is not only because the EU is structurally coupled to a far larger geographical area than any of the MS, but also because the continued enlargement process and the systematic attempt to link neighbouring countries as closely as possible to the EU means that boundaries existing along territorial lines are far less relevant. In addition, due to its status as one of the largest regulatory structures in the world, regulation pursued in the EU is de facto global regulation as EU measures tend to have massive 'extra-territorial effects'. Adaptation to European, instead of national, regulatory reference points therefore increases the possibility of operating globally.

Hence, the societal function of European integration vis-à-vis society as whole is to offer other functional systems the possibility of decreasing their reliance on territorial and stratificatory forms of internal differentiation and/or to ensure a fusion of nation-state subsystems in order to establish territorial differentiation on a regional as opposed to a national level. Obviously, the term integration in this specific case does not refer to the classical sociological understanding of integration. Nor is it aimed at offsetting societal *anomie* in the Durkheimian sense, although that might

[50] The EU has launched a 'social dialogue' with European employers' and employees' organisations through the European Economic and Social Committee. This corporatist attempt, however, remains of limited relevance.

also be a consequence. Instead the EU only reproduces 'European integration' in the form of an increased fusion of previously distinct nationally delineated territorial subsystems. From a sociological perspective the EU therefore exercises a limited and relatively well-defined societal function. It is therefore impossible to view the EU as either a guardian against globalisation or as a driving force of globalisation and therefore as 'part of the problem'. Instead the EU, given to its role as a stabilising hybrid, is at one and the same time one of the clearest and most radical manifestations of the globalisation processes and a structural setting within which legal regulation and political decision-making evolve in accordance with the structural realities of an increasingly global world.[51]

2.8 INTEGRATION AS A REGULATORY IDEA

An important difference between the EU and political and legal systems in their nation-state forms is the specificity of its policy programme (*Zweckprogramm*), as its operations remain subordinated to the regulatory idea of increased integration.[52] Consequently the EU's operations develop within the language of integration and on the basis of a specific logic of integration. The EU cannot extend beyond integration and consequently integration becomes an objective in itself (*Selbstzweck*) achieving the status of *raison d'être*. Hence, the EU's policy programme can be said to be guided by an integration/non-integration distinction.

Subordination to the objective of integration helps explain why the political systems in the nation-state form continuously face disappointment when they try to control the operations of the EU. Even when their priorities seem to be fully accepted, as was the case with the United Kingdom (UK) during the SEA negotiations, such political priorities are merely 'translated' and consequently a completely different meaning and purpose are attributed to them when transferred from the sphere of the MS into the EU sphere. In the specific case of the SEA, and to the surprise of the UK government, the move towards negative integration was intrinsically linked to a move towards positive integration through re-regulation at the European level. Hence, the Thatcher government quite clearly shared the naivety of the intergovernmentalists by believing that the process could

[51] For an analysis of the EU as a 'mediating variable' in between the global and the national contexts exemplified by the processes leading to liberalisation of the telecommunications and electricity industries in Europe see D Levi-Faur, 'On the "Net Impact" of Europeanization. The EU's telecoms and electricity regimes between the global and the national' (2002) 6 (7) *European Integration online Papers (EIoP)*.

[52] For a historical account of the integrationist logic see AS Milward, *The European rescue of the nation-state* (Oxford, Routledge, 2000). For the legal point of view see H Rasmussen, *On law and policy in the European Court of Justice: a comparative study in judicial policymaking* (Dordrecht, Kluwer, 1986).

be controlled on the basis of nation-state priorities even though the integration process is guided by a logic which is substantially different compared to the kind of logic guiding MS politics.[53]

In other words it is possible to observe a deeply rooted division between the forms of policy making in the EU context compared to the MS contexts. Countless attempts have been made to explain that the EU is a 'normal' power-based political system.[54] However, power politics are based on the ability to ensure subordination on the basis of a distinction between superiority and inferiority (*Machtüberlegenheit/Machtunterlegenheit*) through the possible deployment of negative sanctions.[55] But the EU does not possess such power and has therefore been forced to use other means than force in order to achieve its objectives.[56] Moreover, in established democracies the traditional distinction between superiority and inferiority has increasingly been replaced with the distinction between government and opposition. This distinction has not materialised at the EU level. As opposed to the political system in its nation-state form, the measure of success within the EU is not therefore related to the government/opposition distinction but instead concerns whether integration is progressing or at a standstill.[57]

Moreover, the key element of power, namely its exercise, necessitates knowledge of who is exercising power, or at least the existence of a *symbolic* structure which one can assume constitutes the centre of power. The absence of the government/opposition distinction means, however, that there is no clearly identifiable centre of power within the EU. Whether governing (*Regieren*) takes place at all within the EU is therefore remains a relevant question[58] since the kind of Schmittian decisionism, which is an inherent part of the self-understanding of the political system at MS level, does not exist within the EU. Instead, as embodied in the 'Monnet Method', the EU has identified integration as a 'technical task', where traditional power politics are seen as an obstacle to integration rather than

[53] For an intergovernmentalist view on the emergence of the SEA see A Movracsik, 'Negotiating the Single European Act: national interests and conventional statecraft in the European Community' (winter 1991) *International Organization* 19.

[54] Eg S Hix, *The Political System of the European Union* (Basingstoke, Macmillan, 1999).

[55] C Borch, 'Systemic Power. Luhmann, Foucault and Analytics of Power' (2005) 48 (2) *Acta Sociologica* 155; N Luhmann, *Politik der Gesellschaft* (Frankfurt am Main, Suhrkamp Verlag, 2000) 88 and 97; N Luhmann, 'Theorie der Politischen Opposition' (1989) 36 (1) *Zeitschrift für Politik* 13.

[56] C Joerges and M Zürn (eds), *Law and Governance in Postnational Europe. Compliance Beyond the Nation-State* (Cambridge, Cambridge University Press, 2005).

[57] Guy Verhofstadt arrived at similar conclusions in that he compares the integration process with riding a bike. One needs to keep pedalling in order not to fall off. See G Verhofstadt, *Les états-unis d'Europe* (Bruxelles, Luc Pire, 2006).

[58] M Jachtenfuchs and M Knodt (Hrsg.), *Regieren in internationalen Institutionen* (Opladen, Leske + Budrich, 2002).

a tool of integration.[59] Indeed, every time the EU has pursued integration within areas which have been conceived of as politically crucial by the MS, and which they have been strong enough to reproduce within their respective national settings, it has hit a wall of resistance. It is therefore not surprising that the 'technical tools' with which integration has been pursued have been legal instruments, which dominated the 1960s and 1970s, market instruments, mainly during the 1980s and early 1990s, and governance instruments from the mid-1990s onwards. In contrast, genuine political acts in the nation-state sense have largely been avoided and when tried have led to disappointment. Obvious examples of such disappointments are the failure of the European Defence Community (EDC) in the 1950s and the CT. The transformation of the CT into a mere 'technical exercise' through the LRT, moreover, represents a classic circumvention strategy. One of the strongest features of the integration process is in fact the tendency to transform political issues into technical issues in order to allow integration to proceed.[60] For example, the transfer of monetary policy from the national to the European level after Maastricht implied that the majority of the national central banks, which had not been politically independent before the launch of the Maastricht process, gained such independence. Moreover, the independence granted to the European Central Bank (ECB) in the Treaty of Maastricht even exceeds the independence of the German *Bundesbank*.[61]

Another characteristic of EU politics is that the EU takes an 'opportunistic' approach to substantial matters. In the case of the SEA the fiercest resistance came from the UK government and accordingly its liberalist preferences were incorporated to the extent necessary to overcome UK resistance at the same time as the 'hidden' re-regulation agenda was played down. Today, with integration increasingly encroaching on the welfare and labour market regimes of the MS, the strongest resistance seems to come from France. Accordingly the liberalist approach, which emerged in order to overcome UK resistance, is slowly being substituted with a 'flexsecurity' approach that has been specifically invented to overcome French resistance. Seen from the Brussels perspective, continued integration remained the primary objective in both cases, however, and the choice of actual policy therefore remains of secondary importance. On the other hand, this does not mean that economic concerns (eg efficiency and competitiveness), political concerns (eg in terms of influence on and the popularity of specific

[59] Eg R Schmalz-Bruns, 'Deliberativer Supranationalismus' (1998) 6 *Zeitschrift für Internationale Beziehungen* 185.

[60] M Bach, *Die Bürokratisierung Europas. Verwaltungseliten, Experten und politische Legitimation in Europa* (Frankfurt am Main, Campus Verlag, 1999).

[61] G Majone, *Dilemmas of European integration: the ambiguities and pitfalls of integration by stealth* (Oxford, Oxford University Press, 2005) 38 *f*.

measures) or ethical concerns (eg in relation to risk regulation) do not play a role. It only indicates that such concerns are not primary and that they remain subordinated to the integration imperative. Moreover, such subordination is not necessarily problematic since most problems can be addressed in a multitude of ways, and often in a way which will enable the objective of integration and other objectives to be achieved simultaneously. As pointed out by Majone,[62] the primacy of integration does, however, create a structural bias which over time tends to systematically produce sub-optimal outcomes, for example when viewed from an economic perspective.[63]

2.9 THE SOCIETAL STATUS OF THE EU POLITICAL SYSTEM

The differences between EU politics and nation-state politics outlined above indicate that the EU's political system plays a fundamentally different role and takes a different form when compared to the political subsystems in the nation-state context. This difference is directly related to far deeper societal transformation processes in the form of increased substitution of territorial and stratificatory forms of differentiation with functional differentiation outlined earlier on.

In the Hegelian era the political system combined collectively binding decision making with, at the level of self-description, the development of all-encompassing narratives[64] which served as a basis for its claim of superiority compared to other functional systems and the promotion of an organic understanding of society. However, this was only possible because, in effect, the majority of the collectively binding decisions that emerged from the political system in its nation-state form were oriented towards securing national defence and social stability through welfare politics. Hence, the bulk of the collectively binding decisions taken within the realm of the nation-state political system form was (and partly is) oriented towards problems of a territorial and stratificatory nature. In contrast the vast majority of the collectively binding decisions of the EU are oriented towards the reduction of negative externalities; asymmetries and

[62] *Ibid.*

[63] Not surprisingly, the EU has therefore been faced with continued criticism. For example in a critical comment on the European Commission discussion paper on mortgage credit in the European Union entitled 'Integration is not necessarily the right concept to guide integration' David Miles, the Chief Economist from Morgan Stanley, made the following illuminating statement: 'The Commission needs to keep in mind that what matters is efficiency, rather than integration as an end in itself', *Financial Times*, 16 December 2005.

[64] JF Lyotard, *La condition postmoderne: rapport sur le savoir* (Paris, Minuit, 1979).

'crowding-out' effects emerging between functionally differentiated systems (especially between the economic system and other systems).[65] As regards positive integration the substantial task of the EU's political system is therefore to act as an engine of hyper-complex risk regulation. At this level the central contribution of the EU towards society as a whole lies in its attempt to ensure convergence between different forms of rationality, which are reproduced within areas such as economy, health, science and environment. Hence, the EU mainly acts as a coordinator and arbitrator between functionally differentiated systems. This change of substantial function means that the (embryonic) attempts of the EU to describe itself as a mechanism capable of forging substantial unity are bound to remain even more implausible than similar attempts were in the nation-state context.[66]

Given this background it is possible to partly revise the claim made above concerning the EU as a structure which de-politicises the policy areas which are being integrated. One can only come to such a conclusion on the basis of an uncritical transmission of a nation-state vision of politics to the EU realm,[67] or through an insistence on 'radical democracy' as the normative standard from which one starts.[68] Instead, the EU's political system must be seen as a structure which only tentatively relies on the classical modern distinction between state and society (*Staat und Gesellschaft*) and hence as a structure which does not describe itself as a political system that assumes a superior role vis-à-vis other functional systems. It must be understood as a radical modern structure because it is the political subsystem where the general tendency towards the erosion of the (imagined) primacy of the political system is most evident. As already stated, this does not mean the end of politics, however, but merely a change in the substantial function and status of politics. Such a change of status and substantial function means that the majority of EU decisions do not provide a structural basis that can facilitate the development of political narratives capable of reflecting society as a whole at the level of self-description. Consequently, the reference to the concept of the 'people' which guides the direction of decision making within democratic nation states has proved to be a too general a parameter for EU decisions. Instead the concept of 'stakeholders', defined as affected parties operating within a

[65] That is, for example, the case within areas such as consumer policy, environmental policy, competition policy and food safety.

[66] U Haltern, 'Internationales Verfassungsrecht? Anmerkungen zu einer kopernikanischen Wende' (2003) 128 *Archiv des öffentlichen Rechts* 511.

[67] M Zürn, 'Politik in der postnationalen Konstellation. Über das Elend des methodologischen Nationalismus' in C Landfried (Hrsg), *Politik in einer entgrenzten Welt. 21. wissenschaftlicher Kongreß der Deutschen Vereinigung für Politischen Wissenchaft* (Köln, Verlag Wissenschaft und Politik, 2001).

[68] Eg R Schmalz-Bruns, 'Deliberativer Supranationalismus' (1998) 6 *Zeitschrift für Internationale Beziehungen* 185.

formalised institutional framework, has emerged as the functional equivalent to the concept of 'the people' in the EU context. Substitution of the concept of 'the people' with a concept of 'stakeholders' highlights the partiality of EU policies. On the one hand, this partiality means that EU politics are radical anti-totalitarian in nature. On the other hand, the price paid is systematic vagueness as it remains unclear who the binding decisions made within the EU's political system are oriented against.[69]

[69] R Stichweh, *Inklusion und Exklusion. Studien zur Gesellschaftstheorie* (Bielefeld, Transcript Verlag, 2005) 78.

3

The Emergence of Governance

3.1 INTRODUCTION

HOW HAVE GS emerged? In order to answer this question the focus on the overall societal context analysed in the previous chapter should be complemented by a focus on the institutional level. The central feature of the EU remains its integrationist logic. The basis for continued reproduction of this logic is the concept of institutional balance (IB), which is closer to early modern constitutional concepts of mixed government than modern concepts of a functional separation of powers. The EU's reliance on the concept of IB means that its institutional structure assumes an organic character. Consequently, the EU is internally an 'under-differentiated' entity, as is also evident in the subordination of the rationalities of law, politics and bureaucracy to the logic of integration. This is paradoxical given that the EU's function vis-à-vis society as a whole is the expansion of functional differentiation.

As a result of this internal under-differentiation, the EU is characterised by a low level of division of labour, limited cognitive resources and high decisional costs. This is especially the case in relation to implementation and compliance where a permanent imbalance between functions and capacities can be observed. It is this functional imbalance which has created the basis for a logic of 'decisional outsourcing' to institutional structures lying outside the CIS. This development is illustrated through a reconstruction of the overall developments that led to the emergence of Comitology, agencies, and the OMC. This chapter also contains a strong descriptive element as it provides an overview of the evolution of these three forms of governance as well as a description of the various sub-forms which have emerged within them.

3.2 CONCEPTS OF SHARED AND SEPARATED POWERS

The constitutional concepts of shared and separated powers have traditionally mirrored the general structures of society, insofar as they have copied and acted like particularly dense forms of the structures of differentiation that characterise society as a whole. The evolution of the concepts of shared and separated powers from the early modern period on can thus be seen as providing a particularly clear reflection of the broader societal processes that transformed Europe from a stratified to a largely functionally differentiated region. Mixed government, representing a further development of medieval structures, achieved a relatively well-defined constitutional form in 17th-century England and its first precise theoretical basis in the writings of Locke (1632–1704).[1] The concept was based on a mixture of monarchy, aristocracy and democracy, and the objective was to ensure that the stakeholders in society *jointly* shared the functions of government, in order to prevent a single interest from imposing its will. The concept of mixed government can be seen as a transitory concept which on the one hand is feudal, but at the same time offered a response to the rise of functional differentiation and its side effects, as it provided a solution to the problem of maintaining an integrated society within the context of increased functional differentiation. Accordingly, early-modern constitutional structures can be regarded as constructions which were intended to establish unity by framing society as a whole. But constitutions were also intended to ensure a negative limitation of power in order to avoid tyranny. Hence, early-modern constitutional structures promoted a 'brute' form of power sharing aimed essentially at curtailing power by establishing obstacles to its exercise through mechanisms that increased the costs of decision making. In 17th-century England major decisions were therefore conditioned by a steady flow of 'pay-offs', which ensured that the royal executive could only get a limited number of its priorities approved and only by granting advantages to the lower classes.

The concept of mixed government, as developed by Locke, provided the major source of inspiration for Montesquieu (1689–1755), who updated the Lockean insights and adjusted the theory of mixed government to the French context. Consequently, Montesquieu's constitutional theory is, although often referred to as exactly that, not a theory about the separation of powers (*séparation des pouvoirs*) but instead a theory about the distribution of powers (*distribution des pouvoirs*).[2] Montesquieu wrote prior to the French Revolution in a period when the road to modernity was prepared, although no breakthrough had yet occurred. Consequently, his theory remains based on a feudal worldview to the extent that he assumes society is an organism or a holistic entity which is divided into a number of sub-units. This view is in stark contrast to the modern world view, as

[1] In particular J Locke, *Two Treatises of Government* (Cambridge, Cambridge University Press, [1690] 1967); see also JGA Pocock, *The Ancient Constitution and the Feudal Law: A Study of English Historical Thought in the Seventeenth Century* (Cambridge, Cambridge University Press, [1957] 1987).

[2] A Riklin, 'Was Montesquieu noch nicht wissen konnte. Überlegungen zur Revision der Gewaltenteilungslehre' (2006) *Ancilla Iuris* 20.

developed by Kant half a century later for example, according to which society is as anything but a holistic entity. Instead Kant presents the view, which has been taken to its extreme within modern systems theory, that each of the functionally differentiated spheres of society is larger than the sum of those spheres.[3] Thus, Montesquieu's theory is, like Locke's, characterised by a mixture of feudal and modern concepts. On the one hand, he introduces a separation between the legislative, executive and juridical powers. On the other hand, he attributes this *Trias Politica* structure to institutions representing three distinctive social groups: the bourgeoisie, the monarchy and the aristocracy. These institutions thus remain feudal in the sense that they are defined on the basis of stratificatory as opposed to functional differentiation. Moreover, as a consequence of his limited objectives and as a direct result of his pre-modern holistic approach Montesquieu granted the monarchy, representing executive power, a role in legislative power as well. The bi-cameral parliament, in which the two chambers were respectively intended to represent the bourgeoisie and the aristocracy, and which had its main prerogatives within the sphere of the legislative branch, also received a share of the executive power. The second chamber, representing the aristocracy, also acted as a court. Consequently, his theory remains a theory of mixed government (*gouvernement mêlé*) based upon a mixed constitution (*Mischverfassung*) and not a theory concerned with a separation of powers.[4] Montesquieu's theory of the *Trias Politica* is therefore not a democratic theory in the modern sense.[5] Instead the key objective remains early-modern as it is merely aimed at ensuring unity, at the same time as preventing tyranny through the dominance of one social group over others. However, this ambition falls short of the standards imposed by modern democratic theory from Kant onwards.[6]

Owing to their focus on power sharing between different social classes, Locke's and Montesquieu's concepts of mixed government differ substantially from a truly modern concept of a functional separation of powers. A modern constitutional concept of this kind was first developed by Kant

[3] H Baier, Soziologie als Aufklärung, oder die Vertreibung der Transzendenz aus der Gesellschaft (Konstanz, UVK Universitätsverlag Konstanz, 1998).

[4] CL de Secondat Montesquieu, *De l'Esprit des lois* (Paris, Gallimard, [1748] 1995) V/14, XI/6, XI/7, XI/14, XI/18, XI/20, XII/ 1. See also A Riklin, 'Was Montesquieu noch nicht wissen konnte. Überlegungen zur Revision der Gewaltenteilungslehre' (2006) *Ancilla Iuris* 20.

[5] Lenaerts and Verhoeven, for example, seem to assume that Montesquieu's theory is a democratic theory. See K Lenaerts and A Verhoeven, 'Institutional Balance as a Guarantee for Democracy in EU Governance' in C Joerges and R Dehousse (eds), *Good Governance in Europe's Integrated Market* (Oxford, Oxford University Press, 2002).

[6] For an elegant reconstruction of Kant's theory of democracy see I Maus, *Zur Aufklärung der Demokratietheorie. Rechts- und demokratietheoretische Überlegungen im Anschluß an Kant* (Frankfurt am Main, Suhrkamp Verlag, 1994).

and Sieyès (1748–1836).[7] The basic insight of the separation of powers approach is that a specific institution is developed as a response to the handling of a specific function, which then is monopolised by that institution. This permits the establishment of a separation of powers based on a distinction between legislative, executive and juridical branches. These separated powers mirror the functionally differentiated structure of the society to which they correspond and are therefore released from the stratified social classes on which Locke and Montesquieu based their theories.[8] The concept of a functional separation of powers is a far more progressive 'double-edged' structure, aimed not only at ensuring a negative limitation of power through shared government. Instead the foundational element is the simultaneous facilitation and restraint of power through their mutual increase (*Gegenseitiges Steigerungsverhältnis*), in a manner which ideally overcomes the discrepancies between autonomy and interdependency. Consequently, and in contrast to the early modern concepts, the functional separation of powers does not necessarily imply that the limitation and strengthening of power structures must be understood as mutually exclusive objectives. A clear functional differentiation of powers between branches of government, as opposed to a sharing of power between institutions, should therefore strengthen conditions of possibility (*Möglickeitsbedingungen*) that may permit dynamic institutional innovation and adaptation. In the same way, an increased division of labour between branches of government on the basis of functional criteria should increase the processing capacities of the respective branches. *In principle*, the functional separation of powers therefore provides the political and legal systems with a far higher level of decisional capacity, thereby allowing functional needs for political decision making and legal regulation to be channelled into and processed by the institutional context formed by the interlocking relationship of the three branches of power.

In contrast to the concept of mixed government, the modern concept of a functional separation of powers remains an analytical one which has never been applied in its pure form. Instead, and most notably in the constitution of the United States, the concept of a functional separation of powers has been combined with a third element, which is the idea of *checks and balances*. The concept of checks and balances re-introduces the idea of shared powers—albeit without a basis in distinctive social groups—as an attachment to a fundamentally functionally differentiated

[7] A Riklin, *Machtteilung – Geschichte der Mischverfassung* (Darmstadt, Wissenschaftliche Buchgesellschaft, 2005) 269 *ff*.

[8] I Kant, *Die Metaphysik der Sitten* (Stuttgart, Reclam, [1797] 1990) §§ 45, 46 and 49.

structure.[9] Examples of checks and balances in the US constitution are, for example, the prerogative of the president to veto legislative proposals and the duty of the Senate to approve departmental appointments.

As already stated, the evolution described here from mixed government to a functional differentiation of powers, partly limited through checks and balances, can be understood as a symptom of the general transformation of society from a primarily stratified to a primarily functionally differentiated society. This process has resulted in increased differentiation between the functional systems of law and politics, as well as in growing internal differentiation between the legislative and executive dimensions of the political system, combined with greater differentiation between the political and administrative dimensions of the executive body. This development has been conditioned by the evolution of modern constitutional structures, acting as structural couplings between the two differentiated (*Auzdifferenzierte*) systems of law and politics and the different dimensions within the political system. In other words, the development of modern constitutions can also be seen as a direct result of the transformation of society from stratified to being largely functionally differentiated.[10]

3.3 POWER SHARING IN THE EU

In *Köster* the ECJ explicitly recognised the concept of IB as a central constitutional feature of the Community.[11] In the literature this concept is often considered identical to that of a functional separation of powers,[12] just as the basis of this theory is often considered to be Montesquieu's *Trias*

[9] The ideal types presented here must of course be somewhat relative depending on the specific periods and contexts. For further reading see E Klimowsky, 'Die englische Gewaltenteilungslehre bis zu Montesquieu' (1927) *Archiv für Rechts- und Wirtschaftsphilosophie, Beiheft* 22; WB Gwyn, *The Meaning of the Separation of Powers* (The Hague, Martinus Nijhoff, 1965); MJC Vile, *Constitutionalism and the Separation of Powers* (Oxford, Clarendon Press, 1967) especially 25 *ff*; M Rostock, *Die Lehre von der Gewaltenteilung in der politischen Theorie von John Locke* (Meisenheim, Anton Hain, 1974); H Fenske, 'Gewaltenteilung', in O Brunner, W Conze and R Koselleck (Hrsg), *Geschichtliche Grundbegriffe. Historisches Lexikon zur politisch-sozialen Sprache in Deutschland*, *Bd.* 2 (Stuttgart, Klett-Cotta Verlag, 1975); T Koopmans, 'The Birth of European Law at the Crossroads of Legal Traditions' (1991) 39 *American Journal of Comparative Law* 493; M Stolleis, 'Das "europäische Haus" und seine Verfassung' (1995) 78 *Kritische Vierteljahresschrift für Gesetzgebung und Rechtswissenschaft* 275.

[10] N Luhmann, 'Verfassung als evolutionäre Errungenschaft' (1990) 9 *Rechtshistorisches Journal* 176.

[11] *Einfuhrstelle v Köster*, Case No C-25/70 [1970] ECR 1161, 6.

[12] Eg G Haibach, 'Separation and Delegation of Legislative Powers: A Comparative Analysis' in M Andenas and A Türk (eds), *Delegated Legislation and the Role of Committees in the EC* (The Hague, Kluwer, 2000).

Politica.[13] Bearing in mind the two ideal models—mixed government and functional separation of powers—such views can, however, be dismissed as they are based upon a superficial understanding of the concepts. In the EU legislative power is divided between the Commission, the Council and the EP; executive power is divided between the Commission, the Council and the MS; and juridical power is divided between the ECJ, the Court of First Instance (CFI) and the MS courts. Not surprisingly, Lenaerts therefore concludes that 'it simply appears impossible to characterize the several Community institutions as holders of one or the other power since a close analysis of their prerogatives does not indicate a clear-cut line between legislative and the executive branches of the Community government'.[14] Hence, it is futile to claim that the EU is characterised by a functional separation of powers, since none of the institutions monopolises a single function.[15] On the other hand, this does not mean that the functional features of the legislative, executive and juridical forms of communication cannot be identified in relation to the EU. But the functional features are not attached to specific institutions, and it is exactly this lack of attachment of different forms of communication to corresponding organisational structures which makes the existing order different from the vision embodied in the modern concept of a functional separation of powers.

But as pointed out by Majone,[16] Montesquieu's theory does indeed have relevance for the EU, although for reasons that are the opposite of those normally assumed in the literature. Majone argues that the EU is based upon a mixed constitution which bears a striking resemblance to the form of mixed government promoted by Montesquieu, since the main political-administrative institutions *jointly* share decisional and executive powers. Moreover, a fundamental principle of the Community is the principle of institutional autonomy which resembles the autonomy of the 'estates' in the early-modern period, just as the principle of loyal co-operation was an important feature of early-modern mixed polities as well as of the EU today.[17] To these three features one can furthermore add the central importance of the commissioners' office. Not only does the function

[13] Eg K Lenaerts and A Verhoeven, 'Institutional Balance as a Guarantee for Democracy in EU Governance' in C Joerges and R Dehousse (eds), *Good Governance in Europe's Integrated Market*, (Oxford, Oxford University Press, 2002).

[14] K Lenaerts, 'Some Reflections on the Separation of Powers in the European Community' (1990) 28 *Common Market Law Review* 11, 13.

[15] That the Community is not based on a concept of functional separation of powers has also been recognised by the ECJ. See Joined Cases 188 to 190/80, *France, Italy and United Kingdom v Commission* [1982], ECR 2545, 2573. See also G Haibach, 'Comitology after Amsterdam: A Comparative Analysis of the Delegation of Legislative Powers' (1997) 3 *EIPASCOPE* 1.

[16] G Majone, 'Delegation of Regulatory Powers in a Mixed Polity' (2002) 8 (3) *European Law Journal* 319.

[17] *Ibid*.

performed by the commissioners prevent a clear distinction between the political and administrative dimensions of the executive branch, but the very concept of a commissioner is also a distinctively early modern phenomenon. As pointed out by Riekmann, the function of the commissioners' office in the construction of the nation states was, moreover, similar to the function exercised by contemporary European commissioners in the construction of Europe.[18]

The above description of the EU as largely characterised by an 'early-modern' form of power sharing, where the Commission, the Council and the EP respectively seem to fulfil the role of the King, the Lords and the Commons, helps explain the integrationist bias of EU policies. This is because power sharing gives the EU an organic character which is oriented towards establishing unity through the suppression of centrifugal tendencies.[19] In principle, the IB ensures that all stakeholders have a say in the decision-making processes. Hence, the quest for increased integration not only provides a regulatory principle for the EU's policy programmes: integration is also the meta-norm through which the internal unity of the EU universe is established, given that the logic of integration is the mechanism through which cohesion between the legal, political and administrative dimensions of the EU structure is created and continuously reaffirmed.

The price paid for such unity is substantial, however, as power sharing implies that several institutional actors possess the possibility of blocking decision making. Not surprisingly, this has led to the development of a complex system of pay-offs, which are introduced in order to get priorities approved. For example, the CAP was developed as a pay-off to France to guarantee it would accept liberalisation of the market for industrial goods as advocated by Germany.[20] The introduction of the SEA was, moreover, conditioned by the increased introduction of regional and social funds, which served as a system of pay-offs to economically less advanced countries such as Greece, Ireland, Portugal and Spain in the 1980s and 1990s and the Central and Eastern European countries (CEEC) today. This

[18] SP Riekmann, *Die kommissarische Neuordnung Europas. Das Dispositiv der Integration* (Wien, Springer Verlag, 1998). For a historical account of the function of the Commissioners' office see also O Hintze, 'Der Commissarius und seine Bedeutung in der allgemeinen Verwaltungsgeschichte. Eine vergleichende Studie' in O Hintze, *Beamtentum und Bürokratie* (Göttingen, Vandenhoeck & Ruprecht, [1910] 1981).

[19] The organic character of the Community was also acknowledged by Jacques Santer: 'The efficiency of the community method ... reflects the good cooperation and organic complementarity between the institutions' (my translation, PFK); J Santer, *L'avenir de l'Europe . . . Quel rôle pour la Commission? Eloge de la méthode communautaire* (1995) 20 October, European University Institute, Jean Monnet Lecture. Also quoted in G Haibach, 'The History of Comitology' in M Andenas and A Türk (eds), *Delegated Legislation and the Role of Committees in the EC* (The Hague, Kluwer, 2000) 215.

[20] A Moravcsik, *The Choice for Europe: Social Purpose and State Power from Messina to Maastricht* (Ithaca, Cornell University Press, 1998) 159.

also explains why the EU has never confined itself to the role of a 'regulatory state', as advocated by Majone.[21] The reason is that the EU's institutional setting creates a structural frame within which the exercise of regulatory functions is conditioned by the ability, using redistributive policies, to 'bribe' institutional actors who are able to block decision making, and who are most likely to experience a sub-optimal outcome from common regulatory approaches.[22] In terms of policy outcome, strong reliance on mixed government features, which are merely oriented towards the establishment of negative limitations on the exercise of power, also explains the strong orientation towards 'conservation' which characterises policies such as the CAP and the Common Fisheries Policy (CFP). Not only have these policies proved inherently difficult to reform but they also seem to be defended by the Commission for the sole reason that they embody the idea of almost complete integration.[23]

In contrast to the above perspective, gradual expansion of the co-decision procedure and the rise of the EP could be interpreted as a tentative move towards the establishment of a federal two-chamber system with the Council and the EP as the central players. Such a development can, moreover, be interpreted as a first step towards a clearer functional differentiation of powers.[24] But the rise of the EP, increasingly acting on an equal footing with the Commission and the Council, has also augmented the complexity of the institutional setting and reinforced the character of the EU as a structure where all representative institutions have a say in all decisions. This development is, moreover, strengthened by the rise of the European Council, which today shares de facto the right to initiate legislation with the Commission. Consequently, the Community Method (CM) and especially the co-decision variant, acting as the central and most mature element of the EU's legislative structure, might increasingly resemble the constitutional structures of political systems in the nation-state form. Meanwhile, new institutional forms and procedures, which reinforce the characteristics of the EU as an integrationist structure based upon shared powers, continue to emerge.

[21] G Majone, *Regulating Europe* (London, Routledge, 1996). For a critique of Majone in relation to the issue of regulatory and distributive policies see A Follesdal and S Hix, 'Why there is a Democratic Deficit in the EU: A Response to Majone and Moravcsik' (2005) 44 (3) *Journal of Common Market Studies* 533.

[22] See also K Lenaerts, 'Some Reflections on the Separation of Powers in the European Community' (1990) 28 *Common Market Law Review* 11; XA Yataganas, 'The Treaty of Nice. The Sharing Power and Institutional Balance in the European Union – A Continental Perspective' (2001) 1 *Jean Monnet Working Papers*.

[23] These policy areas are probably the only ones where it is possible to apply a concept of 'integrated administrations' in the sense of Hofmann and Türk. See HCH Hofmann and A Türk, 'The Development of Integrated Administration in the EU and its Consequences' (2007) 13 (2) *European Law Journal* 253.

[24] Eg XA Yataganas, 'Delegation of Regulatory Authority in the European Union. The Relevance of the American Model of Independent Agencies' (2001) 3 *Jean Monnet Working Papers* 11 *ff*.

Hence, the EU's institutional development seems to be characterised by a contradictory dual movement whereby the characteristics of power sharing expand continuously while, at the same time, tentative moves towards a clearer functional separation of powers can be observed within the most mature areas of the institutional setting. As analysed by Majone, this tension between shared powers and the tentative move towards a more functionally delineated system also explains the contradictory position of the Commission in relation to institutional reform. On the one hand, in principle the Commission supports the move towards transforming the institutional structures of the EU on the basis of a modern concept of separated powers[25] because its regulatory objective remains the transformation of the EU into some sort of state. On the other hand, it tends to defend the concept of IB as a central safeguard for its own prerogatives, even though this concept runs counter to the ambition of transforming the EU into a structure resembling modern nation states.[26] With these contradictory developments in mind it is therefore not surprising that the 'expanding universe' of the EU seems to be 'stumbling along', as its contradictory 'early-modern' and 'modern' features both seem to be strengthened, thereby creating a setting characterised by constant internal tensions between the two dimensions.

The frequent attempts to compare the development of the EU with the American experience[27] are, moreover, of limited value, since the EU's constitutional structure is precisely the opposite to that of the US constitution.[28] As already mentioned, the US constitution is based on a functional separation of branches, limited by various check and balance mechanisms, which has been placed 'on top' of the functionally differentiated basis. In contrast, the EU's basic structure is characterised by power sharing, while elements that work towards functional separation have emerged within this structure.

[25] Eg in the Commission White Paper on Governance; Commission of the European Communities: *European Governance. A White Paper*, 428 final, 2001, 34 *ff*.

[26] G Majone, *Dilemmas of European Integration. The Ambiguities & Pitfalls of Integration by Stealth* (Oxford, Oxford University Press, 2005) 53 *ff*.

[27] Eg J Habermas, 'Why Europe Needs a Constitution' (2001) 1 *New Left Review* 5; XA Yataganas, 'Delegation of Regulatory Authority in the European Union. The Relevance of the American Model of Independent Agencies' (2001) 3 *Jean Monnet Working Papers*.

[28] For a 'Madison v Montesquieu' analysis see S Smismans, 'Institutional Balance as Interest Representation: some reflections on Lenaerts and Verhoeven' in C Joerges and R Dehousse (eds), *Governance in Europe's Integrated Market* (Oxford, Oxford University Press, 2002).

3.4 DECISIONAL OUTSOURCING

As already mentioned, from an early-modern perspective, constitutional structures can be conceptualised as 'frames' which enclose society as a whole. Needless to say, the EU is far from providing such a framework for Europe as a whole. Rather, the concept of IB acts as a skeleton which ensures the unity of the EU's own legal order and hence the EU's own universe, but not the legal orders of the MS. Hence, the skeleton metaphor implies that the constitutional structure of the EU is less than a frame but more than a mere structural coupling between law and politics. This skeleton-like structure means that the EU has a somewhat static character. Although the rise of the EP has introduced a major qualitative change in the EU's functioning, the fundamental principles guiding its operational mode have only been marginally changed over the years, since the concept of IB remains the basis of its infrastructure. Moreover, the Commission, Council and the ECJ have essentially retained the structure which was developed by the merger of the Communities in 1967. These relatively limited changes are surprising when one takes stock of the massive expansion in the EU's integrative activities over the years.[29] The concept of IB, which was originally imposed by the MS in order to secure the operability of a functionally based international organisation with limited responsibilities, has therefore become a straightjacket, increasingly acting as a hindrance for institutional adaptation of the CIS to the massive expansion of policy activities which has taken place over the years. Moreover, since the main characteristic of modern society is functional differentiation, the reliance on power sharing means that the EU goes 'against the world' instead of reflecting the functionally differentiated structures of the society from which it has developed. In an institutional sense the EU is therefore a holistic phenomenon which operates in an increasingly de-holistic world. Hence, a fundamental discrepancy exists between the EU's archaic 'pre-modern' institutional structure and the mainly risk-regulatory function it fulfils within a radically modern world.

It is against this background that the emergence of GS must be understood since their spontaneous emergence can be described as responses to functional needs related to the handling of increased social complexity. Social complexity can be defined as a paradoxical unity of multiplicity, which implies an imperative need for selection in the sense that not all elements of a given social structure can relate to all other elements of that structure at the same time.[30]

[29] Eg David Coombes' classic study of the Commission still seems remarkably up to date. See D Coombes, *Politics and Bureaucracy in the European Community. A Portrait of the Commission of the EEC* (London, George Allen and Unwin, 1970).

[30] N Luhmann, *Soziale Systeme. Grundriß einer allgemeinen Theorie* (Frankfurt am Main, Suhrkamp Verlag, 1984) 46 *ff*; N Luhmann, *Die Gesellschaft der Gesellschaft* (Frankfurt am

With the continued expansion and deepening of EU policy areas, the workload and resources needed to manage EU policies grew steadily from the 1960s onwards. Given this background, decisional outsourcing to GS can be seen simply as a response to a fundamental asymmetry between the functional demands for European actions and the capability to accommodate these demands within the under-differentiated structure of the EU. Hence, the capacity deficit of the EU has led to the mobilisation of additional resources from outside the existing institutions through GS.

This capacity deficit has three dimensions. First, the EU is characterised by a low level of cognitive resources meaning that it has few instruments which can be deployed 'in the field' or 'on the ground'. This has consequences for information gathering and the ability to react. Valid information about how societal processes develop, potentially the subject of integrative measures through regulation, and a clear picture of problems and obstacles, is vital for establishing and justifying regulative measures. In order to access and process such information the EU has been forced to link up with both national administrations, typically possessing a far higher level of resources and a clearer and more updated picture of concrete issues and problems within their own jurisdictions, and with private actors. As regards the latter it is therefore not surprising that lobbying in the EU context is far from a one-way exercise, since the influence of private actors on EU decisions is conditioned by their ability to provide relevant information to EU institutions which would otherwise be unable to access this information. Hence, the private actors fulfil a functional need which EU institutions are not capable of handling themselves. This also explains why lobbying plays a relatively important role in the EU when compared to the situation in the MS, since MS administrations have larger resources and hence less need to compensate for information deficits through alliances with private actors.

Secondly, the lack of control mechanisms is another characteristic element of the EU. The absence of a Napoleonic system of prefects means that the EU is forced to rely on MS administrations to ensure implementation and compliance. This functional need provides EU institutions with an incitement to establish institutionalised and stable relations with MS administrations in order to ensure that they implement EU law and guarantee compliance.[31]

Main, Suhrkamp Verlag, 1997) 136 *ff*. For the relationship between law and functional differentiation see N Luhmann, *Ausdifferenzierung des Rechts. Beiträge zur Rechtssoziologie und Rechtstheorie* (Frankfurt am Main, Suhrkamp Verlag, 1981) 42 *ff* and 366 *ff* as well as N Luhmann, *Das Recht der Gesellschaft* (Frankfurt am Main, Suhrkamp Verlag, 1993) 112 *ff*.

[31] J Neyer and M Zürn, 'Conclusions. The Conditions of Compliance' in M Zürn and C Joerges (eds), *Governance and Law in Postnational Constellations. Compliance in Europe and Beyond* (Cambridge, Cambridge University Press, 2005).

Thirdly, the relatively strong limitations on EU competencies, and therefore on possible EU action regarding treaties, provide the EU with an incentive to promote the development of GS. This is because these structures can potentially be used to circumvent the cumbersome decision-making procedures of the CM and extend the EU's integration activities beyond the scope of the treaties.

In addition to these three factors, delegation of discretionary power to independent regulators has also been seen as a way of guaranteeing policy credibility. As we will see in more detail in Chapter 5 when assessing Majone's theory of delegation, the question of policy credibility is essentially a problem of time since a contradiction exists between short-term political interests and the functional need for ensuring long-term solutions to functional problems. Accordingly, delegation of discretionary powers to independent institutions can be understood as a strategy aimed at minimising this trade-off.

Bearing in mind these reasons for delegation, it is plausible to argue that GS are reflexive structures, nurtured by the EU in order to off-set its structural deficits. The conditions for the successful establishment of such structures are, however, the existence of 'mutual interests' between the institutions and actors involved.[32] The EU is therefore bound to pay a price when it seeks to off-set its own deficiencies through GS, for example in the form of the heavy influence exercised by MS administrations and private actors on the outcome of EU decision making, or by losing competencies to regulatory agencies.

In order to diminish this trade-off between mobilising external resources and safeguarding its own autonomy, the EU, and most notably the Commission, have deliberately sought to frame their mutual interests in a manner which is supportive of their pro-integrative policy agenda. Consequently they have sought to Europeanise the external actors in question, through, for example, a systematic preference for engaging with pan-European trade associations and lobby groups rather than with nationally organised associations. This preference has provided the European associations with a major argument in favour of stronger pan-European and Brussels-based structures, capable of closer collaboration with the Commission in the constant competence clashes between European and national associations.[33] The Commission has, moreover, supported the development of pan-European networks of MS administrations, as is particularly obvious within the area of Comitology and the 'networked' agencies.

[32] For the relation between resource dependency and the 'logic of access' see P Bouwen, 'A Theoretical and Empirical Study of Corporate Lobbying in the European Parliament' (2003), 7 (11) *European Integration online Papers (EIoP)* 2.

[33] The difference in access between national and European associations is, however, substantially less in relation to the EP. See *ibid.*

Such forms of Europeanisation are only possible because there is a functional need which creates an environment within which the Europeanisation strategy, consciously developed by the Commission, can flourish. When such functional needs emerge, the MS are faced with limited alternatives. They can either support reforms of the CIS and the CM in order to accommodate these needs within the EU's traditional governing structures, as the continued treaty revision processes partly do, or they can support the outsourcing of decisions to various forms of GS such as Comitology, agencies and the OMC. A third option is for the MS to take an 'unreflexive' approach and insist on their prerogatives by refusing common European policies. As previously indicated, the MS are thereby opening the door to the emergence of informal regulative structures capable of ensuring that functional needs for regulation and coordination are fulfilled. An example of such informal structures are the European Electricity Regulation Forum, also known as the Florence Process, which brings together national electricity regulators, national competition authorities, market actors, academic experts, consumer groups and Commission officials for informal consultations, in order to draft guidelines and policy proposals and to ensure that national regulations do not establish barriers to the IM. As illustrated by the 2003 electricity directive and the 2003 Regulation on cross-border trade in electricity,[34] such informal structures tend, however, to be (at least partially) formalised at a later stage,[35] thereby illustrating the earlier observation that MS might be able to slow down the speed of Europeanisation but are rarely capable of bringing the process to a halt.[36]

The term 'decisional outsourcing' implies that we are dealing with more than just a formal delegation of competencies. For example, the OMC implies Europeanisation of the policy areas where it is applied, although no formal delegation of competencies is taking place. But also in relation to Comitology and agencies, where formal delegation of competencies does take place, decisional outsourcing implies that delegation is more than just delegation. Instead each delegation of legal competencies implies a de facto recognition of the autonomy of the structures to which competencies are delegated. Some forms of GS – most notably within Comitology – exercise significant discretionary powers. GS, moreover, tend to frame policy areas in a manner which produces a limited number of options for further policy

[34] Directive 2003/54/EC and Regulation (EC) 1228/2003.

[35] B Eberlein, 'Formal and Informal Governance in Single Market Regulation' in T Christiansen and S Piattoni (eds), *Informal Governance in the EU* (Cheltenham, Edward Elgar, 2004); CF Sabel and J Zeitlin, 'Learning from Difference: The New Architecture of Experimentalist Governance in the European Union' (2006) 18 *La Follette School Working Paper* 16 *ff*.

[36] Another example is the Madrid Process, where gas regulators and their stakeholders meet within a forum exercising the same function as the Florence Process does for electricity.

development, because significant choices are made in the initial phases of policy development. They also tend to develop specific norms and become policy actors in their own right. Moreover, delegation of competencies is always a step into the unknown and the uncontrollable, which potentially can release forces that possess surprising viability, as is illustrated by the unintended expansion of Comitology from the 1960s onwards and the uncontrollable development of agencies and the OMC over the last decade. Accordingly, each act of delegation implies the potential release of forces that are beyond the control of MS and produce results to which the MS will have to react at a later date. In the European context, GS have, moreover, gained a degree of complexity which means that a complete withdrawal of the competencies delegated to GS would be de facto impossible without leading to the collapse of the EU system.

3.5 COMITOLOGY

In the early 1960s the Community began the task of fleshing out the detailed structure and harmonising the measures of the CAP.[37] The Council did not possess the resources needed to process such work, and was equally ill-equipped to carry out day-to-day management. The MS were, however, reluctant to delegate powers of implementation to the Commission. A temporary solution was found with the creation of the first management committees in 1962, consisting of MS representatives who were charged with issuing opinions on implementing measures proposed by the Commission. The Commission was granted the possibility of overriding the committees when a qualified majority vote (QMV) resulted in a negative opinion. In such cases the issue would, however, be referred to the Council, which could then alter the decision within a specified time limit. Through the 1960s the number of management committees grew steadily and in

[37] For different overviews of the evolution of Comitology see C Demmke, E Eberharter, GF Schaefer and A Türk, 'The History of Comitology' in RH Pedler and GF Schaefer (eds), *Shaping European Law and Policy. The Role of Committees and Comitology in the Political Process* (Maastricht, European Institute of Public administration, 1996); E Vos, 'EU Committees: the Evolution of Unforeseen Institutional Actors in European Product Regulation' in C Joerges and E Vos (eds), *EU Committees: Social Regulation, Law and Politics* (Oxford, Hart Publishing, 1999); J Falke, 'Komitologie – Entwicklung, Rechtsgrundlagen und erste empirische Annährung' in C Joerges and J Falke (Hrsg), *Das Ausschußwesen der Europäischen Union. Praxis der Risikoregulierung im Binnenmarkt und ihre rechtliche Verfassung* (Baden-Baden, Nomos Verlag, 2000); G Haibach, 'The History of Comitology' in M Andenas and A Türk (eds), *Delegated Legislation and the Role of Committees in the EC* (The Hague, Kluwer, 2000); AE Töller, *Komitologie. Theoretische Bedeutung und praktische Funktionsweise von Durchführungsausschüssen der Europäischen Union am Beispiel der Umweltpolitik* (Opladen, Leske + Budrich, 2002) esp 231 *ff*; E Vos, 'The Role of Comitology in European Governance' in DM Curtain and RA Wessel (eds), *Good Governance and the European Union. Reflections on concepts, institutions and substance* (Antwerp, Intersentia, 2005).

1963 the first management committee outside the area of agriculture was established, dealing with development aid. In 1969 the committees were made permanent. Moreover, in 1968 a new variant occurred with the introduction of regulatory committees. The first regulatory committee dealt with customs policy and here the Commission was only permitted to implement measures that were positively approved by the committee by QMV. Should a majority be lacking, the issue would also be referred to the Council. However, the Commission maintained the right to implement the measure but only if the Council failed to take a positive decision on the issue within a given time frame. This procedure is also known as the *filet*-procedure (safety-net procedure). In relation to veterinary policy, food-stuffs and plant health yet another variant was introduced called the *contrefilet* procedure (double safety-net procedure). This procedure implied that the Council, by a simple majority vote, could prevent the Commission from adopting a measure, even if the Council failed to make a positive decision.

Although heavily criticised by the EP, which regarded it as a way of undermining its supervisory function vis-à-vis the Commission, the Comitology system underwent massive expansion during the 1970s and especially in the 1980s after the launch of the SEA. The background for this expansion was not only functional but also legal since the SEA determined that the Council *should* confer implementing competencies on the Commission.[38] This was a significant change and was in contrast to the earlier legal basis, which merely stated that the Council *could* confer complementary competencies to the Commission.[39] This provided the background for the *first Comitology decision* in 1987,[40] which established the existing structures and created three general procedures, combined with a number of exceptions:

(1) **The advisory committee procedure**, by which the Commission will be assisted by an advisory committee consisting of MS representatives but chaired by the Commission, which will be entitled to deliver its opinion on draft measures. The Commission will be obliged to take account of these opinions.

(2) **The management committee procedure**, which also foresees a committee chaired by the Commission and consisting of MS representatives. Under this procedure the Commission submits draft measures to the committee, whose opinion will be expressed by QMV. If the committee's opinion is not in line with the position of the Commission, the issue will be referred to the Council, which may formulate a different

[38] Treaty Establishing the European Community, Article 145.
[39] Treaty Establishing the European Community, Article 155.
[40] Council Decision 87/373/EEC of 13 July 1987.

position within a certain time limit. At this point two variants exist: (a) the Commission *can* choose to postpone the application of the proposed measure for a month and the Council, acting under QMV, is entitled to make a different decision within that period; (b) the Commission *must* postpone the application of measures for a maximum period of three months and the Council can, again by qualified majority vote, make a different decision within that time period.

(3) **The regulatory committee procedure** also foresees committees that consist of MS representatives under a Commission chair. The Commission will present draft measures to the committee, which will deliver its opinion on the basis of a qualified majority. Where the Committee is not in agreement with the Commission, or if no opinion is delivered by the Committee, the measure must be submitted to consideration by the Council. Again two options exist: (a) if the Council does not act within a specified period of time (maximum three months) on the basis of QMV the proposed measure can be adopted by the Commission; (b) the Council may act and change the decision within the given time frame on the basis of a simple majority.

Both the Commission and the EP expressed dissatisfaction with this outcome, especially because, when setting up committees related to the completion of the IM, the MS overwhelmingly opted for the most restrictive procedure, namely the second variant of the regulatory committee procedure. The EP continuously and successfully maintained pressure on the Council and the Commission in order to play a stronger supervisory role. As a result, with the Plumb–Delors agreement in 1988, the Commission committed itself to sending all Comitology proposals of a legislative nature to the EP at the same time as they were submitted to the Committees. Moreover with the Maastricht Treaty the EP achieved the status of an equal co-legislator with the Council within those policy areas falling under the new co-decision procedure. Accordingly, the EP achieved equal responsibility with the Council for delegating powers of implementation within these policy areas and thereby the opportunity of jointly deciding which variant of the Comitology procedure should be applied.

Following pressure from the Commission and the EP a *second Comitology decision* was adopted in 1999.[41] The new decision adopted criteria regarding which kind of committee procedure should be applied. The management procedure was reserved for measures related to the CAP and CFP as well as areas with substantial budgetary implications. The regulatory committee procedure was reserved for measures aimed at regulating the provisions of basic instruments, for example through technical standards, and the protection of human, animal and plant health. The advisory

[41] Council Decision 1999/468/EC of 28 June 1999.

procedure could be applied in all areas where it was deemed appropriate. The second Comitology decision changed the regulatory committee procedure so that the Council is no longer able to reject a proposal by a simple majority. The supervisory role of the EP was strengthened as the decision also foresees that it shall receive information regarding the proceedings of the committees on a regular basis (for example agendas, draft measures, voting results, summary records and lists of committee members and information on their organisational affiliation). The EP was entitled to express its disapproval of implementation measures which it considered to be in breach of the Council's and the Commission's powers. The second Comitology decision also strengthened the transparency of the proceedings since it clarified that the provisions for public access to documents applicable to the Commission also applied to Comitology committees, and a list of all committees was published.

In 2006 a *third Comitology decision* was adopted.[42] The major change introduced relates to the regulatory committees and the EP, as its right to supervise the Commission was strengthened. Hence, the procedure has also been dubbed the 'regulatory Comitology procedure with scrutiny'. But the third decision also strengthened the Commission insofar as the ability of the EP and the Council to oppose draft measures proposed by the Commission was made conditional to a justification of their opposition. In the same way, earlier use of time limits regarding the implementation of measures (so-called sunset clauses) will be phased out.[43]

In terms of expansion, the Comitology system has, as already mentioned, experienced constant growth since its emergence. In the early 1960s 10 committees were established. In the mid 1980s the number reached more than 200 and at the beginning of the new millennium the number exceeded 400.[44] This massive expansion reflects the increased complexity of the EU, due to the continued broadening and deepening of integration, which has made it increasingly difficult to process the workload within the CIS. In addition, as indicated, the Community institutions are faced with a structural deficit in terms of cognitive resources. The Commission in particular remains dependent on the possibility of mobilising external resources in terms of expert knowledge and information on the practicalities of implementation and harmonisation.

Although Comitology did circumvent the EP when originally established, this was not its main purpose since the EP at the time did not have the

[42] Council Decision 2006/512/EC of 17 July 2006.

[43] An important reason for the strengthening of the Commission seems to be the need to maintain efficiency after enlargement, thereby illustrating the connection between 'widening' and 'deepening' of the integration process stated earlier.

[44] E Töller, *Komitologie. Theoretische Bedeutung und praktische Funktionsweise von Durchführungsausschüssen der Europäischen Union am Beispiel der Umweltpolitik* (Opladen, Leske + Budrich, 2002) 313 *ff*.

competencies relevant to the implementation of legislation. Comitology does, however, circumvent institutional constraints to the extent that Comitology decisions would have to be transformed into legislative proposals if the Comitology system did not exist; consequently this would activate the Community's rather cumbersome legislative procedures. However, the question of ensuring policy credibility was not a major issue in relation to the emergence of Comitology. Instead, this issue mainly gained momentum as part of a criticism of the system due to the risk-regulation scandals in the late 1990s.

3.6 REGULATORY AGENCIES

Two agencies were established in 1975. In the early 1990s a second wave established further agencies and since then the number has expanded rapidly. Thirty community agencies are currently up and running. In addition, three other agencies have been established under the second pillar of the Union (CFSP) and three under the third pillar of the Union (PJCC).[45] The agencies are very different in nature but share a common basic structure insofar as they have a limited mandate and are equipped with a management board, with a majority of MS representatives, which develops the general guidelines, programmes and priorities. The Commission has no formal control over the agencies, with the exception of the so-called executive agencies, but can exercise influence through its representatives on the boards. All of the agencies are, moreover, assisted by one or more of the committees and are intended to perform tasks of a purely technical, scientific or managerial nature. In terms of functions, Yataganas identifies four types of agencies: (a) quasi-regulatory agencies aimed at administering the IM (for example CPVO, EFSA, EMEA and OHIM); (b) monitoring agencies (for example EEA, EMCDDA, FRA); (c) social dialogue agencies (CEDEFOP, EASHW, EUROFOUND), and (d) executive agencies (for example CdT, EAR, ETF).[46]

The two agencies established in the 1970s (CEDEFOP and EUROFOUND) are social dialogue agencies serving non-distributive social policy objectives and emerged as an attempt to substantiate the EU's social dimension without encroaching on MS competencies within the field of

[45] See annex for a complete list as of 2 July 2009. For an overview see also C Scott, 'Agencies for European Regulatory Governance: A Regimes Approach', in D Geradin, R Muñoz and N Petit (eds), *Regulation Through Agencies in the EU: A New Paradigm of European Governance* (Cheltenham, Edward Elgar, 2005).

[46] XA Yataganas, 'Delegation of Regulatory Authority in the European Union. The relevance of the American model of independent agencies' (2001) 3 *Jean Monnet Working Papers* 25 *ff*.

social policy.[47] The second wave was triggered by two developments: first, the finalisation of the IM in 1992, which created a massive demand for re-regulation at the European level. This could only be achieved through the mobilisation of additional resources and more detailed day-to-day management. Hence, the IM implied a massive increase in regulatory complexity which deepened the already existing gap between the resources of the Commission and the Council and the regulatory tasks which had been Europeanised. Since the issue of complexity was particularly apparent within policy areas related to the IM, it is not surprising that it was within this area that quasi-regulatory agencies were first established as they are largely aimed at producing technical assessments of a highly complex nature, to provide a basis for decision making within the CIS or Comitology. Besides increased complexity, the related problem of insufficient cognitive resources also played a major role in the establishment of agencies. This is especially, but not only, relevant for the monitoring agencies which have been established with the objective of organising information gathering and problem identification, thereby providing an informed basis for EU decision making as well as being a tool for increased coordination and learning between MS. The question of circumventing institutional constraints to decision making does not, however, seem to have played a major role in the establishment of agencies since the exercise of discretionary power has largely remained with the CIS and Comitology. Instead of regulatory agencies with discretionary power, the agencies dealing with regulatory tasks have become 'network secretariats' which provide the existing policy networks (especially Comitology) with information and also coordinate their day-to-day operations. Information sharing and network management are also important elements for the social dialogue agencies, whose central task is to provide and maintain platforms facilitating an ongoing exchange among the MS, European institutions and social partners on relevant issues. With the passing of time this function has, moreover, evolved into a broader and more proactive form of activity which has been labelled 'persuasive policy-making'.[48] The executive agencies have been established in order to carry out well-defined and usually rather technical tasks, such as the administration of EC programmes, which, because of their heavy use of resources, are difficult for the Commission to carry out.

Another reason for the establishment of agencies is the question of policy credibility or credible commitment. As mentioned, this issue is of particular relevance to risk regulation. One way to ensure policy credibility

[47] S Smismans, *Law, Legitimacy and European Governance. Functional Participation in Social Regulation* (Oxford, Oxford University Press, 2004) 255 *ff*.

[48] S Smismans, *Law, Legitimacy and European Governance. Functional Participation in Social Regulation* (Oxford, Oxford University Press, 2004) 105 *ff*.

is to increase the functional differentiation between risk assessment and risk management, with the former responsible for information gathering and scientific advice, and the latter for legislation and control. The establishment of the EMEA in 1993, when risk assessment was outsourced to the agency whereas risk management was largely retained within the CIS and the Comitology structure, can be interpreted as a desire to increase policy credibility. A weaker variant of the distinction between risk assessment and risk management also played a central role in the establishment of the European Food Safety Authority (EFSA) in 2002,[49] which was part of a more general attempt to overhaul the risk regulation structure in the food and foodstuffs sector.[50]

3.7 THE OPEN METHOD OF COORDINATION

The OMC was officially baptised by the European Council in Lisbon in 2000 and was presented as the central tool for realising the Lisbon agenda. Elements of this method, however, have a longer history within transnational governance. Benchmarking and evaluations, for example, have been central tools for the IMF and the OECD for decades.[51] In the EU context, structures resembling the OMC already emerged with the Broad Economic Policy Guidelines (BEPG), developed in order to coordinate the economic polices of the MS after ratification of the Maastricht Treaty in 1993.[52] Moreover, the strong focus on achieving fulfilment of the criteria established for entrance to the EMU created the impression that the EU was heedless of unemployment. Hence, the European Employment Strategy (EES) was launched in 1997 in order to show that the EU did indeed care about unemployment.[53] Given this background the method has been

[49] For a comparison of the institutional structure of EMEA and EFSA see S Krapohl, 'Credible Commitment in Non-Independent Regulatory Agencies: A Comparative Analysis of the European Agencies for Pharmaceuticals and Foodstuffs' (2004) 10 (5) *European Law Journal* 518.

[50] European Commission: 'White Paper on Food Safety', COM (1999), 719 final, 14 *ff*.

[51] A Schäfer, 'A New Form of Governance? Comparing the Open Method of Coordination to Multilateral Surveillance by the IMF and the OECD' (2005) 4 *MPIFG Working Papers*. It has, however, been pointed out that the 'political atmosphere' within which OMC processes are carried out are significantly different from the OECD setting insofar as the OECD largely remains an expert organisation. See N Noakson and K Jacobsson, 'The Production of Ideas and expert Knowledge in OECD. The OECD Jobs Strategy in contrast with the EU employment Strategy' (2003) 7 *SCORE Rapportserie*.

[52] The BEPG procedure, which is based on Article 99 of the Treaty, is as follows: on the basis of a Commission recommendation, the Council, by a qualified majority vote, produces draft BEPGs that are submitted to the European Council, which adopts a conclusion. On this basis the Council, again acting by QMV, adopts the relevant recommendations. The EP is informed of the recommendations.

[53] The procedure of the EES, on the basis of Articles 125–30, is as follows: the Commission proposes guidelines, which then are sent to hearing in a committee of MS and

dismissed as a mere policy scam consisting of nothing more than 'cheap talk'.[54] But within the last decade the OMC has gained a life of its own and expanded rapidly, and is now beginning to have a significant, although mostly indirect, impact. Today different versions of the OMC are applied within a wide range of policy areas.[55] Borrás and Jacobsson distinguish three main groupings:

(a) social policy (pensions and social inclusion) and research and technological development. A shared characteristic of these areas is that earlier attempts to transfer competencies from the MS to the EU have failed. Accordingly, the OMC was introduced as a substitute for increased competence transfer;
(b) policy areas where public involvement on the EU level is relatively new. This is the case for employment policy and policies related to the information society;
(c) policy areas which do not fall under the CM but possess strong interdependencies with other EU policy areas which are themselves subject to the CM. The prime example here is the coordination of the economic policies of the MS and their relation to EMU.[56]

These different versions of the OMC all rely on comparisons, evaluations, benchmarking and peer reviews as their main policy instruments. These instruments are seen as process-oriented tools whose substance is continuously revised via the incorporation of new knowledge and lessons learned. Consequently, deployment of these instruments is intended to foster policy experimentation and knowledge creation, flexibility and revisability of normative and policy standards. Furthermore the OMC aims to achieve

Commission officials, in the EP and among the social partners represented by the European Economic and Social Committee (EESC) and the Committee of the Regions (CoR). Subsequently the revised guidelines are forwarded to the Council, which will adopt them with qualified majority. If adopted the MS then develop national action plans which are reviewed by the Commission on a yearly basis. A joint report from the Commission and the Council on best practices is then produced and can lead to recommendations concerning specific actions for bad performers.

[54] D Chalmers and M Lodge, 'The Open Method of Co-ordination and the European Welfare State' (2003) 11 *ESRC Discussion paper*; S Borrás and B Greve, 'Concluding Remarks: New Method or Just Cheap Talk?' (2004) 11 (2) *Journal of European Public Policy* 329.

[55] Budgetary policy: Stability and Growth Pact, launched in 1997, based on Article 104. Macro-economic policy: BEPG, launched in 1993, based on Article 99. Employment policy: Luxembourg Process, launched in 1997, based on Articles 125–30. Social inclusion policy: launched in 2000, based on Articles 136–37 and 144. Pension reform: launched in 2001, based on Article 140. Information society: the eEurope action plan, launched in 2000, no direct treaty basis. Research and innovation: the European Research Area Plan, characterised as an OMC process since 2003, no direct treaty basis. See also S Borrás and K Jacobsson, 'The open method of co-ordination and new governance patterns in the EU' (2004) 11 (2) *Journal of European Public Policy* 185, 193 *f*.

[56] *Ibid*, 191.

the highest possible level of participation and diversity, as well as radical decentralisation.[57] In terms of substance the method is aimed at achieving increased coordination and, in the longer term, convergence of the policy regimes of the MS. In its pure form the method does not involve a formal transfer of competencies to the EU and is therefore often characterised as a 'soft mode of governance' or as an example of 'soft law'.[58] The legal basis is, however, stronger in some areas than others and hence 'the shadow of hierarchy' is longer in some policy areas than in others. The Stability and Growth Pact (SGP) has a clear legal basis whereas the OMC in the information society and research and innovation areas has no direct legal basis. Moreover, the SGP envisages the imposition of sanctions in the sense that MS with excessive budget deficits can be fined. In the other versions of the OMC, however, peer pressure and public 'shaming' remain the only ways to impose adjustments. Policy recommendations under the SGP, the BEPG and the EES are decided upon by QMV. In the remaining areas unanimity applies.

After the 're-launch' of the Lisbon Process in 2005, on the basis of the recommendations of the Wim Kok report[59] the various versions of the OMC were all officially integrated under the Lisbon umbrella and became subject to the policy objectives of the Lisbon Process, with its focus on competitiveness through increased innovation, and social cohesion through higher employment rates. This does not, however, explain why the OMC emerged as the institutional response. One reason is that the policy areas where the OMC is applied tend to be characterised by substantial divergences in their organisation across the MS; this is especially true within the area of welfare policies and higher education. Additionally, within national political discourses the specific way in which these policy areas are organised, and the policy objectives they embody, are often considered to represent the inner core of MS national identities, and as expressing essential characteristics of those nations. Such idealised views can of course be easily dismissed by observing that the different welfare systems of European nation states are evolutionary phenomena resulting from contingent and uncontrollable processes.[60] In terms of political realities, nationally embedded welfare regimes are, however, linked to

[57] For the link between the OMC and the Lisbon Process see MJ Rodrigues, *European policies for a knowledge economy* (Cheltenham, Edward Elgar, 2003).

[58] For an analysis of OMC in relation to hard and soft law see DM Trubek and LG Trubek, 'The Open Method of Co-ordination and the Debate over "Hard" and "Soft" Law' in J Zeitlin and P Pochet (eds), *The Open Method of Co-ordination in Action. The European Employment and Social Inclusion Strategies* (Brussels, Peter Lang, 2005).

[59] 'Facing the Challenge. The Lisbon strategy for growth and employment', November 2004. Available at http://europa.eu.int/comm/lisbon_strategy/index_en.html.

[60] N Luhmann, 'Wohlfahrtsstaat zwischen Evolution und Rationalität' in P Koslowski u. a. (Hrsg), *Chancen und Grenzen des Sozialstaats* (Tübingen, Mohr Siebeck, 1983).

substantial socio-economic interests and strong ideological and emotional forces, making attempts to increase EU competencies within such areas extremely difficult. These difficulties are increased even further since the EU's classical integration strategy, which was applied during the launch of the IM and the EMU, namely to de-politicise the areas in question, as done, for example, through the outsourcing of monetary policy to the ECB and the national central banks through the European System of Central Banks (ESCB), does not seem to be a viable option within the area of welfare polices. It is against this background—large differences in organisational mode and policy objectives, high levels of political sensitivity and the absence of de-politicised alternatives—that the deployment of OMC instruments should be understood. Accordingly the OMC is a subtle instrument, used to achieve convergence between policy objectives and organisational methods in policy areas where political resistance and technical difficulties obstructing harmonisation are substantial.

This does not, however, mean that the OMC does not facilitate integration. On the contrary, the method is used to 'upload' policy areas which to date have not been subject to common European approaches, and which mainly are falling outside the CM. So even though the partial lack of formal competence transfers means that the method only produces 'light integration', the application of the method does imply increased Europeanisation and continued expansion of the scope of the integration process. This also explains why the Commission has chosen to 'go along'. The OMC represents a win-win situation for the Commission since the alternative to 'weak' integration through the OMC probably would be the absence of integration within the policy areas in question.

Hence, when compared to Comitology and agencies, the main reason for the emergence of the OMC seems to be the MS' desire to circumvent the CM, and the Commission's objective to expand the scope of the integration process. Again, however, it is important to emphasise the existence of a functional pressure for Europeanisation, which means that some sort of policy reply had to be developed. For example, the functional 'spill-over' effect arising from the strong focus on fulfilling the entrance criteria for the EMU created a relatively urgent need to develop a European employment policy which could complement the increased Europeanisation of monetary and fiscal policy.[61] The rapid technological transformations from the 1990s onwards, most notably within the area of information technology, and the massive expansion in globalisation and therefore in global economic competition, also created the need for coordinated European responses within areas such as R & D and the information society. The MS have

[61] A Schäfer, 'Beyond the Community Method: Why the Open Method of Coordination was introduced to EU Policy-making' (2004) 8 (13) *European Integration online Papers (EIoP)* 8 *f*.

therefore 'merely' been able to decide whether the Europeanisation of these policy areas should take the form of 'hard' integration, through competence transfer, or 'soft' integration through the OMC. Complexity, on the other hand, does not seem to have played a direct role, insofar as the bulk of the work is still being done by the Commission. Indirectly, however, one can argue that it has played a role in the choice of the OMC as a policy instrument, since the alternative would have been to 'communitarise' the policy areas in question. The administration of welfare policies tends, however, to be a very intensive resource task which the Commission, in its present form, would be ill-equipped to carry out. The Commission also possesses insufficient cognitive resources to play such a role, insofar as efficient employment strategies, for example, are conditioned by detailed local knowledge and the ability to continuously update such knowledge. Policy credibility, on the other hand, does not seem to be an issue in relation to the choice of the OMC as a policy instrument.

3.8 RECOGNISING GOVERNANCE

For a long time GS constituted the unrecognised 'underworld' of the EU.[62] In the early decades of their existence Comitology committees were merely conceived of as pragmatic and ad hoc institutional forms which were convenient second-best options for the Commission as well as the Council. For the Commission they were merely a temporary stepping stone towards its transformation into a unified executive acting within the framework of a federal state. For the Council it was an unwelcome necessity due to its own capacity problems. However, it was an acceptable arrangement for the Council because it gave the impression that the MS were somehow still in control. The two agencies established in the 1970s could, moreover, be considered as 'abnormalities' due to the specific characteristics of labour and social regulation.

The 'breakthrough' in terms of recognition of their importance and independent impact first came in the 1990s following the explosion in the number of Comitology committees after the introduction of the SEA and the continued expansion of agencies from the mid 1990s onwards. This development was complemented by the emergence of the OMC in the same period. As is often the case, a scandal, or rather a series of scandals, led to the exposure of GS. First, the fall of the Santer Commission. The maladministration that led to the fall of the Commission was not directly associated with the operation of GS, but led to a general awareness of the need to reform the administrative structures of the EU. These reforms inevitably had to include the GS. Secondly, the food and risk regulation

[62] JHH Weiler, 'In der Unterwelt der Ausschüsse' in *Die Zeit* (22 October 1998) 9.

scandals of the late 1990s were to a great extent related to the administrative practices of Comitology.[63] The culmination of this development was the adoption of the Commission White Paper on governance in 2000 by which the adoption of governance semantics became official community policy. This move entailed de facto recognition of GS as a phenomenon which is here to stay and which in one form or another will continue to play a central role in the European context.

This development also resulted in the increased interest of academics, who sought to establish what these theoretical 'misfits'[64] actually are, and to transform the theoretical basis for analysis of the EU accordingly. As indicated in the introductory chapter no clear picture has emerged so far, however. The multiplicity of GS and their different functions and maturity, combined with the immense dynamic by which they evolve, means that it has been almost impossible to establish a clear-cut concept capable of framing the new complexity. In addition, policy proposals such as Majone's theory of the regulatory state and the attempt of mainly American scholars to describe the OMC as Europe's new 'magic bullet' (*Wunderwaffe*) have not been realised, thereby contributing even further to the confusion. At present it is therefore still uncertain whether we will see a move towards some sort of unified and coherent system of GS in a relatively stable form, or if the current explosion in the multiplicity of GS will continue. As a preliminary conclusion, however, one can state that GS are spontaneous structures which have emerged due to the discrepancy between the strong societal forces pushing Europeanisation ahead and an underdeveloped institutional structure which is incapable of handling the functional demands facing it. Hence, the organic institutional structure has burst, thereby creating a highly complex conglomerate of regulatory structures and mechanisms which are not framed by a coherent regulatory philosophy.

[63] S Krapohl and K Zurek, 'The Perils of Committee Governance: Intergovernmental Bargaining during the BSE Scandal in the European Union' (2006), 10 (2) *European Integration Online Papers (EioP).*

[64] R Dehousse, 'Misfits: EU Law and the Transformation of European Governance' in C Joerges and R Dehousse (eds), *Good Governance in Europe's Integrated Market* (Oxford: Oxford University Press, 2002).

4

The Networks of Governance

4.1 INTRODUCTION

ALTHOUGH THE THREE modes of governance outlined in the previous chapter are highly complex and contain several subcategories, one element common to all is that they rely on networks. Whereas the previous chapter focused on the institutional setting leading to the emergence of GS, an exploration of the network phenomenon will provide an increased clarification of their substantial functions. It will be argued that the common feature of the three forms of governance is the establishment of structural couplings between organisational systems. These couplings lead to reductions in complexity, stabilisation of expectations, and the activation of resources produced by other organisational systems. In addition, they provide channels through which collisions of rationality, developed at the level of functional systems, can be minimised as they fulfil the function of 'bundling' a multiplicity of rationalities.

This line of thought is not new. Not only has the network concept been *en vogue* throughout the last two decades, but it has even been claimed that the network concept grasps the most fundamental characteristics of late-modern society, which has accordingly been dubbed a 'network society'.[1] In contrast to such broad approaches more narrow variants focus on networks as phenomena which mainly emerge in between market and hierarchy. However, none of these existing approaches is adequate for describing intermediate structures such as the governance phenomenon. The objective of this chapter is therefore to develop an additional variant of the network concept, which not only is directly aimed at describing the function of GS but can also serve as a basis from which a positive definition of GS can be developed.

[1] M Castells, *The Information Age: Economy, Society and Culture. Volume 1. The Rise of the Network Society* (Oxford, Blackwell, 1999).

4.2 THE RE-EMERGENCE OF NETWORKS

Before we examine the existing theoretical positions, however, another central distinction needs to be clarified. This distinction relates to the time horizon inherent in the different network approaches. One possible approach is to view networks as an entirely new phenomenon reflecting a transition from a modern to a post-modern society.[2] The alternative is an interpretation of the network phenomenon as a partial 'return' to a medieval and hence pre-modern order.[3] Neither of these two perspectives is adequate, however. Although networks have gained renewed relevance, current networks have little in common with pre-modern structures since the kind of networks related to that period fulfilled a fundamentally different societal function to that of present-day networks. In addition, it is problematic to argue that the fundamental structures of society have changed to such an extent that it is possible to postulate a fundamental break with modern structures. Hence, in order to gain an understanding of the network phenomenon which reflects more than merely the latest fashion, a deeper historical understanding of the transformations of the network function is essential. Working with ideal types, three periods can be distinguished: (i) the pre-modern, (ii) the modern and (iii) the present radical modern period.[4]

In feudal pre-modern Europe, networks were arguably a widespread phenomenon, since networked structures such as guilds, orders of chivalry and monastic orders all had an important role. At first glance these structures seemed to reproduce functions equivalent to those performed by hierarchical organisations within the modern functionally differentiated society. In particular, their emergence seems to have been closely related to the internal creation of stability within their respective segmented layers of society on the basis of inclusion/exclusion mechanisms. However, the function of ensuring integration for society as a whole was mainly centred on the household, an institution that acted as a container for members of different layers of the stratified society; households could therefore act as structural couplings between these layers.[5] Moreover, in terms of internal organisation, pre-modern network structures were fundamentally different

[2] K-H Ladeur, 'Towards a Legal Theory of Supranationality – The Viability of the Network Concept' (1997) 3 (1) *European Law Journal* 33.

[3] M Wind, 'The European Union as a polycentric polity: returning to a neo-medieval Europe?' JHH Weiler and M Wind (eds), *European Constitutionalism Beyond the State* (Cambridge, Cambridge University Press, 2003).

[4] For a historical overview see A Karsten and H von Thiesen (Hrsg), *Nützliche Netzwerke und korrupte Seilschaften* (Göttingen, Vandenhoeck & Ruprect, 2006).

[5] MM Knight, *Economic History of Europe. To the End of the Middle Ages* (London, George Allen & Unwin LTD, 1928) 162 *ff*; R Latouche, *Les origines de l'eéconomie occidentale, IVe-XIe sieècle* (Paris, A Michel, 1956) 221 *ff*; N Luhmann, *Die Gesellschaft der Gesellschaft* (Frankfurt am Main, Suhrkamp Verlag, 1997) 678 *ff*.

from modern organisations, in that their internal structure reflected that of the society they operated within as they were based on a mixture of hereditary positions and the occasional inclusion of newcomers. Moreover, this mixture reflected the hybrid nature of a society which was partly based on stratificatory and partly centre/periphery differentiation. With regard to the specific problem of market regulation one could also be tempted to consider the pre-modern guilds as market-regulating institutions operating in between markets and hierarchy, similar to late-modern GS.[6] However, this description does not capture the importance of the distinction between centre/periphery and stratification which existed within all layers of pre-modern society. Modern markets do not have a centre and a periphery in the pre-modern sense[7] and modern hierarchal organisations are not based on stratificatory differentiation in the form of a largely hereditary and religiously embedded order. Moreover, the breakthrough of modernity, through functional differentiation, must be regarded as a paradigmatic shift. This makes attempts to establish direct links between pre-modern and modern elements a futile exercise. Even if a continuity of structures can be observed,[8] such structures are likely to fulfil significantly different societal functions and to be ascribed radically different meanings when operating within a fundamentally different societal setting.

The emergence of modern structures through the increasing primacy of functional differentiation can, as described by Hegel, be understood as oriented towards the systematic breakdown of pre-modern feudal networks in all areas of society and the replacement of such networks with modern hierarchical organisational structures.[9] In Continental Europe and in contrast to the shared Liberalist and Marxist myth regarding the supremacy of the economic system vis-à-vis the political system, this development first occurred within the area of public administration. Hence, the introduction of modern organisational structures to the economic sphere in Continental Europe was achieved through mercantilism and—later on—state capitalism.[10] Industrial organisations were often established on the basis of government decrees and usually in order to fulfil military needs. Hence, industrial organisations in Continental Europe

[6] S Deakin, 'The return of the guild? Network relations in historical perspective' in G Teubner and M Amstutz (eds), *Networks: Legal Issues of Multilateral Co-operation* (Oxford, Hart Publishing, 2009).

[7] N Luhmann, *Die Wirtschaft der Gesellschaft* (Frankfurt am Main, Suhrkamp Verlag, 1998) 91 *ff.*

[8] S Deakin, 'The return of the guild? Network relations in historical perspective' in G Teubner and M Amstutz (eds), *Networks: Legal Issues of Multilateral Co-operation* (Oxford, Hart Publishing, 2009).

[9] GWF Hegel, 'Die Verfassung Deutschlands' in GWF Hegel, *Gesammelte Werke, Band 1* (Frankfurt am Main, Suhrkamp Verlag, [1800–02] 1971) esp 467 *f.*

[10] M Weber, *Wirtschaftsgeschichte* (Leipzig, Duncker & Humblot, 1923) 289 *ff.*

copied the organisational structures of the state, thereby making the organisation of state administration the role model for industrialists. This was, moreover, one of the reasons why public law became the role model for private law within Continental European legal systems during the 19th century. One of the many consequences of the rise of modern state organisation was that the state took over the functions which previously had been handled by the guilds and other forms of private networks. Security issues became the exclusive purview of the state, which had gained the monopoly of power. The regulation of the economy became a primary concern of the state. Issues such as setting standards therefore became a public function.[11] A similar development can be observed in relation to the regulation of competition and price setting. The state, moreover, played a central role in the secularisation of society, thereby contributing to the breakdown of the religious embeddedness of the economy.

As already indicated, a central characteristic of modern society is the counterbalancing of functional differentiation by territorial differentiation, insofar as the nation state acted as a container for the modern functionally differentiated society. But, as we have also seen, the frame was not only territorial. A central function of the modern state was to ensure sufficient stabilisation of the new stratified class structures which emerged as a consequence of industrialisation and urbanisation.[12] In practice, this meant that whereas pre-modern economic structures in Continental Europe had been framed by a religious universe, the rationality of the modern economy was—at the organisational level—subsumed under the larger frame of *Étatisme*.[13] Firms and other economic organisations became subject to a 'double-binary coding'. They were reproducing themselves on the basis of the profit-oriented distinction property/non-property, at the same time as they faced the demands of operating in accordance with the rationality of the state, which was based on the distinction between the ruler and the ruled. Consequently, the distinction between state and society was largely reduced to a distinction between state and economy, thereby creating the basis for the establishment of structural couplings through the kind of corporatist economic constitutions that developed over the course of the 19th and early 20th centuries in most Continental European countries. Such constitutions ensured the legal stabilisation of the triangular relations

[11] H Schepel, *The Constitution of Private Governance: Product Standards in the regulation of integrating markets* (Oxford, Hart Publishing, 2004).

[12] GWF Hegel, *Grundlinien der Philosophie des Rechts. Oder Naturrecht und Staatswissenschaft im Grundrisse. Werke Band 7* (Frankfurt am Main, Suhrkamp Verlag, [1821] 1970) § 250–6.

[13] The state-centredness in the 19th and 20th centuries was not only confined to the economy as is also indicated by, for example the existence of organisations such as state churches, public universities, research institutes and public broadcasting corporations.

between the state, employers and employees. Moreover, economic constitutions served as a frame for society as such, in that virtually all areas of society from health and education to sport were reorganised and subsumed under the umbrella of the welfare states which were their practical manifestation. Hence, the economic constitutions served not only as stabilisers of the relationship between the state and the economy but also between the social classes of the industrial society. In organisational terms the economic constitutions were, however, intrinsically state-centred, in that the labour market organisations which evolved tended to mirror the organisational forms of the state administrations or even to see themselves as parts of the state.[14] Consequently, there was little room for non-hierarchical organisational structures in the modern period. The network phenomenon was therefore confined to the margins of modern society.[15] Hence, in the context of modernity the concept of networks was only useful to describe the kind of policy networks that tend to surround the hierarchical peaks of modern organisations.[16]

The Hegelian nation-state society achieved its zenith with the expansion of the welfare societies in the 1960s. Since then, the nation-state container has increasingly been broken down just as class society has been increasingly dissolved through the replacement of class distinctions with inclusion/exclusion mechanisms, emerging along the borders of functionally differentiated systems.[17] In other words, the level of functional differentiation has been radicalised, and territorial as well as stratificatory forms of stabilisation have increasingly, although not completely, lost their relevance. Consequently, what is often described as post-modern society is, in fact, only a society where the intrinsic modern logic of functional differentiation has become an even stronger characteristic of society than before.[18] In addition, the state is increasingly facing 'capacity problems' in relation to its ability to operate the societal functions that it used to monopolise. Moreover, the other functional systems, and in particular the economic system, are ever less confined within the nation states. The state, which for Hegel had three meanings: (i) the political system; (ii) the 'broad' societal system established through economic constitutions; and (iii) the nation state, understood as a container demarcating one society from other

[14] A Brodocz, 'Strukturelle Kopplung durch Verbände' (1996) 2 (2) *Soziale Systeme. Zeitschrift für Soziologische Theorie* 361.

[15] S Deakin, 'The return of the guild? Network relations in historical perspective' in G Teubner and M Amstutz (eds), *Networks: Legal Issues of Multilateral Co-operation* (Oxford, Hart Publishing, 2009).

[16] G Grabher (ed), *The Embedded Firm* (London, Routledge, 1993).

[17] N Luhmann, 'Inklusion und Exklusion' in N Luhmann, *Soziologische Aufklärung Band 6* (Opladen, Westdeutscher Verlag, 1995).

[18] N Luhmann, *Die Gesellschaft der Gesellschaft* (Frankfurt am Main, Suhrkamp Verlag, 1997) 1143 *ff*.

societies,[19] is increasingly being reduced to one functional system among others.[20] As already illustrated, in relation to the difference in function between the EU's political system and the political system in the nation state form, only the first of Hegel's three meanings of the state therefore have empirical validity in relation to a radical modern structure such as the EU. As has also been described, the relative weight of the political system in relation to other functional systems is therefore steadily diminishing.

Although the increasingly functionally differentiated world society is based in principle on heterarchy, since no functional system is directly subsumed under the rationality of another, the economic system has progressively emerged as the 'market leader' among functional systems. This final victory of the commercial spirit (*Handelsgeist*) as foreseen by Kant[21] means that the form of economic reproduction has become the ideal model which organisations operating within other functional systems seek to imitate. Consequently, private law has increasingly become the role model for public law. The organisations of the political system, and especially of its bureaucratic subsystem, are therefore undergoing profound changes due to their adoption of the economic semantics of efficiency, market orientation and customisation. This move from Bismarck to benchmark profoundly undermines the modern illusion of the state as a unity because public institutions more and more operate within a competitive context as they increasingly compete with other public institutions as well as with private organisations. Hence, the reorganisation of political-bureaucratic organisations on the basis of economic rationality means that the policy programmes of the political system are faced ever more with a double binary coding. The functional system of politics continues to operate on the basis of the recognised distinctions between the ruler and the ruled and the related parasitic distinction between government and opposition at the same time as the political-bureaucratic organisational systems adopt the logic and semantics of the economic system. This changes the way these organisational systems engage with their environments. They increasingly act as societal coordinators or 'market brokers' and much less as Weberian instruments of rule (*Herrschaftsinstrumenten*). Accordingly, public organisations are more inclined to align themselves with concepts such as corporate social responsibility (CSR) and self-regulation rather than exclusively with hard legal regulation, thereby

[19] GWF Hegel, *Grundlinien der Philosophie des Rechts. Oder Naturrecht und Staatswissenschaft im Grundrisse. Werke Band 7* (Frankfurt am Main, Suhrkamp Verlag, [1821] 1970) § 257–360.

[20] N Luhmann, *Politik der Gesellschaft* (Frankfurt am Main, Suhrkamp Verlag, 2000).

[21] I Kant, 'Zum Ewigen Frieden' in A Buchenau, E Cassirer and B Kellerman, *Immanuel Kants Werke, Schriften von 1790–1796* (Berlin, Bruno Cassirer, [1795] 1914) 454 *f.*

providing a challenge for the way the legal system has traditionally sought to regulate interaction between public and private structures.

But the reorganisation of public organisations on the basis of economic rationality also has an impact on the economic system itself as it is faced more and more with a need to perform functions that are no longer handled exclusively by public organisations. An important example, as illustrated by Schepel, is standard setting, which is increasingly outsourced to private actors because it is becoming difficult for public authorities to handle the complexity of such issues.[22] In fact, the safeguarding of competition seems to be the only area where the state continues to hold a strong position and even in this area it is possible to observe an increased reliance on the concept of efficiency rather than the concept of fairness. It is, therefore, not surprising that almost the only area where the EU, as an emerging late-modern public structure, possesses exclusive competencies is in the area of competition policy.[23]

In addition, although the political system seeks to frame relations between the economic system and its broader social environment by reproducing indirect structural couplings between the economic system and, for example, the functional systems of science, education and the environment at the organisational level, this process is also being increasingly eroded. Hence, organisations operating within the economic system have not only been forced to seek alternative ways of ensuring compatibility with the political system, but have also been forced to adopt new strategies towards its wider social environment. More practically, the economic system is faced with a functional need to substitute the indirect structural couplings, established through the political system, with direct structural couplings. It is against this background that the expansion of the phenomenon of networks within the area of market regulation should be understood. The establishment of network-based 'partnerships' between firms and other organisational systems, which are often reproduced within the spheres of other functional systems, is one of the strategies invoked by economic organisations to ensure embeddedness in society. In particular, larger companies no longer engage only with traditional corporatist organisations but actively seek to participate in networks concerned with, for example, self-regulation of marketing norms, standard setting, and dialogue with a multiplicity of public authorities, research institutions, environmental groups, advocates of fair trade and so forth.[24] Accordingly,

[22] H Schepel, *The Constitution of Private Governance: Product standards in the regulation of integrating markets* (Oxford, Hart Publishing, 2004).

[23] Treaty establishing the European Community § 81 and 82.

[24] Royal Dutch/Shell's change of communication strategy after the Brent Spar affair is a very good illustration. See: www.shell.com/home/Framework?siteId=uk-en&FC2=/uk-en/html/iwgen/zzz_lhn.html&FC3=/uken/html/iwgen/about_shell/brentspardossier/dir_brent_spar.html.

representation within the wider social environment is now more often handled directly by the firms in question. In other words, any major economic entity is increasingly faced with the need to actively develop reflexive strategies to handle uncertainty and irritations that originate from its social environment.

Thus, in the era of radical modernity networks are acquiring a fundamentally different role from that of the Hegelian era, when the concept was no more than a useful tool for describing the very limited kind of interaction systems which tend to surround the peaks of hierarchical organisations. In addition, present-day networks are also fundamentally different from the pre-modern networks since their main function is to act as integrative measures within the context of radical functional differentiation. Applying the metaphor of a 'return to medieval times' to describe contemporary networks is therefore not particularly useful, as it tends to evoke connotations which provide little understanding of the operating conditions within radical modernity. Instead, networks must be seen as inter-hierarchical phenomena that link modern organisations. The intrinsically modern concept of hierarchical organisation remains, therefore, the central body[25] on which parasitic networks can thrive.

4.3 METAPHORICAL NETWORKS

The above historical reconstruction is a useful basis for contextualising the distinction between 'broad' and 'narrow' network concepts. In relation to the former approach, the works of Ladeur appear as particularly central. He developed his network concept in contrast to the Habermasian vision of modernity as an 'incomplete' and therefore ongoing project.[26] Habermas' position is based on the assumption that the societal processes of the 21st century are a repetition, at a higher level, of the kind of societal processes which led to the establishment of the nation states. Based on this assumption, Habermas claims that Europe must utilise the logic of the circular creation of state and society that shaped the modern history of European countries.[27] In contrast, Ladeur focuses on the massive increase in the complexity of contemporary society and the consequent much higher level of uncertainty and risk. Applying the rationalising principles of the nation states to a higher level will therefore not lead to the creation of a supranational legal and political order, since the context within which the

[25] The vision of Piore and Sabel concerning a possible breakdown of the vertical integration of production has therefore not materialised. See MJ Piore and CF Sabel, *The Second Industrial Divide: Possibilities for Prosperity* (New York, Basic Books, 1984).

[26] J Habermas, *Die Moderne, ein unvollendetes Projekt. Philosophisch-politische Aufsätze 1977–1990* (Leipzig, Reclam, 1990).

[27] J Habermas, 'Why Europe Needs A Constitution' (2001) 11 *New Left Review* 17.

European nation states were created was completely different to the context within which the processes of European integration and constitutionalisation are evolving.[28]

On a more concrete level, a main difference between Habermas' intrinsically modern perspective and the post-modern perspective presented by Ladeur is how the latter views the structural changes taking place in the economic system. The economy, one of the prime spheres of legal regulation, is rapidly being transformed from an industrial to a knowledge-based and more dynamic entity.[29] This transformation, taking place through the increased temporalisation of society, not only increases the need for regulatory schemes which can operate in the context of increased uncertainty, but also the need for far more flexible rules aimed at regulating 'micro-structures'. The ideal of constructing general rules applicable to particular cases is therefore increasingly placed under pressure because the maintenance of the kind of *Weberian* administrative structures based upon a *Kelsenian* legal hierarchy which is a precondition for the realisation of Habermas' vision is becoming less and less viable. Instead, far more fluid and flexible administrative structures are needed. The law must therefore adapt itself to the existence of a wide variety of overlapping and multi-level networks, which are not only profoundly a-hierarchical but also encompass a wide variety of actors, both public and private. It is against the background of this transformation of the economy that Ladeur calls for the development of a legal concept of networks.

A network is, according to Ladeur, more 'than a variously densified grouping of negotiated relations among stable subjects'.[30] This does not mean that subjects are irrelevant, only that a network cannot be reduced to a mere expression of co-operation and bargaining between subjects. Subject relations are therefore only one of many components of a network in which the multiplicity of interdependent and complementary components provides a basis for continued re-combination. This creates synergy effects and produces new options which are only accessible through the network in question. Synergy effects are therefore conditioned by an

[28] K-H Ladeur, '"Deliberative Demokratie" und "Dritter Weg" – eine neue Sackgasse? Transformation des "alten" Sozialstaats in den "aktivierende" Staat?' (2002) 41 *Der Staat*, 3. More generally see also K-H Ladeur, *Postmoderne Rechtstheorie – Selbstreferenz – Selbstorganisation – Prozeduralisierung* (Berlin, Duncker & Humblot, 1995) and K-H Ladeur, *Negative Freiheitsrechte und gesellschaftliche Selbstorganisation. Zur Erzeugung von Sozialkapital durch gesellschaftliche Institutionen* (Tübingen, Mohr Siebeck, 2000).

[29] Another and perhaps even more important change lies in the absence of serious military conflict. The *Étatisme* of the nation states emerged as a result of fierce military competition and almost constant war. Hence, the context within which the EU has emerged is fundamentally different from the context within which the European nation states emerged. See also U Beck, *Die Feindlose Demokratie* (Stuttgart, Reclam, 1995).

[30] K-H Ladeur, 'Towards a Legal Theory of Supranationality – the Viability of the Network Concept' (1997) 3 (1) *European Law Journal* 33, 47.

acceptance of the logic regulating the evolution and functioning of the network itself. This is also the case for the results of bargaining, deliberation or co-operation between subjects within a given network. Their results can only be externalised through the network structure and not by the subjects themselves. Another central feature of networks is their 'fluid' character. This fluidity makes the outcome of network operations radically open-ended, as the number of possible recombinations among the elements of a given network is almost infinite. A network cannot therefore be seen as a stable unity, even though it can briefly become denser and easier to distinguish in the case of collisions with other decisional structures.[31]

The rise of networks is taking place at all levels – locally, at the nation-state level, regionally as well as globally; the result is the emergence of a system of multi-level networks. The evolution of networks at the EU level is, however, far more advanced than at other levels, which is why Ladeur characterises the EU as an 'avant-garde structure' with respect to the development of polycentric and heterarchical legal structures. One other important feature of networks is that they tend to break down the distinction between the public and private spheres. The function of many networks is indeed to combine public and private elements, thereby stabilising relations between the political and administrative systems and those to which they relate, such as the economic system. The main objective of networks acting between the private and public spheres is therefore to ensure correspondence between private and public policy objectives. In practice, such networks are typically aimed at ensuring a high level of self-regulation by the private parties, while the public authorities that participate in the network tend to assume a supervisory role.[32] In relation to the EU, Ladeur therefore proposes that the Commission should restrain its activities and focus on its supervisory function, as well as on the production and sharing of information, thereby contributing to the creation of discursive contexts within which networks can evolve.[33]

Information gathering is also becoming more crucial due to the increased complexity of society. Legislators find themselves increasingly taking decisions under conditions of uncertainty, which in turn means that they must be systematically modified in the light of new knowledge and on the basis of trial and error. Consequently, an ex ante formulation of the 'public interest' is becoming more and more difficult. Instead, political and

[31] *Ibid*, 46.

[32] For a number of instructive examples of network regulation within the areas of information technology law and environmental law see K-H Ladeur, 'Regulierte Selbstregulierung als Steuerungskonzept des Gewährleistungsstaates' (2001) *Die Verwaltung, Beiheft 4* 59.

[33] K-H Ladeur, 'The Changing Role of the Private in Public Governance – The Erosion of Hierarchy and the Rise of a New Administrative Law of Cooperation. A Comparative Approach' (2002) 9 *EUI Working Papers Law*.

administrative systems will have to ex post re-formulate the public interest based on processes of continued learning and evaluation.[34] In practice, network structures therefore tend to evolve without any clear legal basis. Instead, ex post legitimisation of network structures is ensured through a mutual adaptation of law to the network and of the network to law on the basis of new information.

From a 'traditional' legal perspective the focus on simple ex post formulation of the public interest makes it possible to question whether Ladeur's network concept qualifies as a legal concept at all. The impression that his approach is 'beyond law' is further reinforced by his minimal interest in the question of legitimacy. His focus on ex post reformulation, however, seems to be compatible with Luhmann's concept of legitimacy. Luhmann identifies the institutionalisation of legitimacy as a legal undertaking aimed at achieving societal learning processes through which social expectations are continuously re-structured.[35] Such learning processes are based on 'proceduralisation', a specific method for binding decision making which is substantially open-ended but based on specific values which can be deployed to evaluate unknown future developments.[36] The legitimising function of procedures is derived from a double-edged differentiation of roles between participants. On the one hand, the variety of roles represented develops according to the specific function which the institutional structure in question is handling. Thus the number of relevant roles is limited and the possible themes which can be dealt with are indirectly reduced. Moreover, each role has a certain perspective attached to it. Therefore only issues which are of relevance to the particular role assigned can be raised and all other issues excluded. All in all, negative limitation through role differentiation leads to a reduction in complexity. Such limitations can be seen as a requirement for the successful handling of a certain function. Hence, the limitation of roles can be seen as a tool aimed at achieving output legitimacy. On the other hand, the differentiation of roles is also intended to ensure representation of all the relevant perspectives. In this way each role also has a positive obligation assigned to it, since the representative of the role is obliged to promote a specific interest or to develop an opinion based upon a specific type of professional knowledge. This positive obligation should ensure inclusion in the decision process of all relevant perspectives. Potentially, this will guarantee that the outcome is in accordance with the interests of all the parties concerned.

[34] *Ibid*, 32 *ff*.

[35] N Luhmann, *Legitimation durch Verfahren* (Berlin, Neuwied, 1969) 34 *ff*; T Würtenberger, 'Legitimität, Legalität' in O Brunner, W Conze and R Koselleck (Hrsg), *Geschichtliche Grundbegrieffe, Bd. 3* (Stuttgart, Klett-Cotta, 1983) 737 *f*.

[36] N Luhmann, *Politik der Gesellschaft* (Frankfurt am Main, Suhrkamp Verlag, 2000) 124.

The positive obligation therefore serves as a specific form of input legitimacy as the organisational structures develop specific roles which they consider representative of the interests involved.[37]

Without applying the Luhmannian insights above, Ladeur's network concept remains very general. One reason is that it serves mainly as a formula for the self-description of society, as his aim is to present it as radically decentralised and heterarchical and therefore beyond control or steering. Accordingly, he is rarely using the network concept as a basis for empirical examinations or detailed mappings of the functioning of specific institutional forms. Instead, the network concept becomes a metaphorical concept used to describe processes of mutual adaptation under conditions of societal anarchism. Ladeur's concept of network seems, in other words, to act as a substitute for the concept of societal heterarchy. Moreover, his generalisation of the network concept seems to radically overemphasise their importance, in that he sees them as the main building blocks of society. Instead networks should simply be seen as a specific institutional form which operates alongside a range of other forms and fulfils very specific societal functions. The main use of the network concept developed by Ladeur is therefore to serve as a general frame which sets the scene for the development of more concrete approaches.

4.4 NETWORKS BETWEEN MARKET AND HIERARCHY

In contrast to Ladeur, Teubner has developed a narrow network approach. His point of departure is private law and he aims mainly to explore the rise of networks within the economic area, particularly in the form of virtual companies, intranets, extranets, franchising, just-in-time and outsourcing.[38] He sees networks as a third form of coordination which differs from both private contracts and the state/society contract between rulers and ruled. Accordingly, he defines networks as a third form which is neither market nor hierarchy.[39] Hence, in the terminology of systems theory, Teubner claims that networks are a special type of system which does not fall within any of the three 'classical' categories: functional systems (for example law, politics and economy), organisational systems (public bureaucracies, firms etc.) or interaction systems.

[37] N Luhmann, *Rechtssoziologie, Band 2* (Berlin, Rowohlt Taschenbuch, 1972) 259 *ff*; N Luhmann, *Ausdifferenzierung des Rechts, Beiträge zur Rechtssoziologie und Rechtstheorie* (Frankfurt am Main, Suhrkamp Verlag, 1981) 132 *f*.

[38] G Teubner, *Netzwerk als Vertragsverbund. Virtuelle Unternehmen, Franchising, Just-in-time in Sozialwissenschaftlicher und juristischer Sicht* (Baden-Baden, Nomos Verlag, 2004).

[39] M Hutter and G Teubner, 'The Parasitic Role of Hybrids' (1993) 149 (4) *Journal of Institutional and Theoretical Economics* 706.

A central feature of networks is the existence of reciprocal trust, repeated interaction and observation by third parties. Networks are, however, different from purely informal relations between subjects, as a minimum of institutionalisation is needed. Furthermore, they have the character of 'parasites' in the sense that they are conditioned by attachment to a market or a hierarchical organisation. A typical function of networks is to create structural couplings between market and hierarchy, especially in situations where collisions of rationality occur, leading to paradoxical, ambivalent and contradictory demands. As an alternative to suppressing such ambiguities, networks can be seen as an attempt to use them positively. As a consequence triangular hybrids, which combine markets, hierarchies and networks, might emerge. Such hybrids are characterised by 'co-optition', as they combine competition and co-operation, and by 'double inclusion', in that the linking of markets and hierarchies through networks creates triangular structures which permit the simultaneous inclusion of subjects in a market and in a hierarchy.[40] Accordingly, Teubner argues that, from a legal perspective, the main challenge is to develop a concept of 'network interest', which differs from the concept of 'contract objective' as well as from the concept of 'organisational interest'.

It is clear, therefore, that Teubner sees networks as being able to act as buffers, contributing to the dissolution of collisions between market and hierarchy. This gives them a potentially legitimising function for the hierarchies and markets involved, since they tend to contribute positively to the integration of society through their decentralised processing and regulation of externalities. Given the fluid nature of networks, such striving for compatibility can only take place in a punctual form and only when already existing factual ramifications are consolidated normatively. A network can therefore ensure the normative compatibility of legal orders but cannot establish a unified hierarchical legal order. Consequently, legal orders are established through reciprocal irritation, observation and reflexivity between partial legal orders covering specific policy areas.[41] Following Teubner's network logic, the only legal method suitable for handling collisions is therefore a decentralised one aimed at achieving a limitation of harmful externalities which in most cases do not imply a reconciliation of rationalities through a Hegelian *Aufhebung*. According to Teubner, a state theory suitable for the 21st century will therefore have to be based on

[40] G Teubner, 'Das Recht hybrider Netzwerke' (2001) 165 *Zeitschrift für das gesamte Handelsrecht und Wirtschaftsrecht* 550, 563.

[41] Fischer-Lescano and Teubner give a number of instructive examples concerning transnational copyright, patent rights in the medical area and *Lex Constructionis*. See A Fischer-Lescano and G Teubner, 'Regime-Collisions: The Vain Search for Legal Unity in the Fragmentation of Global Law' (2004) 25 (4) *Michigan Journal of International Law* 999, 1019.

heterarchy and not hierarchy, on the institutionalised inclusion of private actors in the state, and on the constitutionalisation of networks.[42]

4.5 THE MARKETISATION OF THE PUBLIC SECTOR

Teubner's approach is largely confined to the relationship between markets and hierarchies and private law. However, the perspective can be somewhat expanded as marketisation, and with it hybriditisation as already indicated, have increasingly become central features of the public sector as well. Markets can be defined as the 'internal environment' of the economic system which ensures that economic organisations operate in a competitive context. Since the 1980s, NPM strategies have increasingly served as instruments for the transformation of the public sectors through the introduction of economic rationality. The NPM revolution does not, however, only affect the area of public administration in the narrow sense but also has profound indirect effects on systems such as education, science, health, media and art, since public organisations such as schools, universities, hospitals, public media and museums increasingly operate under market conditions.[43] The marketisation of the public sector is based on two variants since it partly consists of subcontracting public functions to private enterprises and partly the establishment of 'internal markets' within the framework of vertical public organisations. In the latter form organisations are 'mimicking' contractual relations in the sense that a multiplicity of subunits are forced to bid on specific assignments in competition with other subunits of the organisation in question, thereby creating a sense of competition within the framework of vertical organisations.[44]

The development towards marketisation can be seen as a response to the overburdening of the welfare state. This has created a functional need for the mobilisation of external resources, and especially resources from the economic system, in order to maintain the public sector's ability to function. Public–private partnerships (PPPs) as a way to ensure private financing, especially within the area of infrastructure development, are an obvious example here. In addition, the introduction of 'pseudo-markets'

[42] G Teubner, *Polykorporatismus: Der Staat als 'Netzwerk' öffentlicher und privater Kollektivakteure* in H Brunkhorst and P Niesen (Hrsg.), *Das Recht der Republik* (Frankfurt am Main, Suhrkamp Verlag, 1999) 347 *ff*.

[43] H Wilke, *Global Governance* (Bielefeld, Transcript Verlag, 2006) 42 *f*.

[44] For an instructive example concerning the development of 'internal markets' within the BBC see S Deakin, 'The return of the guild? Network relations in historical perspective' in G Teubner and M Amstutz (eds), *Networks: Legal Issues of Multilateral Co-operation* (Oxford, Hart Publishing, 2009).

within the framework of public institutions is envisaged as increasing productivity and hence reducing costs.

But at the same time as the move towards marketisation is being introduced to solve one type of problem it also creates new problems. The increased breakdown of the (perceived) unity of the state by marketising the public realm means that the need to ensure a reduction of complexity, stabilisation of expectations and coordination between the different units increases. This is evident for example in relation to the PPP phenomenon where intensified co-operation between public and private organisations is conditioned by a stabilisation of relations through an intentional institutional framing of the relationship. Within public organisations similar needs arise as a result of the establishment of internal markets, since economic rationality is thereby introduced as an intermediate layer between the rationality of the political-bureaucratic system and the rationality of systems such as science, education, art and health. Hence, present trends in the public sector go in precisely the opposite direction to the trends that characterised the Hegelian era when the political system served as the intermediary through which the economic system was linked to other social systems, thereby creating a state-centred society. Today marketisation is therefore extending beyond the boundaries of the economic system in the same way as the vertical organisation of state bureaucracy extended beyond the borders of the political-bureaucratic system in the 19th and 20th centuries. Consequently, public organisations are increasingly faced with the complex task of ensuring convergence between at least four forms of rationality: political-bureaucratic, legal, economic as well as the rationality of the specific policy area(s) such as health, environment, education or science. Hence, public organisations are increasingly forced to deal with complex clashes of rationality and are therefore not only forced to engage in hybrid forms of co-operation by establishing networks with external private partners who operate within a market but, within the framework of vertical organisations, are also establishing internal hybrids. Such hybrids are partly characterised by hierarchy and partly by heterarchy, as they combine internal markets and organisational subunits within institutional structures which are specifically developed to link the market element with the organisational element.

4.6 EMBEDDING THE EU

For the specific purpose of conceptualising GS in the EU context Teubner's approach is only useful to a certain extent. As noted earlier, the EU is itself a hybrid operating in between an 'anarchic' world society and hierarchically organised MS. Mature GS such as the framework for the regulation of the European chemicals market can also be characterised as hybrids and this will be discussed in due course. However, the concept of networks which underpins Teubner's approach is problematic. His attempt to see networks as a 'fourth form of system', in addition to functional, organisational and interactive systems, is based on an unclear mixture of action and systems theory. Secondly, the attempt to conceptualise networks as a phenomenon beyond hierarchy, the key element of organisational systems, as well as beyond contracts, the legal form of market transactions, profoundly limits the reach of his approach since, in spite of continued marketification, far from all networks involve links with the economic system. Hence, Teubner's network concept cannot be considered a general concept capable of encompassing the phenomenon in its entirety since that would necessitate the ability to describe intra- as well as inter-systemic networks as such.[45]

It is beyond the scope of this study to identify a general theory of networks, however. Instead we will limit ourselves to presenting an approach which is specifically aimed at clarifying the role of inter-hierarchical networks. This choice is based on the understanding that the central characteristic of GS is that they are inter-organisational phenomena. Such networks do not necessarily imply links with the economic system, although this is often the case. Within Comitology, for example, the vast majority of the committees involve only representatives of the Commission and national administrations. The limited relevance of the market/hierarchy distinction in the EU context is furthermore underlined by the modest impact of the NPM revolution on the European institutions establishing the CIS. At first glance this is surprising when one takes into account the massive reform efforts undertaken within EU institutions since the administrative scandals of the late 1990s. A central reason for the resistance of EU institutions vis-à-vis NPM may, however, be found in the character of EU activities. In spite of the need to develop 'pay-offs' the EU's central task is to perform regulatory functions and, only to a very limited extent, the kind of redistributive functions that characterise modern welfare states. Hence the possibility of introducing marketisation is relatively limited. As noted earlier, the heavy emphasis on regulation means, moreover, that the EU's relations with the economic system and other parts of its environment are regulated mostly through lobbying networks. These networks also fulfil the function of linking organisations as their primary function is to link firms with the EU institutions. The triangular interaction between public structures and hierarchical corporatist organisations representing employers and employees is thus circumvented. It is therefore more

[45] For a somewhat similar critique of Teubner see E Kämper and JFK Schmidt, 'Netzwerke als strukturelle Kopplung. Systemtheoretische Überlegungen zum Netzwerkbegriff' in J Weyer (Hrsg), *Soziale Netzwerke – Konzepte und Methoden der sozialwissenschaftlichen Nertzwerkforschung* (München, Oldenbourg Verlag, 2000) 220 *ff*.

viable to conceive of networks as a *specific form* of structural couplings between organisational systems in the EU context. As networks imply communication 'among those present' (*unter Anwesenden*), these couplings are dependent on the simultaneous activation of interaction systems.[46]

As seen earlier, structural couplings can be defined as institutionalised forms which generate and stabilise expectations between social systems, be these functional, organisational or interaction systems. The stabilisation of relations between organisational systems through structural couplings in the form of networks therefore enables organisation A to assume that organisation B is conducting operations which are necessary for the continued functioning of organisation A. Accordingly, networks can be conceived of as a specific form through which organisations observe the environment within which they operate, leading to a reduction of complexity in the sense that the institutionalisation of expectations partly enables a substitution of cognition with trust. Engagement in the network form therefore reduces the level of cognitive capacities which an organisation needs to deploy in order to continue operating. However, structural couplings do not only enable organisations to synchronise their operations but more importantly also make it possible for a system to rely on elements produced by other organisations. A further characteristic of structural couplings is indeterminacy in that they cannot be ascribed to only one of the organisations involved. Instead, both the organisations involved tend to operate under the assumption that they control the coupling in question, thereby indicating a certain tendency to 'pretentiousness'; as Weiler puts it when commenting on Comitology and making a reference to John Le Carré: 'One gets the impression, by the cosy convenience between Commission and Council that each think *Comitology* is their own Smiley or Karla.'[47] Following the logic of the mutual increase in autonomy and interdependency, symmetric structural couplings can furthermore be seen as strengthening everyone involved. This also seems be to the case with GS as, in many instances, re-regulation at the European level has not led to reductions in the regulatory capacities of MS administrations.[48] Instead, the demands for increased European regulation have been conditioned by

[46] N Luhmann, *Die Gesellschaft der Gesellschaft* (Frankfurt am Main, Suhrkamp Verlag, 1997) 812 *ff*.

[47] JHH Weiler, 'Epilogue: "Comitology" as Revolution – Infranationalism, Constitutionalism and Democracy' in C Joerges and E Vos (eds), *EU Committees: Social Regulation, Law and Politics* (Oxford, Hart Publishing, 1999) 342.

[48] These couplings do, however, tend to lead to a reconfiguration of the internal balance between the legislative and the executive dimensions of MS governments as these structures are, to a large extent, by-passing national parliaments.

simultaneous increases in national capacities to handle the flow of decisions channelled through the GS; they also provide a means through which MS administration can channel their input into the European regulatory machinery.[49]

One of the main functions of organisations is to implement policy programmes. Accordingly, structural couplings between organisational systems typically occur as a result of policy failures, or more generally in cases where organisations are prevented from producing elements essential for the fulfilment of their policy programmes.[50] As seen earlier, the EU is faced with a number of structural deficits regarding the mobilisation of cognitive resources, implementation and compliance. These deficits are in many ways similar to the 'capacity problems' faced by the political-bureaucratic systems of the nation states. In relation to the EU, however, these problems are more pronounced and fundamental.

In addition, GS combine perspectives emerging within different functional systems and can therefore be seen as directly oriented towards achieving a reconciliation (*Hegung*) of such differences. Not only are GS characterised by a specific form of 'political administration' which blurs the distinction between the political and the bureaucratic dimensions of the political-bureaucratic system;[51] in most cases GS also serve as 'hubs' where the information that emerges from different functional systems is gathered, organised and redistributed. The attempt to increase convergence between the scientific system and the economic system through the deployment of OMC instruments is a good example. As we will see in Chapter 6, this process is directly oriented towards increasing the ability of the economic system to rely on the scientific system and vice versa. For the economic system, this attempt is justified under the slogan of 'increasing competitiveness'. Within the scientific system, the same process is seen as a push towards 'further innovation'. In Chapter 7, moreover, we will see that risk regulation is another and particularly clear example since such structures are aimed at linking scientific, medical, environmental, economic, legal and political rationalities within a specific descriptive frame and specific practice, intended to reduce negative externalities.

[49] An anecdotal but still highly representative example of the strengthening of MS administrations is the establishment of the *Banque centrale du Luxembourg*. Prior to the EMU, Luxembourg did not have a central bank and it was the move towards monetary union which made it necessary for Luxembourg to establish one.

[50] E Kämper and JFK Schmidt, 'Netzwerke als strukturelle Kopplung. Systemtheoretische Überlegungen zum Netzwerkbegriff' in J Weyer (Hrsg), *Soziale Netzwerke – Konzepte und Methoden der sozialwissenschaftlichen Nertzwerkforschung* (München, Oldenbourg Verlag, 2000) 229.

[51] A Bücker and S Schlacke, 'Die Entstehung einer politischen Verwaltung durch EG-Ausschüsse – Rechtstatsachen und Rechtsentwicklungen' in J Falke and C Joerges (Hrsg.), *Das Ausschußwesen der Europäischen Union. Die Praxis der Risikoregulierung im Binnenmarkt und ihre rechtliche Verfassung* (Baden-Baden, Nomos Verlag, 2000).

Another central but more general difference is that national political systems are part of larger national configurations. As illustrated earlier, they are therefore embedded in society in a manner which is fundamentally different from the way in which the EU is. Even though the nation states have undergone a massive opening during the last half of the 20th century, they remain embedded in economic constitutions and corporatist systems just as 'national universes' in terms of relatively homogenised spaces which have been purposefully constructed through century-long processes of reiteration continue to exist.[52] The concrete manifestation of such universes is the existence of different political and legal cultures. These cultures are an expression of the substantially different political and legal practices which characterise the different nation states and serve as frames which, by their very existence, lead to enormous reductions in complexity while also ensuring the stabilisation of expectations. The EU operates only within a very embryonic universe and hence lacks the 'symbolic-aesthetic dimension'[53] and societal anchoring which characterise national legal and political systems. Hence, as a phenomenon which is much less embedded than the national political and legal systems, the EU has been forced to develop strategies enabling it to compensate for the absence of this kind of frame. The strategic promotion of GS in the network form fulfils precisely this function in that they act as structural couplings which not only facilitate a systematic increase in the reflexivity of EU institutions but also serve as channels through which the EU can ensure convergence between its operations and the operations of other social structures, thereby ensuring it is, itself, embedded.

The functional need to ensure that the EU is embedded is expressed in several ways. For example, OMC processes act as a specific form of structural coupling mainly oriented towards compensating for a lack of cognitive resources. OMC networks in effect link MS administrations within specific policy areas thereby enabling these administrations to mutually observe each other. Hence OMC processes increase reflexivity and potentially facilitate mutual adaptation and learning.[54] Ideally, therefore, OMC processes are oriented towards 'transplanting' experiences from one setting to another. These processes are 'intergovernmental' in nature and are mainly oriented towards increasing the reflexivity of the MS by enabling them to increase the intensity of their mutual observation. The role of the Commission is therefore mainly to provide the necessary

[52] For the concept of reiteration see P Kjaer, 'Systems in Context: On the Outcome of the Habermas/Luhmann-debate' (2006) *Ancilla Iuris* 66, 70 *f.*

[53] U Haltern, 'Internationales Verfassungsrecht? Anmerkungen zu einer Kopernikanischen Wende' (2003) 128 *Archiv des Öffentlichen Rechts* 511, 512.

[54] For the problematic use of the concept of learning in relation to the OMC see S Kröger, 'When learning hits politics or: Social policy coordination left to the administrations and the NGOs?' (2006) 3 *European Integration Online Papers (EioP).*

infrastructure for these processes and to act as a container within which their institutional memory can 'reside'. The Commission does, however, also play a more active role in OMC processes since it acts as a broker and actively engages in 'persuasive policymaking'. Hence, as we will return to in detail when deconstructing the theory of Directly-Deliberative Polyarchy (DDP), the role of the Commission is not as innocent as it looks. Indeed, the role of broker provides the basis for instrumentialisation of the processes involved by transforming the OMC activities into tools of increased integration. From the perspective of the Commission, OMC processes therefore provide a means of pushing the Europeanisation processes forward within the policy areas where the method is applied. The barriers erected by the MS through their refusal to transfer formal legal competencies to the Commission are thereby circumvented. The Commission is supported in this endeavour by the very nature of social processes as the central lesson arising from those of the OMC is that aperture of the contexts in question is a necessary but insufficient condition for the successful 'transplantation' of knowledge from one context to another. Instead, successful transplantation remains conditioned by the establishment of shared frames. The proactive creation of common areas through an increased substitution of 'national universes' with common 'European universes' is, however, only achievable through far more fundamental and intrusive processes of 'social engineering' which reach far beyond the kind of increased mutual observation initiated through the OMC processes. The failure of the OMC to 'deliver' has therefore provided the Commission with arguments supporting its continued push towards increased harmonisation and detailed regulation.

Comitology structures also serve as instruments that increase reflexivity insofar as they institutionalise forms of mutual observation and information sharing between MS. Partly due to the legal framing of Comitology these structures tend, moreover, to be more stable and dense compared to the OMC processes. In addition, many committees have operated for several decades and have increasingly turned into 'epistemic communities'. The majority of Comitology committees deal with highly complex and technical matters. Hence, the committees tend to be characterised by practices related to specific professions, thereby providing a certain 'common ground'. From the perspective of the Commission, Comitology committees also serve as 'reservoirs of knowledge' and hence as a way of mobilising expertise which the Commission itself does not possess. Apart from offsetting structural deficits in terms of cognitive capacities, Comitology also serves as a way to ensure implementation. As noted earlier, one of the major differences between MS administrations and the Commission is the latter's profound lack of implementation tools. The emergence of Comitology can indeed be seen as a direct response to this deficit insofar as the Comitology structures enable the Commission to rely on the resources of the MS administrations to ensure implementation. However, it is not just a simple question of resources. Rather, Comitology gives MS administrations a stake in the implementation of EC legislation and hence provides the Commission with the possibility of ensuring their commitment. Comitology is therefore heavily based on persuasive policymaking and 'soft power' which, in the absence of the necessary competencies and resources, serve as functional equivalents to traditional demand and control mechanisms. The Comitology machinery is thereby directly oriented towards the generation of norms which underpin the Commission's efforts to ensure compliance with EC legislation, thus reducing the structural deficit of the EU as regards implementation and compliance mechanisms.

Agencies represent another and somewhat special variant. As illustrated in the previous chapter, several kinds of agencies have emerged over the last decade with, however, the common feature that they are networked. Agencies tend to be established within policy areas which have gained a high level of complexity thereby making it increasingly difficult for the Commission to exercise its role as secretariat and ensure the necessary stability of the networks in question. Hence, the secretarial tasks and role as network coordinators have been outsourced to agencies which assume the role of 'mini-Commissions' in relation to these specific tasks. Their intrinsic lack of discretionary competencies, however, largely limits their role to the generation of information and to network coordination. The role as initiator and developer of policy has largely remained with the Commission. Networks therefore seem to fulfil the same function in policy areas with agencies as in the areas dominated only by Comitology as they link hierarchical organisations—Commission, agencies and MS administrations—thereby ensuring that these organisations are embedded within the broader social realm.

It follows from the above that GS can be positively defined as institutional formations relying on the network form and characterised by organisational and legal heterarchy, which act as structural couplings between hierarchically organised organisations, increasing the reflexive capacities of the organisations in question and thereby offsetting the structural deficits of one or more of those organisations.

In addition, and especially in those areas where agencies have emerged, Teubner's distinction between networks and hybrids gains renewed relevance. Whereas OMC processes can be understood as 'pure' networks which merely link organisations, the more mature policy areas—especially those where agencies have emerged—are increasingly characterised by GS which go 'beyond networks'. Such hybrids combine hierarchical models of organisation with heterarchical structures such as Comitology and OMC instruments. Hence, ongoing developments point in the direction of the development of an 'integrated model' of governance which includes elements from all three forms of GS—agencies, Comitology and the OMC.

This is, for example, the case of EFSA, EMEA and the European Chemicals Agency (ECA). These conglomerates consist of elements derived from MS administrations, the Commission, the agency secretariats, agency committees, so-called forums which serve as a basis for OMC-like processes, Comitology committees as well as private actors. None of these structures can, however, claim to be the decisional 'centre'. In organisational terms the agencies tend to act as the centre, while the formal competence of decision making tends to rest within Comitology. But the continuing struggle between the MS and the Commission concerning 'ownership' looms behind Comitology. Hence, such conglomerates cannot be considered either 'intergovernmental' or 'supranational' since they are neither a mere extension of the Commission nor of the MS. Instead these structures are a third form which evades the increasingly desperate attempts to make them 'fit' within the old intergovernmental/supranational paradigm.

In a legal sense these structures are also partly based on hierarchy and partly on heterarchy. They operate within the framework of the 'semi-hierarchy' of community law and can therefore rely on 'direct effect' and 'supremacy' but not on competence-competence (*Kompetenz-Kompetenz*). In the same way as the ECJ depends on the active engagement of national courts and has therefore been forced to develop a strategy of 'persuasive jurisprudence' in order to operate effectively, these conglomerates are characterised by the need to combine elements of command and control with persuasion and the ensurance of commitment by intentionally developing norms which sanction obstruction of the conglomerate's ability to operate. Hence, the existing distinction is increasingly blurred between the OMC, Comitology committees, which the CFI has ruled are structures that do not constitute another Community institution or body just as they do not fall within the third-party category,[55] and agencies, which are bodies with their own legal personality. The emergence of such conglomerates therefore indicates a move towards increased fusion of 'hard' and 'soft' law in the EU context.[56]

As GS combine different forms of rationality and thus serve as buffers which contribute to the dissolution or softening of discourse collisions, it is therefore not surprising that the 'turn to governance' has been characterised as a move towards 'de-differentiation' (*Entdifferenzierung*).[57] It is indeed possible to understand GS in this way and, as the food scandals of the late 1990s illustrate, such de-differentiation is inherently dangerous. GS

[55] *Rothmans v Commission* T-188/97 [1999] ECR II-2463.

[56] DM Trubek, P Cottrell and M Nance, '"Soft Law", "Hard Law" and EU Integration' in G de Burca and J Scott (eds), *New Governance and Constitutionalism* (Oxford, Hart Publishing, 2005).

[57] Eg C Joerges, 'Integration through de-legalisation? An irritated heckler' (2003) 7 *European Governance Papers (EUROGOV)*.

are grey areas and are 'unfortunate' pragmatic solutions which will never gain the 'purity' that characterises most hierarchical organisations. Thus even though they fulfil pivotal functions they are bound to provoke some discomfort and uneasiness because they challenge borders and hence the consistency of meaning (*Sinn*) producing social systems such as the scientific, the economic and the political systems.

On the other hand, coordination of different types of rationality is not only inevitable but is also a necessary function which must be reproduced in order to ensure the integration of society. The function of GS as buffers between different systems and hence different discourses is therefore a positive aspect in their favour. Hence, the discussion of GS can be reduced to the paradoxical problem of functional differentiation. On the one hand, functional differentiation is synonymous with modernity and hence with the concepts of rationality and freedom. On the other hand, it poses a problem because it raises the issue of how society can remain integrated under the condition of functional differentiation. As we will return to in detail later, the key objective should therefore be to develop an institutional design for hybrid structures which are capable of ensuring convergence between different forms of rationality at the same time as maintaining functional differentiation. In addition, focus on the 'totality' of hybrids should be increased, thereby facilitating recognition of their autonomous nature and their reproduction of specific functions necessary for society as such to continue to operate. Hence, the development of a concept of the 'conglomerate interest' would be much more in line with the function and actual operational form of these structures.

5

The Power of Governance

5.1 INTRODUCTION

FOR EACH OF the three forms of GS—agencies, Comitology and the OMC—corresponding theories have been developed. Majone's theory of the regulatory state focuses on regulatory agencies; Joerges and Neyers' theory of deliberative supranationalism explores the Comitology phenomenon, and with various other scholars, Sabel has developed the theory of DDP which is close to the OMC.

But these theories are not only aimed at analysing how the three forms of governance have come into existence and evaluating the way they function. The proponents of the three theories are de facto acting as advocates for the respective forms of GS on which they focus. Hence, the three theories can also be understood as policy proposals which have been developed in order to underpin and promote specific forms of governance. To a certain extent the three theories can therefore be understood as reflecting the self-descriptions of those structures. A 'de-construction' of the theories will therefore indirectly support the attempt to gain a deeper knowledge of the 'self-understanding' inherent in the different forms of GS.

It will be argued that the three theories rely on different assumptions of rationality and three different concepts of power: steering, consensus and conduct of conduct. Hence the proponents of the three theories are inclined to talk at cross-purposes. They therefore fail to recognise that the three forms of GS should be understood as complementary rather than mutually exclusive structures.[1]

[1] See also PF Kjaer, 'Three Forms of Governance and Three Forms of Power' in EO Eriksen, C Joerges and F Rödl (eds), *The Unsettled Political Order of Europe* (Oxford, Routledge, 2008).

5.2 THREE FORMS OF POWER

Three concepts of power can be delineated: (i) a liberalist concept; (ii) a communicative, or reformist, concept; and (iii) a radical concept.[2] The liberalist concept is often associated with the behaviourist tradition within American political science, and especially Dahl's definition, of A's power over B so that A can get B to do something B would otherwise not do.[3] The origins of this concept can be traced to Weber, who stated that 'Power means every chance within a social relationship to assert one's will even against opposition'.[4] Both definitions are methodologically focused on observable behaviour—actual decisions and clear causality. Furthermore, both definitions adopt a pluralist view, in the sense that each assumes a multiplicity of individual actors competing with each other to further their interests on the basis of strategic rationality. Power is not an end in itself, but a teleological tool, a means to achieve certain objectives. One can therefore claim that the liberalist concept of power is essentially an extrapolation from a unidimensional concept of strategic rationality.

In contrast, Habermas, strongly influenced by Arendt, develops a concept of communicative power. This arises out of a criticism of Weber's concept of strategic (cognitive-instrumental) rationality. Habermas views Weberian rationality as too narrow. Consequently, he adds social (moral-practical) and dramaturgical (aesthetic-expressive) forms of rationality to the strategic.[5] However, his main emphasis, again influenced by Arendt, is on that which he labels social rationality. It is from this dimension that Habermas derives the central elements of his concept of power. Accordingly, he does not see power as the instrumentalisation of another's will, but rather as aimed at forging a common will on the basis of consensus established through intersubjectivity.[6] Consequently, consensus becomes an objective in itself within this dimension. But Habermas recognises the extent to which the modern social world consists of systemic structures, more or less autonomous, such as state bureaucracy and the economy, which he argues is dominated by strategic rationality. He therefore

[2] In his classic work on power Steve Lukes also delineates three concepts of power. His distinctions do not, however, correspond to the distinctions presented here. See S Lukes, *Power: A Radical View* (Hampshire, Palgrave, 1974).

[3] R Dahl, 'The Concept of Power' in J Scott (ed), *Power. Critical Concepts* (London, Routledge, 1994) 290. For a similar perspective see HA Simon, 'Notes on the Observation and Measurement of Political Power' (1953) 15 *Journal of Politics* 500.

[4] M Weber, *Wirtschaft und Gesellschaft, 2 vols* (Tübingen, JCB Mohr, 1925) 1, 16 and 2, 1. Also quoted in J Habermas, 'Hannah Arendt's Communications Concept of Power' (1977) 44 (1) *Social Research* 3.

[5] J Habermas, *Theorie des kommunikativen Handelns, Band 2: Zur Kritik der funktionalistischen Vernunft* (Frankfurt am Main, Suhrkamp Verlag, 1981) 304 *ff*.

[6] J Habermas, 'Hannah Arendt's Communications Concept of Power' (1977) 44 (1) *Social Research* 3.

seeks—in contrast to Arendt—to balance strategic and social rationalities. He accepts that the exercise of power often fulfils instrumental objectives, but he argues that these objectives tend at the same time to be embedded in the kind of communicative understanding which derives from the social dimension of rationality.

The radical concept of power, which also can be labelled post-structuralist, is associated with a large number of mainly French theories of society.[7] Here Foucault stands out as the central thinker. Foucault's concept of power is based on a critique of early modern concepts of sovereignty in Europe. These he identifies as based on the following four assumptions: (i) power can be possessed; (ii) power is clearly located in specific organisations, positions and geographical places; (iii) power is a zero-sum phenomenon; and (iv) power represses, and stands in opposition to freedom.[8] Foucault questions these assumptions. He sees power as intrinsic to all forms of communication. Consequently, power can neither be seized nor clearly located. This means that the application of power in any one area does not necessarily lead to its decline in other areas. Freedom and power are intrinsically linked, in that power exists precisely because the subject possesses a choice, which then can be changed through power. Hence, more freedom of choice creates more room for the exercise of power. Against this background, Foucault defines power as the 'conduct of conduct', thus identifying it as the ability to define the field of possible action for others. Not contained within the juridical-political sphere, the conduct of conduct moreover evolves within all kinds of social relations.[9]

In Luhmann's variant of post-structuralism, power is, following Parsons, perceived as a symbolically generalised medium of communication. An intermediary handles the problem of 'double contingency' between *ego* and *alter*. Both *ego* and *alter* possess the ability to make choices, and the symbolically generalised medium of communication reduces contingency by facilitating coordination between the two.[10] All functionally differentiated systems continuously reproduce their respective media (for example, money in the economic system, law in the legal system, love in the intimacy system, truth in the science system and belief in the religious system). The medium of the political system is power and its function is to ensure that *ego* uses *alter* as the premise for its own actions.[11] Luhmann's position

[7] For the best introduction and overview see U Stäheli, *Poststrukturalistische Soziologien* (Bielefeld, Transcript Verlag, 2003).

[8] M Foucault, 'The Subject and Power' in HL Dreyfus and P Rabinow (eds), *Michel Foucault: Beyond Structuralism and Hermeneutics* (Chicago, University of Chicago Press, 1982).

[9] *Ibid*, 221.

[10] R Vanderstraeten, 'Parsons, Luhmann and the Theorem of Double Contingency' (2002) 2 (1) *Journal of Classical Sociology* 77.

[11] N Luhmann, *Politik der Gesellschaft* (Frankfurt am Main, Suhrkamp Verlag, 2000) 31 *ff*.

differs here from Foucault's, which would ascribe power to all symbolically generalised media of communication, since all reduce and normalise communication. Luhmann's argument for reserving power for the political system is that power not only performs the task of coordinating *ego* and *alter* but does this in a specific way: bureaucratic power is based on the ability to impose negative sanctions. Accordingly, Luhmann introduces a distinction between power and influence, restricting the former to the political system.[12] The linking of power to negative sanctions and the focus on the concept of influence makes Luhmann's position somewhat 'less radical' than Foucault's. Luhmann does, however, state that power is not a zero-sum game, and that power cannot be seized or clearly located within specific physical locations.[13] Luhmann and Foucault also correspond regarding the 'old-European' (*Alteuropäische*) origin of prevailing concepts of power and sovereignty and both, as a result, develop a relational concept of power freed from its 17th- and 18th-century ontological roots.

As also pointed out by Göhler, on the basis of the distinction's intransitive/transitive power and regulative/productive power, the three approaches outlined above describe different aspects of power thereby indicating that the power phenomenon cannot be adequately understood through a reliance on only one of the three approaches. Rather they should be understood as complementary approaches, just as the relative weight which the different dimensions of power obtains within a specific social setting remains contingent.[14]

5.3 THE REGULATORY STATE

In his theory of the regulatory state, Majone advocates delegation of discretionary power to non-majoritarian institutions in the form of regulatory agencies. Majone argues that delegation offers solutions to the problem of time: he presents it as an institutional response to the contradiction between the short-term operational perspective of politics and the need in practice for long-term solutions to problems in many policy areas, ranging from central banking and competition policy to risk

[12] Ibid, 45 *f*. The restriction of power to the political system does not, on the other hand, imply that the political system cannot exercise influence as well.

[13] Hence a certain contradiction seems to exist between Luhmann's focus on negative sanctions and his claim that power cannot be located within specific institutions. For an elegant analysis of the affinities and differences between Foucault's and Luhmann's concepts of power see also C Borch, 'Systemic Power: Luhmann, Foucault and analytics of power' (2005) 48 (2) *Acta Sociologica* 155.

[14] G Göhler, 'Constitution and Use of Power' in H Goverde, PG Cerny, M Haugaard and H Lentner (eds), *Power in Contemporary Politics. Theories, Practices, Globalizations* (London, Sage Publications, 2000).

regulation.[15] But Majone emphasises that the problem of time is not only a problem of the short-term in politics. Even if regulation is deemed appropriate, problem solving via political intervention in discretionary policy areas often leads to the application of policies that are already outdated by the time they take effect. Thus, Majone suggests, interventionist measures are typically sub-optimal as policy instruments; they may even tend to do more harm than good. Besides in-built tendencies to opportunism and short-termism, the political system is therefore also characterised by a structural deficit, namely that it does not possess the instruments necessary for undertaking rapid and precise regulation (for example, to adjust interest rates in the area of monetary policy).[16]

The restricted effectiveness of political intervention due to time lags might be thought to indicate that the root problem is caused by limits to the cognitive resources of politicians and political institutions. But Majone dismisses this and instead argues the need for policy credibility as the most important explanation for the delegation of power to non-majoritarian institutions. Politicians delegate competencies to protect specific policy areas from their own short-sightedness. Thus while Majone points out two time-related reasons for delegation he ultimately identifies the 'real' reason as political short-sightedness, thereby subscribing to an 'anthropological' understanding of the *homo politicus*.[17]

According to Majone, non-majoritarian institutions avoid political short-sightedness because such institutions are characterised by three elements: (i) a strong sense of purpose based upon functionality since, at least ideally, only one institution is assigned the task of regulating a well-defined policy area; (ii) strong professional norms, such as expertise, professional discretion, policy consistency, fairness and independence of judgement;[18] (iii) a long-range institutional perspective, tending to imply a strategy for long-term survival, which provides an incentive for the adoption of policies that may be maintained consistently over time. For Majone, a mixture of these three characteristics provides the optimal basis for policy interventions. Their absence at the political level provides the argument for delegation of discretionary powers to non-majoritarian institutions.

Applying the theory of the regulatory state to the EU, Majone further reacts to a problem of space, in that regulatory regimes need to take account of structural changes to the economy through internationalisation.

[15] G Majone, 'Temporal Consistency and Policy Credibility: Why Democracies Need Non-Majoritarian Institutions' (1996) 57 *RSC Working Paper, European University Institute*.

[16] *Ibid*; G Majone (ed), *Regulating Europe* (London, Routledge, 1996).

[17] G Majone, 'The Regulatory State and its Legitimacy Problems' (1998) 56 *IfHS Working Paper, Institut für Höhere Studien* 3.

[18] G Majone, *Dilemmas of European Integration: The Ambiguities and Pitfalls of Integration by Stealth* (Oxford, Oxford University Press, 2005) 37.

Functionally, this creates a need for the transfer of competencies from the national to the European setting. But Majone argues that the delegation of powers to the EU in many areas exceeds what is required in order to establish an IM (e.g. environment, consumer protection, health and safety at work). Majone views this as a result of regulatory competition which provides the sovereigns, that is, the MS, with an incentive to agree on common rules while partly delegating rule-making to a 'neutral broker'. This avoids a situation where other MS impose less costly standards, thereby achieving comparative advantage: common rules are made to preclude the famous race to the bottom. Majone thus sees game-theoretical positioning in the capitals of MS, in pursuit of the objective of ensuring optimal conditions for the economic development of individual states in relation to each other as the primary driving force behind European integration.

The form and content of Majone's theory of the regulatory state clearly shows that he subscribes to the mainstream self-understanding of the political science discipline originally developed in the US context, as well as to the particular version of Weberian thinking which was more or less consciously adopted in its formative period.[19] Not only does he assume the act of delegating power to be straightforward—a consequence of his conception of power as residing in a clearly identifiable sovereign (in the case of the EU, in a number of well-defined MS sovereigns). His understanding of politics—at the national level, as well as between the MS of the EU—is furthermore derived from the pluralist assumption of several actors strategically competing for power. He also presumes that power may be reduced to a zero sum game, and that it is used to further interests of a largely economic nature. He also sees power as opposed to freedom: in general, markets should be left to regulate themselves and only in the event of market failure do the 'unfortunate' necessities of state intervention and regulation come into play.

Adopting this classical liberalist understanding of power, Majone is an obvious potential target for the critique advanced by Foucault and Luhmann of the 20th-century tendency to adopt, in a non-reflexive manner, the conceptual tools of power and sovereignty developed in the period prior to the French Revolution. But the affinity of Majone's analysis with 'old-European semantics' does not stop here: his concept of bureaucracy also displays a clear Weberian heritage. The professional norms Majone refers to—expertise, professional discretion, policy consistency, fairness and independence of judgment—are almost identical to the norms Weber highlighted as essential elements of modern bureaucracy.[20] However,

[19] J Bartelson, *The Critique of the State* (Cambridge, Cambridge University Press, 2001).

[20] M Weber, 'Bureaucracy' in H Gerth and CW Mills (eds), *From Max Weber* (Oxford, Oxford University Press, 1946).

Weber's theory of bureaucracy has become rather 'old-fashioned', in the sense that it does not take into account the autonomous role and self-interest of bureaucracies, the partial breakdown of hierarchy, or the erosion of limits on external contacts. In classic concepts of bureaucracy, such contacts were the exclusive reserve of the hierarchical peak whose main function was to represent organisations towards their environment.[21]

Moreover, the EU context differs profoundly from that of the nation state. As illustrated earlier, the cognitive resources of the EU differ radically from those possessed by MS just as the EU is characterised by an almost complete lack of implementation and compliance tools.[22] Moreover, it is precisely to compensate for this structural deficit in information-gathering capabilities and control mechanisms that the EU system and MS administrations are linked through GS such as Comitology and 'networked' agencies. While Majone rejects the cognitive explanation as unsophisticated,[23] it may, on the contrary, be argued that a quest for increased cognitive resources is a central reason for the emergence of GS at European level.

Overall, the evolution of the European integration processes, and especially the 'turn to governance', illustrate that Majone's Weberian approach is based on outdated theoretical premises and, seen as a policy proposal, is a construction out of touch with reality. This is also illustrated by the fact that only a few of the EU agencies possess discretionary powers and none of them have complete independence.

Yet the more fundamental problem with Majone's theory of delegation to non-majoritarian institutions is that it presupposes the EU's transformation into a state (although only a regulatory state): a massive transfer of competencies to EU level would be needed to realise Majone's presupposition that regulatory agencies should possess exclusive competency in their respective fields, since delegation to agencies is conditioned by previous delegation of competency from the MS to the EU. Currently, however, the EU only possesses exclusive competence in the realms of competition policy and evaluation of fish stocks. It is therefore not surprising that EU competition policy serves as a role model for Majone's theory.[24] But this is problematic given the particular nature of competition policy which makes

[21] The fact that Hegel in his Philosophy of Rights developed a theory of bureaucracy which is basically identical with Weber's much later theory also highlights the 'old European' and early modern origin of Weber's theory of bureaucracy. See GWF Hegel, *Grundlinjen des Philosophie des Rechts, Werke Band* 7 (Frankfurt am Main, Suhrkamp Verlag, [1821] 1970) § 287–97.

[22] C Joerges and M Zürn (eds), *Law and Governance in Postnational Europe. Compliance Beyond the Nation-State* (Cambridge, Cambridge University Press, 2005).

[23] G Majone, 'The Regulatory State and its Legitimacy Problems' (1998) 56 *IfHS Working Paper, Institut für Höhere Studien* 3.

[24] G Majone, 'Temporal Consistency and Policy Credibility: Why Democracies Need Non-Majoritarian Institutions' (1996) 57 *RSC Working Paper* 47.

it impossible to extrapolate from it a general regulatory model for Europe. Moreover, recent reform of EU competition policy points towards the establishment of a network of competition regulators,[25] with the potential to soften the existing principal–agent structure and thereby weaken the last stronghold of the classic liberalist perspective on regulatory measures in the EU context.

In conclusion, Majone's analysis goes several bridges too far. The conditions under which his policy proposal might be realised require substantial further centralisation of policy making at EU level as well as an increase in vertical governing as opposed to horizontal GS. Moreover, the unreflexive approach of the concept of state evinces commitment to an outdated ontological heritage, while methodological nationalism results from his uncritical transfer of concepts from the nation state to the EU context.[26]

Yet current trajectories of integration and constitutionalisation processes indicate that single European statehood, whether of modern, post-modern or regulatory form,[27] is out of reach for the foreseeable future. Majone acknowledges this in his latest work, which abandons the earlier concept of the regulatory state based on competition policy, and instead finds in the CFSP a new model for establishment of a European Confederation.[28] Attempting to scale back his ambitions, Majone nevertheless remains committed to a classical liberalist concept of power, seeing it as a principal–agent structure which makes governing—as opposed to governance—the most suitable way to steer social interaction in the European context.

5.4 DELIBERATIVE SUPRANATIONALISM

Important parts of Majone's theory were advanced before the establishment of a large number of European agencies. Accordingly, his work can be seen as a deductive exercise intending to develop a theory, or policy plan, which would be put into practice. Joerges and Neyer have taken another route. Their analysis of Comitology, devised within the parameters of their theory of deliberative supranationalism, aims to illuminate an already existing but frequently disregarded structure. In combination, they

[25] I Maher, 'Competition Law in the International Domain: Networks as a New Form of Governance' (2002) 29 (1) *Journal of Law and Society* 112.

[26] M Zürn, 'Politik in der postnationalen Konstellation. Über das Elend des methodologischen Nationalismus' in C Landfried (Hrsg), *Politik in einer entgrenzten Welt* (Köln, Verlag Wissenschaft und Politik, 2001).

[27] JA Caporaso, 'The European Union and Forms of State: Westphalian, Regulatory or Post-Modern' (1996) 1 (34) *Journal of Common Market Studies* 29.

[28] G Majone, *Dilemmas of European Integration: The Ambiguities and Pitfalls of Integration by Stealth* (Oxford, Oxford University Press, 2005).

undertake an inductive investigation of the extent to which this structure provides a framework for deliberation. In doing so, they adopt Habermas' normative objectives for the development of legitimate structures of political deliberation at European level.[29] However, Joerges and Neyer reject Habermas' rather traditional agenda for the replication of national constitutional structures at European level. In their view, the construction of a European federal state has not and cannot be expected to be realised. The EU's current status as a hybrid—it is more than an international organisation, but less than a federation—appears to have acquired a certain permanence. Joerges and Neyer's project can be seen as a pragmatic attempt to explore how far Habermas' normative objectives concerning the establishment of deliberative structures beyond the nation-state setting can be achieved in the context of hybridisation.

Their first claim is that the normative ideal of ensuring legitimacy of supranational structures via deliberation is not just an ideal: elements of deliberation are already embedded in the political and administrative practices of the EU, most notably Comitology. Comitology is seen as a potential area for deliberation because it is embedded in a robust legal framework establishing a procedural infrastructure that facilitates arrival at consensus through deliberation. On the other hand, this ideal is not fully realised in Comitology's political-administrative practices. Deliberative supranationalism is therefore developed as a partly descriptive and partly normative concept, embodying the intention to bridge the gap between normative discourse and political realities.[30] Accordingly, deliberative supranationalism can be characterised as a hybrid concept developed for a hybrid structure, in that it not only describes how 'real-world' political and administrative processes develop in the European context, but also act as a regulatory idea.

In contrast to Majone, Joerges and Neyer explain why the evolution of the processes of European integration and constitutionalisation have not led to a regulatory state, with the establishment of regulatory agencies as a logical consequence of the transformation of the EU into a conglomerate with massive regulatory functions. They argue that the reason that the Commission and MS have retained discretionary competencies within Comitology structures, and only half-heartedly support the establishment

[29] J Habermas, 'Why Europe Needs A Constitution' (2001) 11 (5) *New Left Review* 5; J Habermas, 'Euroskepsis, Matkteuropa oder Europa der (Welt-)Bürger', in UK Preuß and T Maak (Hrsg.), *Die Wirtschaft in der Gesellschaft* (Bern, Paul Haupt Verlag, 2000); J Habermas, *Die postnationale Konstellation* (Frankfurt am Main, Surhkamp Verlag, 1998).

[30] C Joerges and J Neyer, 'Transforming Strategic interaction into deliberative problem-solving: European comitology in the foodstuffs sector' (1997) 4 (4) *Journal of European Public Policy* 609, 610 *ff*; C Joerges and J Neyer, 'From Intergovernmental Bargaining to Deliberative Political Processes: The Constitutionalisation of Comitology' (1997) 3 *European Law Journal* 273.

of regulatory agencies (though they were proposed in the Commission's White Paper on Governance), is that the concept of the regulatory state does not sufficiently acknowledge the normative-political aspects of regulation. These are especially strong in the area of risk regulation, on which Joerges and Neyer focus.[31] No constitutional state so far has completely delegated risk regulation to non-majoritarian institutions.[32] The political dimension is accentuated where regulation imposes substantial economic costs (costs which de facto are distributive, in the sense that the costs are not equally divided)[33] on industry and consumers. Classic principal-agent concepts, such as Majone's, fail to realise that social constructions are more than the sum of their parts, and have an autonomous impact on their constituent units. It is this additional element which leads to the need for autonomous justification of their operations, beyond the kind of output legitimacy, which offers the sole justification for agreements reached by bargaining.[34] Again, risk regulation offers an obvious example, since here scientific knowledge acts as a filter for strategic objectives. Joerges and Neyer argue that proponents of classic principal-agent theories fail to adequately recognise the role of commonly accepted scientific knowledge and scientific argumentation in day-to-day decision making in risk regulation.

As already seen, Habermas' normative objective of promoting rational political outcomes on the basis of consensus-oriented deliberation and the 'non-forced force of the better argument', serves as the guiding principle for the theory of deliberative supranationalism. It aims to highlight the limitations of a one-sided focus on strategic interaction, which is seen as neither corresponding to reality, nor normatively satisfactory.[35] In this light it is relatively straightforward to conclude that deliberative supranationalism is based on Habermas' concept of rationality and an understanding of power as communicative power, driven just as much by consensus as by strategic interaction.

Though their Habermasian foundations are not systematically scrutinised or evaluated by Joerges and Neyer, the theory of deliberative supranationalism still indirectly (and probably unintentionally) launches a

[31] European Commission: *European Governance. A White Paper*, COM (2001) 428 Final 24. Available at http://eur-lex.europa.eu/LexUriServ/site/en/com/2001/com2001_0428en01.pdf.

[32] C Joerges and J Neyer, 'From Intergovernmental Bargaining to Deliberative Political Processes: The Constitutionalisation of Comitology' (1997) 3 *European Law Journal* 273, 278.

[33] *Ibid*, 278.

[34] C Joerges and J Neyer, 'Transforming Strategic interaction into deliberative problem-solving: European comitology in the foodstuffs sector' (1997), 4 (4) *Journal of European Public Policy* 609, 615 *ff*.

[35] C Joerges, 'Deliberative Supranationalism – Two Defences' (2002) 8 (1) *European Law Journal* 133 and 140.

severe critique of Habermas' deliberative theory. One main problem with the latter is that it remains too close to Arendt's concept of the political. Arendt conceptualises the political sphere and the social sphere as opposed, with power strictly reserved for the former. Owing to a nostalgic attachment to this thinking, Habermas continues to regard bureaucratic structures as inherently problematic rather than as potential spaces for deliberation in their own right. This view is not only expressed in Habermas' legal and political philosophy, but also leads to the distinction between system and lifeworld in his theory of communicative action, with the lifeworld understood as the context of culturally and linguistically organised patterns of interpretation within which subjects find themselves.[36] This common ground consists of 'implicit or unimpaired beliefs' ('*Selbstverständlichkeiten oder unerschütterten Überzeugungen*'),[37] which make it possible for two or more subjects to form a common understanding of the world on the basis of an already-existing shared interpretation. Negatively reserving the concept of lifeworld to the non-bureaucratic and non-economic spheres of society, Habermas implies a very simplified understanding of the function and self-understanding of bureaucrats (as well as of private sector actors), and a very limited view of social practice occurring within bureaucratic structures.

In developing his concept of trust as a substitute for the Habermasian lifeworld, Luhmann focuses on the concept of reiteration. Every social operation which is repeated is a condensing operation which increases the 'pre-knowledge' available for future social operations.[38] Given the strong role of procedures in bureaucratic organisations, a consequence of Luhmann's position is that he can argue that the lifeworld actually becomes a strong feature of the social operations of such organisations.[39] In turn Luhmann can therefore claim that the potential basis for evolution of the social dimension of rationality is in fact relatively stronger within the realm of bureaucracy than elsewhere. This then allows Luhmann to argue that social norms, and not only the kind of 'pre-knowledge' which Habermas focuses on, play a substantial role within bureaucratic structures.

From this Luhmannian perspective, Joerges and Neyer's attempt to expand the empirical validity and normative reach of Habermas' theory so as to encompass bureaucratic structures can be seen as an important

[36] J Habermas, *Theorie des kommunikativen Handelns, Band 1: Handlungsrationalität und gesellschaftliche Rationalisierung* (Frankfurt am Main, Suhrkamp Verlag, 1981) 386.

[37] J Habermas, *Theorie des kommunikativen Handelns, Band 2: Zur Kritik der funktionalistischen Vernunft* (Frankfurt am Main, Suhrkamp Verlag, 1981) 189.

[38] N Luhmann, 'Die Lebenswelt – nach Rücksprache mit Phänomenologen' (1986) 72 (2) *Archiv für Rechts- und Sozialphilosophie* 176, 177; N Luhmann, 'Familiarity, Confidence, Trust: Problems and Alternatives' in D Gambetta (ed), *Trust: Making and Breaking Cooperative Relations* (New York, Basil Blackwell, 1988).

[39] N Luhmann, 'Lob der Routine' (1964) 55 *Verwaltungsarchiv* 1.

reinforcement.[40] Habermas has, however, rejected the concept of deliberative supranationalism due to the lack of input-legitimacy within regulatory structures such as Comitology,[41] and instead continues to maintain that bureaucratic structures need to be kept under 'permanent siege' by the public sphere[42] if the normative ideal of achieving legitimacy through deliberation is to have any chance of realisation. This perspective is also supported by Habermas' followers, such as Schmalz-Bruns, who has argued that deliberative supranationalism favours technocratic regulation at the cost of 'true politics'.[43]

Instead of engaging in debate on the theoretical implications of their approach, Joerges and Neyer have concentrated on providing empirical evidence to support their claim that most Comitology decisions issue from consensus achieved via deliberation rather than through strategic bargaining.[44] Thereby they have sought to undermine the empirical validity of Majone's assumption concerning the dominance of strategic interaction and at the same time corroborate their own claim about the autonomous value of Comitology deliberations. Though their findings have been supportive on both counts,[45] given the limited extent of their empirical investigations, it remains difficult to extrapolate from them to the broader range of committees in the EU system. As a result, the extent to which the theory of deliberative supranationalism can be generalised remains uncertain. Both the theory and empirical investigations relating to it need to be expanded in scope and refined if deliberative supranationalism is to develop into a general theory of Comitology or of committees across different phases of the European policy cycle.

[40] For further elaboration see P Kjaer, 'Systems in Context: On the Outcome of the Habermas/Luhmann-debate' (2006) *Ancilla Iuris* 66.

[41] J Habermas, 'Why Europe Needs A Constitution' (2001) 11 (5) *New Left Review* 5, 7.

[42] J Habermas, 'Further Reflections on the Public Sphere' C Calhoun (ed), *Habermas and the Public Sphere* (Cambridge, MIT Press, 1992) 452. Also quoted in J Cohen and C Sabel, 'Directly-Deliberative Polyarchy' (1997) 3 (4) *European law Journal* 313, 339.

[43] R Schmalz-Bruns, 'Grenzerfahrungen und Grenzüberschreitungen: Demokratie in integrierten Europa?' in B Kohler-Koch (Hrsg.), *Regieren in entgrenzten Räumen* (Opladen, Westdeutscher Verlag, 1998); R Schmalz-Bruns, 'Deliberativer Supranationalismus' (1999) 6 (2) *Zeitschrift für Internationale Beziehungen* 185.

[44] C Joerges and J Neyer, 'Transforming Strategic interaction into deliberative problem-solving: European comitology in the foodstuffs sector' (1997) 4 (4) *Journal of European Public Policy* 609, 610; C Joerges and J Neyer, 'From Intergovernmental Bargaining to Deliberative Political Processes: The Constitutionalisation of Comitology' (1997) 3 *European Law Journal* 273.

[45] C Joerges and J Neyer, 'Transforming Strategic interaction into deliberative problem-solving: European comitology in the foodstuffs sector' (1997) 4 (4) *Journal of European Public Policy* 609, 610; C Joerges and J Neyer, 'From Intergovernmental Bargaining to Deliberative Political Processes: The Constitutionalisation of Comitology' (1997) 3 *European Law Journal* 273.

5.5 DIRECTLY-DELIBERATIVE POLYARCHY

Sabel, together with Cohen, Gerstenberg and Zeitlin, has developed the theory of DDP. DDP, it is argued, provides theoretical underpinning for the OMC. DDP proponents distance themselves from the positions of Habermas and Arendt, arguing their own theory to be more radical in seeking to extend the sphere of deliberation and participatory democracy to the bureaucratic and economic areas of society, as well as to civil society and thereby to society as a whole.[46] The theory of DDP emphasises direct participation, the independent value of deliberation, pluralism, and concrete problem solving. Starting from the US context, they emphasise civil society, comprising family, church and voluntary associations, as a third sphere for the production of social capital besides the state and the market. Accordingly, they regard 'street actions' where citizens 'come together' in partnership with public authorities to solve practical problems in the local area (for example, crime control and renewal of neighbourhoods) as a deliberative democratic ideal.[47] While they assume the continued presence of institutional structures such as legislators, courts, executives and administrative agencies, they nevertheless shift the focus away from institutions towards concrete problem solving. In doing so they highlight the limited nature of institutional problem-solving capacities and accentuate the role of the third sphere as a repository of problem solving outside state and market.[48]

Claiming that this inherently optimistic theory has anything in common with a Foucauldian perspective might seem surprising. But the advocates of DDP build, more or less consciously, on the basic elements of the poststructuralist concept of power at the same time as they invert it. On the one hand, like Foucault, they assume that power is 'everywhere', and accordingly, they reject the assumption that it may be found only in specific institutional structures. Moreover, they do not view power as a zero-sum phenomenon: the focus on the development of a third dimension between state and market suggests potential for an increase in citizens' power without any claim of a concomitant reduction in power produced in other areas. Further, DDP proponents do not claim that power opposes freedom. Instead, power is an ability-enhancing tool. Bearing in mind that post-structuralism partakes in broader themes in post-modernist thinking, it is also notable that their theory has a post-modernist undertone, in

[46] J Cohen and C Sabel, 'Directly-Deliberative Polyarchy' (1997) 3 (4) *European Law Journal* 313; J Cohen and C Sabel, 'Sovereignty and Solidarity: EU and US' in J Zeitlin and DM Trubek, *Governing Work and Welfare in a New Economy. European and American Experiments* (Oxford, Oxford University Press, 2003).

[47] J Cohen and C Sabel, 'Directly-Deliberative Polyarchy' (1997) 3 (4) *European Law Journal*, 313–42, 315.

[48] *Ibid*, 334.

explicitly renouncing concern with principles, identity, solidarity or ideology. Instead, it is a 'pure' problem-solving tool, without modernist nation-state or welfare-society-based connotations.[49] Despite such affinities with the Foucauldian concept of power, as already indicated, DDP turns the former concept upside down. Whereas Foucault regards power as an intrusion, the proponents of DDP see it as an inherently positive concept. A reduction of the differences between continental-European post-structuralism and the theory of DDP into a distinction between pessimism and optimism is of course an oversimplification.[50] Nonetheless, the difference between the concept of power developed by Foucault and the perspective taken by promoters of DDP can be largely boiled down to a fundamental distinction between 'anthropological' views about the 'true' nature of social practices, while paradoxically seeming to agree on the structure of those practices.

Whether one can find a basis for the optimism of DDP advocates in the United States is not an issue for debate here. Instead, the issue is their attempt to combine the theory of DDP with the concept of the OMC in the European context. As indicated, a common feature of the different versions of the OMC is that they all rely on comparisons, evaluations, benchmarking and peer reviews as their main policy instruments. These instruments are seen as process-oriented tools whose substance is continuously revised via incorporation of new knowledge and lessons learned. Consequently, deployment of these instruments is intended to foster policy experimentation and knowledge creation, flexibility and revisability of normative and policy standards. The OMC furthermore aims to achieve the highest possible level of participation and diversity, as well as radical decentralisation.[51]

Sabel and Zeitlin argue that these characteristics mean that the OMC expresses the very essence of DDP. The OMC is deliberative, they claim, because it deploys arguments to disrupt settled practices and redefine interests. It is directly deliberative because it involves actors with direct 'field experience' to generate different reactions and open up new possibilities. And it is polyarchic because it is a system where local units can learn, discipline and set goals for each other.[52]

Several instructive studies have been conducted regarding the OMC's operational mode. Their findings suggest that although free discussion,

[49] J Cohen and C Sabel, 'Sovereignty and Solidarity: EU and US' in J Zeitlin and DM Trubek, *Governing Work and Welfare in a New Economy. European and American Experiments* (Oxford, Oxford University Press, 2003) 362.

[50] J Baudrillard, *America* (London, Sage Publications, 2000).

[51] MJ Rodrigues, *European Policies for a Knowledge Economy* (Cheltenham, Edward Elgar, 2003).

[52] CF Sabel and J Zeitlin, 'Learning from Diffference: The New Architecture of Experimentalist Governance in the European Union' (2006) 18 *La Follette School Working Paper* 7.

exchange of ideas and deliberation appear to be relatively strong features of the operational mode of the committees created to facilitate the OMC, the deliberative element tends to decline as the initial problem-identifying phases expire. Further, the processes tend to be institutionalised and 'framed' as workload expands, and the level of deliberation seems to decline the more the process moves away from 'cheap talk' and the closer it gets to 'real' decisions with important policy implications.[53] It has also been observed that participating civil servants often act on rather narrow mandates, tending to exclude deliberation, and are inclined to adopt 'defensive' positions because they are charged with defending the way a given policy area is organised in their home state.[54]

In addition, as Smismans has illustrated, the idea that participation of actors with 'hands-on' experience is particularly strong within the OMC is largely a myth.[55] Rather than being a process whereby new knowledge is continuously derived from actors on the ground, the OMC works on ideal models which enable ongoing evaluation of the MS performance. The ideal model in the area of the EES consists of a mixture of the Nordic and Anglo-Saxon labour market paradigms. Within the area of social inclusion, the ideal model comprises Nordic and corporatist elements as found, for example, in Germany and the Netherlands.[56] Such ideal models have been developed within rather closed policy circles composed of civil servants from the Commission and MS ministries. The influence of the Commission in this context should not be underestimated, as ideal models tend to be developed principally by Commission officials, followed by minor amendments introduced by MS civil servants.

Overall the discovery of gaps between the ideals of the DDP concerning deliberation, participation and pluralism and the actual operational mode of the OMC undermines the latter's definition as a polyarchic process. But a more fundamental problem looms. The DDP was developed in and for the US context and its application to the European setting has so far remained an essentially ancillary exercise. The problem, however, is that transferring the theory from one setting to another restricts its value. For example, DDP advocates emphasise that their theory aims to complement the classical institutions of power, which they assume continue to exist and—within limits—to function. But at EU level, institutions characterising democratic nation states are absent or still 'under construction'. This is

[53] S Borrás and B Greve, 'Concluding remarks: new method or just cheap talk?' (2004) 11 (2) *Journal of European Public Policy* 329.

[54] *Ibid.*

[55] S Smismans, 'New Modes of Governance and the Participatory Myth' (2006) 1 *European Governance Papers (EUROGOV)*.

[56] C de la Porte, 'Is the Open Method of Co-ordination Appropriate for Organising Activities at the European Level in Sensitive Policy Areas?' (2002) 8 (1) *European Law Journal* 38.

true in particular of political institutions that mediate between governors and governed, be it via political parties or otherwise. It therefore remains impossible to define the EU in its present form as a democracy, since there is no clear *locus* of power and no possibility of ousting those who govern by means of general elections. Deployment of DDP-inspired modes, such as the OMC in the EU context, therefore threatens to produce radically different and unintended results compared to the US setting, where they serve mainly as constructive 'jesters', continuously challenging the assumptions on which advanced democratic institutions operate. That DDP-inspired modes exert a fundamentally different impact on basic institutional structures in the EU setting is already apparent. Whereas DDP methods have never been considered as actually or potentially undermining the separation of powers on which the political and the legal system of the United States rests, the evolution of the OMC has already thrown substantial elements of the EU's IB, which absent of alternatives must be considered a crucial safeguard measure in the EU context, into question. This is so because the OMC, in the policy areas where it is applied, breaks down institutional borders between Council and Commission, while the EP remains excluded from OMC processes. In addition the OMC is not subject to juridical review.

The OMC's actual impact also remains difficult to assess. This is a result of the very nature of its process, since it is not intended to produce 'real' decisions, but rather to ensure continued transformation of discursive structures. The main outcome of OMC processes is a common language in the form of key concepts, classifications, indicators and a common knowledge base, which is followed up by strategic diffusion of knowledge and evaluation of results.[57] With their strong emphasis on ideal models, OMC processes can also be described as oriented towards the establishment of discursive hegemony (Gramsci) and 'voluntary' internalisation of preferences and norms associated with these models amongst relevant actors in the MS. In other words, and bearing in mind that the vast majority of policy areas in which it is applied have only recently been 'uploaded' to the European level, the OMC can be defined as an instrument for 'entrepreneurial discourse construction'. It is a method which creates common European universes within policy areas which until now have been dominated by separate, nationally embedded discourses. From the Brussels perspective, the OMC has therefore become an instrument that can be used to create new 'fields of action'.

Still, its effects are to a large extent 'invisible', as they are achieved by reiteration. The message contained in the ideal models developed is

[57] K Jacobsson, 'Soft Regulation and the Subtle Transformation of States: The Case of EU Employment Policy' (2004) 14 (4) *Journal of European Public Policy* 355.

repeated over and again within ongoing evaluation processes. Such repetitive exercises tend to subsume the message as part of an unquestioned normality. As already stated, the OMC does not aim to intervene directly in the selection of social operations, but rather seeks to alter the perspective and reality of the social structures in question by encouraging the internalisation of objectives developed within the scope of the method. The OMC can therefore be considered an instrument which expresses the essence of Foucault's definition of power as the conduct of conduct. With its emphasis on soft, indirect and invisible power, largely deployed beyond the shadow of hierarchy, the OMC also illustrates the continued relevance of Luhmann's distinction between power, with its foundations in negative sanctions, and influence. From a Habermasian perspective, the form of soft power produced by the OMC can in addition be seen as based on a dramaturgical (aesthetic-expressive) concept of rationality, insofar as it is concerned more with form than substance.

5.6 COMPLEMENTARY FORMS OF GOVERNANCE

The three theories of governance respectively associated with the regulatory state, Comitology and the OMC emerge from different schools of thought and different assumptions about rationality and power. As the majority of the proponents of the different theories are pragmatists, preferring to focus on the development of concrete policy proposals rather than on clarifying their theoretical basis, they are inclined to talk at cross purposes. Within the larger context of European integration they also tend to focus on different policy areas and regulatory structures, with the result that their theories remain partial, none being sufficiently complex to encompass the whole range of regulatory measures at the European level.

Developing such a general theory is of course difficult, given the complexity of issues in question and the extreme dynamism of the evolution of regulatory measures at European level. Nonetheless, a clearer picture can be developed through contextualisation of the different modes of governance within the larger realm of the European integration process, and by strengthening the focus on the societal functions which different forms of GS reproduce within this setting. The basis of such a theory would have to be a multidimensional concept of rationality, which is not only capable of incorporating the functional, social and time dimensions of social structures but also acknowledges that they are, in principle, of equal importance although the relative weight of each dimension differs within different contexts and in relation to the reproduction of different societal functions. In addition, the diverse characteristics of power, as highlighted by Foucault, should be acknowledged at the same time as the higher density of power within formalised institutional forms should be taken into consideration. Hence, departing from a broad concept of power encompassing all forms of communication, it would be necessary to develop a concept of power capable of highlighting the graduated differences in the density of power. A concept capable of encompassing the differences between, for example, OMC and full-blown regulatory agencies, by emphasising the differences in the societal functions produced, also implies that social relations are characterised by different degrees of asymmetry and differences in the relative weight between different forms of power.

In addition, such a concept would have the advantage that it would provide a basis for understanding the three forms of GS as complementary rather than mutually exclusive. Although the three modes of governance are complex phenomena, with several subordinate forms identifiable within each, a bird's eye view shows that the societal functions of the three forms embody three different modes of regulating social interaction: respectively, they describe themselves as oriented towards achieving convergence, harmonisation and steering. In addition, all three forms of governance are intrinsically linked to the attempt to achieve increased integration, in that they can respectively be labelled as pre-integrative, integrative and post-integrative forms of governance.

As previously seen, the OMC is de facto used to 'upload' policy areas which have not to date been subject to common European approaches, and is deployed mainly within policy areas falling outside the CM. In addition, due to substantial divergences in the organisation of the policy areas in question across the MS, the OMC process can be considered as reflecting attempts to achieve increased convergence in policy areas where political resistance and technical difficulties facing harmonisation are substantial. From this perspective, and to the extent that it succeeds in terms of outputs, the OMC is likely to provide a structural basis for increased integration through competence transfers at a later date.

In contrast to the OMC's role as a soft mode of governance which, in its pure form, does not imply any formal transfer of competencies, Comitology serves as the engine room of integration, in that its main task has been harmonisation and continued evaluation and revision of standards in the wake of competence transfers. As a result, Comitology has traditionally been activated in the more intense phases of integration when the 'technical specifications' of new harmonising initiatives needed to be fleshed out.

Although as a policy proposal the concept of the regulatory state remains largely unachieved, were it to be introduced by the establishment of regulatory agencies with full discretionary powers, the EU would possess state-like powers in those policy areas which would consequently represent the 'completion' of integration processes. This would imply a move towards a post-integrative phase, where the main policy concern would no longer be the question of increased integration but rather the day-to-day exercise of top-down steering in the relevant policy area. As the latest reform of EU competition policy indicates, such forms of steering are, however, unlikely to prevail as a dominant mode of regulation in a hybrid structure such as the EU. On the contrary, a scaling back of centralisation remains a possible long-term outcome within competition policy as well as within the CFP.[58]

[58] For the CFP see G Majone, *Dilemmas of European Integration. The Ambiguities and Pitfalls of Integration by Stealth* (Oxford, Oxford University Press, 2005) 111.

6

The Governance of Knowledge

6.1 INTRODUCTION

THE VIEW OF the OMC as a 'pre-integration' instrument presented in the previous chapter can be further demonstrated through a reconstruction of its mode of operating in an existing setting. The policy area of R&D is a good candidate for two reasons. First, R&D is linked to the more fundamental societal transformation processes characterising late modernity and is thus an area where societal pressure for the development of new policies and policy tools is very high. Second, as noted earlier, R&D is one of the policy areas where the OMC was introduced because earlier attempts to achieve integration through traditional means had failed. Consequently, it is a policy area with a lengthy European history, thus facilitating an evaluation of the 'added value' introduced by the OMC when compared to previous policy efforts. The findings indicate that the 'direct effect' of the OMC is rather limited. The main change brought about by introduction of the OMC is a semantic shift as the process has supported a 're-framing' through a substitution of 'science' with 'R&D' and 'innovation'. The OMC in R&D thereby highlights the general societal move towards an adoption of economic semantics within areas that lie outside the economic system.[1]

The case study will, moreover, modify the earlier claim that the OMC was introduced in the 1990s. The deployment of OMC instruments in the area of R&D policy was by no means limited to the 1990s and the new millennium. Developments within the area of R&D illustrate instead that such instruments have been deployed from the very beginning of the integration process, with the objective of preparing the ground for 'real' integration. The findings thereby substantiate the previous claim that the OMC serves as a 'pre-integration' mechanism and does not as such imply de-formalisation.[2] On the contrary, the OMC have contributed to a

[1] See also PF Kjaer, 'Formalisation or De-formalisation through Governance?' in R Nickel (ed), *Conflict of Laws and Laws of Conflict in Europe and Beyond – Patterns of Supranational and Transnational Juridification* (Oslo, ARENA Report Series, 01, 2009).

[2] For an understanding of the OMC as a deformalising measure see C Joerges, 'Integration durch Entrechtlichung? Ein Zwischenruf' (2007) 1 *ZERP-Diskussionspapier*.

systematisation, intensification and professionalisation of already existing informal modes of 'pre-integration activities'—policy activities which have evolved prior to formal competence transfers throughout the history of the integration process.

6.2 THE EXPANSION OF KNOWLEDGE

R&D policy is linked to profound societal changes expressed in fashionable terms such as the 'information society' and the 'knowledge society'. The term 'information society' implies that a tendency towards increased temporalisation can be observed, in that the time interval occurring between the introductions of distinctions is continually reduced. In practice, this means that the period over which scientific knowledge, news, legal regulations, political decisions, products and other social manifestations remain relevant is continually diminishing because the pace with which they are being replaced is increasing.[3] This is not a new phenomenon since increased temporalisation has been a key characteristic of modernity since Kant praised the ability of the emerging modern states to pursue constant reform.[4] We are thus merely experiencing an intensification of distinctively modern processes. Increased temporalisation does, however, mean that all sectors of society are faced with an increased demand for continual change and adaptation. Hence, the related term 'knowledge society' implies that the constant and systematic ability to produce new knowledge, and especially the ability to proactively use such knowledge in the development of products, decisions, regulations and so forth, is a key characteristic of present-day society. But knowledge is not only being used proactively to 'drive development forward', it is also being deployed reactively to produce adequate responses to new knowledge developed in other spheres of society. Public authorities, for example, are continuously faced with a demand to develop new knowledge in order to maintain their ability to assess the risks involved in relation to the

[3] For a critical theory perspective on the acceleration of time see H Rosa, *Bechleunigung. Die Veränderung der Zeitstrukturen in der Moderne* (Frankfurt am Main, Suhrkamp Verlag, 2005) and WE Scheuerman, *Liberal Democracy and the Social Acceleration of Time* (Baltimore, Md, Johns Hopkins University Press, 2004); for a systems theory perspective see N Luhmann, *Soziale Systeme. Grundriß einer allgemeinen Theorie* (Frankfurt am Main, Suhrkamp Verlag, 1984) 253 *ff*; N Luhmann, 'The Future Cannot Begin: Temporal Structures in Modern Society' (1976) 1 (43) *Social Research* 130; N Luhmann, 'Die Knappheit der Zeit und die Vordringlichkeit des Befristeten' in N Luhmann, *Politische Planung* (Opladen, Westdeutscher Verlag, 1971). For a poststructuralist perspective see P Virilio, *Vitesse et Politique: essai de dromologie* (Paris, éd. Galilée, 1977).

[4] For a Kantian analysis of organisation as reorganisation see G Harste, *Modernitet og Organisation* (København, Forlaget Politisk Revy, 1997).

introduction of new products on the market. These products are themselves the result of the transformation of new knowledge into new products. Consequently, the ongoing transformation processes imply that structures with strong cognitive features such as science, technology and economics become increasingly important relative to normatively based structures such as law, politics and morality.[5]

These developments means that political decision making, legal judgments, interpretations of events by the media, product development and so forth increasingly rely on scientific knowledge and the advice of experts.[6] The 'competitive advantage' of private and public organisations, as well as cities, states and regions such as Europe, therefore becomes more dependent on the existence of well-developed research environments, and the strategic fostering of such environments becomes an increasingly important activity of public organisations.

6.3 THE EVOLUTION OF EUROPEAN SCIENTIFIC CO-OPERATION

The evolution of R&D policies in the EU to a great extent reflects a general development towards increased reliance on knowledge in radicalised modernity. European co-operation in the broader realm of science has, however, a long history which goes beyond the present focus on R&D, and beyond co-operation within the framework of the community and the Union. The European Nuclear Research Centre (CERN) was founded in 1953 on the basis of an intergovernmental convention. Euratom was launched with the second Treaty of Rome in parallel with the EEC in 1957. The European Southern Observatory (ESO) was established in 1962 and the European Molecular Biology Organization (EMBO) in 1964, both on the basis of intergovernmental agreements. As early as 1965 the EEC, perceiving a 'technology gap' vis-à-vis the United States, set up a committee dealing with research, science and technology policies and the potential impact of the IM on these policy areas. The committee was charged with a systematic comparison of national research activities and proposed stronger coordination within a wide range of research areas.[7] In 1967 the

[5] N Luhmann, *Soziale Systeme. Grundriß einer allgemeinen Theorie* (Frankfurt am Main, Suhrkamp Verlag, 1984) 436.

[6] H Schelsky, *Die Soziologen und das Recht. Abhandlungen und Vorträge zur Soziologie von Recht, Institution und Planung* (Opladen, Westdeutscher Verlag, 1980).

[7] T Banchoff, 'The Politics of the European Research Area' (2002) 3 *ACES Working Paper*, 7; Y Okubo, A de Miranda and P Senker, *European Scientific Co-operation and its significance for new EU Member States* (2005) Paper prepared for the 5th Triple Helix Conference, Turin, Italy, 18–21 May, 3; P Papon, 'L'Europe de la recherche: une réponse aux defis de l'avenir' (2006) 12 (2) *Revue d'Histoire de l'Integration Européenne* 11, 14; JA Stein, 'Science, Technology and European foreign policy: European integration, global interaction' (2002) 29 (6) *Science and Public Policy*, 463.

Institut Laue-Langevin (ILL), a European neuron science institute, was set up and in 1971 an intergovernmental framework for European co-operation in the field of Scientific and Technical Research (COST) was established. COST was originally initiated by the EEC but most Western European countries were included. In 1972 the EC Heads of State and Government expressed their support for the increased coordination of national research policies. The European University Institute (EUI) was established the same year. In 1973 the Commission established the Directorate General for Research, Science and Education. In addition, the 1973 action programme of the Commission for the first time called for a harmonisation of national procedures on R&D funding as well as systematic exchange of information between MS within the area of R&D. These objectives were formulated under the first Commissioner of Research, Ralf Dahrendorf, who also launched the concept of a 'single European science area', to be achieved by lowering national barriers within the area of science and research.[8] As part of these efforts, CREST (Committee on Science and Technical Research) was established in 1974. CREST is a consultative body of the Commission consisting of MS representatives who monitor R&D polices within the MS, and serves as a platform for developing common approaches. In addition, and on the suggestion of the Commission, the European Science Foundation was established in 1974 as an umbrella structure for national research organisations. However, none of these initiatives were greeted with much enthusiasm by the MS, and they did not significantly transform the national R&D systems, nor did any major move towards integration of those systems take place. Intergovernmental co-operation continued to expand, however, with the creation of the European Molecular Biology Laboratory (EMBL) in 1974 and the European Space Agency (ESA)[9] in 1975.

In the 1980s EUREKA, an intergovernmental programme for technological development, was launched. In addition, the Community changed its strategy with the launch of funding schemes such as ESPRIT, RACE and BRIDGE. These programmes were aimed at strengthening Europe's position within specific research areas by mobilising increased funding. An additional objective was to minimise the 'technology gap' between the different MS. These programmes were later incorporated into the framework programmes (FP), which the Community has maintained and continuously expanded since 1984. The development of the FP was strengthened with the SEA which, relying on unanimity in the Council, granted the Community the competence to coordinate national R&D

[8] T Banchoff, 'The Politics of the European Research Area' (2002) 3 *ACES Working Paper* 8.

[9] The ESA was a merger of the European Launch Development Organisation (ELDO) and the European Space Research Organisation (ESRO), which were both established in 1964.

policies in 1987.[10] Today the FP is the third-largest budget item of the EU after the CAP and the Structural Funds.

In the early 1990s the Commission re-launched the idea of a common European science area. But again the attempt foundered due to the reluctance of MS and the failure of the Commission to ensure backing from other players such as industry and the national research communities.[11] In 1993 the Maastricht Treaty introduced co-decision to the area of R&D but maintained the unanimity required by the Council. Decisional procedures therefore became more complex since the number of institutional actors increased while existing barriers to decision making in the Council were maintained. When the Treaty of Amsterdam entered into force in 1997, the Council switched to QMV on R&D at the same time as the development of an R&D policy was made an objective of the Union.[12] In parallel to the gradual communitarisation of R&D policy intergovernmental co-operation continued to expand within the area of basic science, for example through the establishment of the European Synchrotron Radiation Facility (ESRF) in 1988.

6.4 THE EUROPEAN RESEARCH AREA

In January 2000 the Commission, under the label of the European Research Area (ERA), made a new attempt.[13] This time the plan was endorsed by the European Council at the by now famous Lisbon summit in March 2000, where it became a cornerstone of the Lisbon Process and its strategic objective of revitalising Europe through the transformation of its economy into a 'knowledge-based' economy.[14]

In the academic literature the new offensive has been presented as based on a 'whole new vision'.[15] However, the ideas were virtually identical to those presented 30 years earlier since the focus was on the establishment of

[10] Single European Act: Title VI (Arts 130f–130q).

[11] T Banchoff, 'Institutions, Inertia and European Union Research Policy' (2002) 40 (1) *Journal of Common Market Studies* 1.

[12] Ch XVIII (Arts 163–73) of the Treaty of the European Union; G Boussuat, 'Les coopérations européennes pour la researche scientifique et technique' (2006) 12 (2) *Revue d'Histoire de l'Integration Européenne* 5.

[13] Commission of the European Communities (2000): Communication from the Commission to the Council, the European Parliament and Social Committee and the Committee of the Regions. Towards a European Research Area. Com (2000) 6, 18 January.

[14] Presidency Conclusion (2000) Lisbon European Council, 23 and 24 March 2000.

[15] For such a historically unfounded perspective see Á de Elera, 'The European Research Area: On the Way Towards a European Scientific Community?' (2006) 12 (5) *European Law Journal* 559, 563. For a more sober analysis see R Kaiser and H Prange, 'A New Concept of Deepening European Integration? The European Research Area and the Emerging Role of Policy Coordination in a Multi-level Governance System' (2005) 3 (3) *Comparative European Politics* 289.

a 'common research space' through the increased mobility of researchers, increased linking of national research communities, common projects and the establishment of common laboratories within specific fields.[16] In fact, the only difference from the earlier attempts seems to lie in the framing of the proposal. The Commission aligned itself with the fashionable concept of the knowledge society just as it also joined the general trend to increasingly embed public activities in economic semantics.[17] This time the Commission called for the creation of a 'common market' for R&D, rather than for a common science area. The explicit objective was to achieve for the area of R&D what the SEA had achieved for the economic area. The principles of the IM regarding free movement, non-discrimination and so on, therefore served as the role model for the ERA approach developed by the Commission. In addition, the change of focus from basic research towards innovation enabled the Commission to highlight the explicit economic gains which can potentially be derived from a stronger research policy.[18]

The new framing of the old approach also found support because it corresponded to ongoing reform efforts in leading MS, thereby creating compatibility between MS and European perspectives.[19] In addition, the increasing internationalisation of science and research began to have profound effects, thus creating structural conditions which increased the possibility of acceptance of the Commission's proposals for MS governments and other stakeholders. But the Commission was not only riding on a wave of profound structural changes within the area of science and research, it was also acting as a central entrepreneur within the broader realm of internationalisation processes. Indeed, since the introduction of the FP in the mid-1980s the Commission has systematically used the funding programmes to open up national R&D environments. Hence the Commission, with support from the EP, deployed its classic strategy for circumventing opposition from MS governments by systematically linking up with 'lower-level' organisations, thereby transforming them into advocates of increased Europeanisation. The number of research institutions which acted as partners in the FP, for example, was increased from 13,000

[16] Commission of the European Communities (2000): Communication from the Commission to the Council, the European Parliament and Social Committee and the Committee of the Regions. Towards a European Research Area. Com (2000) 6, 18 January, 8; M André, 'L'espace européen de la recherche: histoire d'une idée' (2006) 12 (2) *Revue d'Histoire de l'Integration Européenne* 131, 133.

[17] PF Kjaer, 'Post-Hegelian Networks: Comments on the Chapter by Simon Deakin' in M Amstutz and G Teubner (eds), *Networks: Legal Issues of Multilateral Co-operation* (Oxford, Hart Publishing, 2009).

[18] This approach has also been coined a 'From invention to invoice' policy.

[19] T Banchoff, 'The Politics of the European Research Area' (2002) 3 *ACES Working Paper* 11.

to 18,000 between 1987 and 1994,[20] thereby creating ever-denser European networks. In addition, the Commission systematically promoted the establishment of European associations and Brussels-based representation offices within the area of science and R&D. The semantic shift from science to R&D, moreover, ensured full support from European business associations, which again exercised considerable pressure on MS governments.

The efforts of the Commission in relation to the ERA have further been complemented by the heightened expectations created through the massive increase of available funding under the 7th funding period (2007–13) compared with earlier FPs. Moreover, in institutional terms the FP has been stabilised through the establishment of the European Research Council (ERC), a permanent funding agency, which will hand out €7.5 billion to specific projects between 2007 and 2013 (compared to €4 billion under the previous framework programme).[21] The outsourcing of funding activities to the ECR also means that DG Research, which was bogged down by the heavy emphasis on the rather technocratic administration of the FP in the 1980s and 1990s, can increasingly devote its attention to the strategic objective of building the ERA. With the launch of the Galileo satellite navigation project in 2003 and the signing of the treaty establishing the International Thermonuclear Experimental Reactor (ITER) in 2006 between China, the EU, India, Japan, Russia, South Korea and the United States, the EU also made a decisive move towards replacing the MS as the key players in the establishment of new research infrastructures and facilities.

6.5 THE OMC IN RESEARCH AND DEVELOPMENT

The adoption of the ERA concept at Lisbon also marked the introduction of the OMC to the R&D area. The Lisbon summit initiated the deployment of OMC tools in order to ensure the realisation of the ERA through benchmarking of national practices, facilitation of cross-border mobility for researchers and the improvement of research infrastructures. In addition, it was agreed at the Barcelona summit in March 2002 that all MS should increase R&D spending from an average of 1.9 per cent of GNP in 2000 (EU 15) to 3 per cent of GNP by 2010 and that the process towards realisation of this objective also should be achieved using OMC methods.

At the organisational level these ambitious targets were followed by a merger of the three Council configurations for IM, Industry and Research into a single Competitiveness configuration in 2002, thereby strengthening

[20] *Ibid*, 18.
[21] The European Research Council website (http://erc.europa.eu/) visited 6 July 2009.

the economic framing of R&D policy. Hence, in their attempt to implement the process, the Council chose to emphasise (i) human resources, (ii) investment productivity, (iii) impact on competitiveness and (iv) impact on employment. Under these headings the first OMC cycle within R&D was carried out between 2000 and 2003. The main focus was on the development of indicators by which national performance in R&D could be assessed. A high-level working group with MS representatives was entrusted with this task. For each of the four themes five indicators were selected; however, 15 of the 20 indicators already existed within EUROSTAT or the OECD. Thus the process only added five additional indicators to an already well-established system. This was followed up by the establishment of five expert groups, which were respectively charged to (i) describe good practices, (ii) how they had been achieved, (iii) the potential for transferring such practices from one MS to other MS and (iv) the development of policy recommendations. These groups consisted mainly of academics who were partly appointed by the Commission and partly by the MS. Officially the MS representatives did not act as national representatives.

The second cycle started with the agreement in 2002 that R&D spending should be increased to 3 per cent of GNP by 2010. The task of carrying out the OMC processes was outsourced to CREST. As noted, CREST is an advisory committee under the Commission, consisting of MS representatives, which was established in 1974 with the task of assisting the Commission in its efforts to coordinate national R&D policies. CREST is therefore a network which serves as a structural coupling between MS authorities and between them and the Commission; its function is to increase the reflexivity of these structures by enhancing the level of mutual observation. Under the auspices of CREST five working groups were established which continue to promote progress towards the 3 per cent target.

A third cycle was started in mid-2006. The main focus of this cycle remains the 3 per cent target. In addition, it has been proposed that the cycle should involve areas such as 'globalisation and R&D' and the use of structural funds to support research.[22] In an attempt to programme future work the Commission adopted a Green Paper entitled 'The European Research Area: New Perspectives,[23] in spring 2007, which served as the basis for a fourth cycle covering 2007–2008.

[22] Presidency Conclusions: Conference on 'Improving Research Policies in Europe through the Open Method of Coordination', Brussels, 18 May 2006, 3; 'Improving Research Policies through the Open Method of Coordination', Speech by European Commissioner for Science and Research Janez Potočnik (SPEECH /06/311), European Commission conference on the open method of coordination in research, Brussels, 18 May 2006.

[23] Commission of the European Communities: The European Research Area: New Perspectives, COM (2007) 161 final.

Apart form the merger of the council configurations, the evolution of the OMC within the area of R&D indicates that it is difficult to identify institutional innovations which are specific to the OMC. This is also confirmed by the effective use of OMC tools. The Commission foresaw use of the OMC within five areas: (i) the '3 per cent action plan', (ii) human resources and mobility, (iii) science and society, (iv) networking of national research programmes and (v) research infrastructure.[24] In practice, however, OMC tools have been deployed in other areas, while in some of the five specific areas the OMC instruments have been only partly adopted. In addition, the overall objective in establishing the ERA is now more than 30 years old. The introduction of the OMC has therefore simply led to 're-branding' of already existing activities and efforts. The outsourcing of the OMC processes to CREST confirms this since CREST has used processes not unlike the OMC for the last three decades. When taking into account that the Commission and the OECD have tried to systematically identify best practices and to achieve convergence between national research systems since the 1960s it is difficult to see any difference between EU R&D policies prior to and after the introduction of the OMC. The OMC in R&D amounts to little more than an attempt to breathe new life into old, and not particularly dynamic, structures. Such attempts to establish increased momentum were, however, already apparent given the launch of the European Science Area and CREST in the mid-1970s, the launch of the FP in the mid 1980s, and the attempt to re-launch the idea of a Common European Science Area in the early 1990s. These attempts, however, all ran out steam after a short period.

6.6 THE FUNCTION OF THE OMC

Deployment of OMC instruments is not, therefore, a new phenomenon within the context of European integration processes, and so far only modest results have been achieved. That the OMC is a 'new mode of governance'[25] possessing the potential to radically improve the problem-solving capacity of the EU and thus represents a real alternative to the classical CM is therefore a rather questionable claim.

[24] Draft Summary Conclusions of the 288th meeting of the Scientific and Technical Research Committee (CREST) held in Iraklion, Greece, 27–28 March 2003. CREST 1203/2003, 7; Å Gornitzka, 'Coordinating policies for a "Europe of Knowledge". Emerging practices of the "Open Method of Coordination" in education and research' (2005) 16 *Arena Working Paper*, Oslo, 23.

[25] Eg CF Sabel and J Zeitlin, 'Learning from Difference: The Architecture of Experimentalist Governance in the European Union' (2007) 2 *European Governance Papers (EUROGOV)*; MJ Rodrigues, *European Policies for a Knowledge Economy* (London, Edward Elgar, 2003).

Another possibility is, however, to understand the introduction of the OMC as representing a systematisation, intensification and professionalisation of 'pre-integration': systematisation because it frames existing soft law activities linking them to the overall policy objectives of the EU; intensification because it increases the level of mutual observation between MS and hence the reflexivity of MS administrations; professionalisation because it somewhat formalises existing instruments and procedures for 'soft' policymaking. From this perspective, and as long as the OMC is not used as a substitute for the CM, it increases rather than decreases the formalisation of policy making just as it increases the possibility of 'exercising critique'[26] insofar as it makes already existing structures more visible.

The introduction of the OMC should thus be seen as reinforcing the policy practices which tend to take place prior to formal transfers of competences. In the case of R&D this is also illustrated by the slow but steady densification of policies at the European level over the last decades. This densification also has organisational consequences. The establishment of an agency in the form of the ERC, for example, indicates that GS in the area of R&D are mutating away from being pure networks that bind Commission and MS administrations together, into a conglomerate combining a multitude of heterarchical and hierarchical elements. Consequently, the policy area assumes a hybrid character that reflects the nature of the EU. Although no major breakthrough has yet occurred in terms of competence transfers within the particular area of R&D, the OMC can be seen as providing a structural basis which increases the probability of integration through formal competence transfers at a later date.

The main problem of the OMC in the specific case of R&D is the rationality bias. The process is framed by economic rather than scientific rationality. This is also illustrated through the merger of the council configurations, which de facto subsumed science under the economic rationality guiding the new competitiveness configuration. Not surprisingly, the promotion of economic competitiveness therefore remains the central objective of the process. But the scientific community will probably continue to see the process as one intended to increase scientific innovation. Hence, they are apt to frame their work in a way which is compatible with economic language without, however, changing their scientific objectives. Both sides are suffering from self-deception, however, since the economist tends to believe he can direct scientific processes and the scientists believe they can remain uninfluenced by the economic frame. Systematic misunderstandings between the two sides are therefore the most

[26] J Habermas, 'Der philosophische Diskurs der Moderne – Zwölf Vorlesungen' (Frankfurt am Main, Suhrkamp Verlag, 1985).

likely outcome. Apart from the functional failures occurring from such misapprehensions the more profound problem is that the asymmetry between economic and scientific rationality represents an over-reduction of meaning (*Sinn*) in the sense that crowding-out effects are likely to occur because the reproduction of scientific rationality is being systematically limited by the economic framing. The central problem of the OMC on R&D, as an instrument operating outside the realm of law, is therefore that it leads to de-differentiation (*Entdifferenzierung*) between economic and scientific rationality.

7

The Governance of Risk

7. 1 INTRODUCTION

WITHIN THE REALM of market regulation the new regulatory system for the EU chemicals market, REACH (Registration, Evaluation, Authorisation and Restriction of Chemicals) is the largest single reform of market regulation undertaken to date within the EU.[1] In addition, the reform can be seen as a 'finalisation' of integration within this particular area, in that it represents a stabilisation of the institutional structure which is likely to achieve permanence for the foreseeable future.[2]

Against this background the policy process which led to the establishment of REACH is analysed with the objective of assessing to what extent the governing dimension is 'in control'. In order to counter the idea that the 'turn to governance' *necessarily* implies de-formalisation, this chapter also reconstructs the extensive legal provisions on which the institutional and decisional structure of REACH is based. In addition, it will be argued that REACH can potentially provide a role model for hybrid structures in the EU context as such. This is possible not only because REACH is substantially a risk-regulating structure which reflects the general transformation of society away from a danger- (*Gefahr*) to a risk-producing structure,[3] but also because it combines the three forms of governance

[1] According to industry sources, the chemicals sector is one of the largest industries in the EC. It employs around 4 million people directly and indirectly. The EC chemicals industry has a global market share of 30% making it the world leader. In 2005 the EC exported chemicals for €110 billion and imports were €72 billion, creating a trade surplus of €38 billion. The EC chemicals industry comprises around 27,000 companies but is dominated by a few multinational companies which produce some 70% of output. In 2004 the main producers were Germany (25% of EC total), France (16% of EC total), Italy (12% of EC total) and the UK (10% of EC total). Source: European Chemical Industry Council website www.cefic.org visited on 5 July 2009.

[2] See also P Kjaer, 'Rationality within REACH? On Functional Differentiation as the Structural Foundation of Legitimacy in European Chemicals Regulation' (2007) 18 EUI Working Papers (Law).

[3] U Beck, *Risikogesellschaft. Auf dem Weg in eine andere Moderne* (Frankfurt am Main, Suhrkamp Verlag, 1986); N Luhmann, *Soziologie des Risikos* (Berlin, de Gruyter, 1991).

within a coherent legal framework. In addition REACH provides a legal answer to the problem of asymmetries between several functionally differentiated forms of communication.[4]

7.2 THE EVOLUTION OF EUROPEAN CHEMICALS LEGISLATION

Chemicals regulation has a long history in the European context. The first directive relating to the classification, packaging and labelling of dangerous substances was adopted in 1967,[5] and has been amended seven times. The most important changes were adopted in 1979 when a harmonised notification system was introduced for all new substances being placed on the market from 1981 onwards[6] and in 1992 when risk assessments were introduced for new substances.[7] In 1976 another directive imposed specific restrictions on the marketing and use of a large number of substances.[8] In 1988 an additional directive was introduced on the classification and labelling of dangerous preparations (mixtures of two or more substances).[9] In 1993 a regulation introduced measures for the evaluation and control of existing substances, defined as those available on the market before 1981.[10] This regulation initiated a process aimed at testing and evaluating these substances in order to assess their potential risks. Apart from these major pieces of legislation, industry sources state that more than 500 additional items of Community legislation are related to or have an impact on the EC chemicals industry.[11]

[4] Hence, the objective is not to evaluate whether the substantial mission of REACH is a meaningful enterprise, but merely to reflect on the possible value of its regulatory model within the wider context of the integration process.

[5] Directive 67/548/EEC of the Council of 27 June 1967 on the approximation of laws, regulations and administrative provisions relating to the classification, packaging and labelling of dangerous substances.

[6] Directive 79/831/EEC of the Council of 18 September 1979 amending Directive 67/548/EEC of the Council of 27 June 1967 on the approximation of laws, regulations and administrative provisions relating to the classification, packaging and labelling of dangerous substances.

[7] Directive 92/32/EEC of the Council of 30 April 1992 amending Directive 67/548/EEC of the Council of 27 June 1967 on the approximation of laws, regulations and administrative provisions relating to the classification, packaging and labelling of dangerous substances.

[8] Directive 76/769/EEC of the Council of 27 July 1976 relating to restrictions on the marketing and use of certain dangerous substances and preparations.

[9] Directive 88/379/EEC of the Council of 7 June 1988 relating to the classification, packaging and labelling of dangerous preparations, revised by Directive 1999/45 EC of the European EP and the Council of 31 May 1999.

[10] Regulation (EEC) No 793/1993 of the Council of 23 March 1993 on evaluation and control of risks of existing substances.

[11] European Chemical Industry Council website www.cefic.org visited on 31 January 2007.

7.3 THE REACH POLICY PROCESS

The policy process leading to REACH was initiated by an alliance consisting of DG Environment (formerly DG XI), a number of MS—most notably Austria, Denmark, Finland, the Netherlands and Sweden—and a wide range of environmentalist groups, who argued that the existing level of risk regulation in the chemicals area was insufficient and outdated. This triggered an informal meeting of the Council group of Environmental Ministers in April 1998 at which the Commission committed itself to performing an extensive review of existing chemicals legislation,[12] in order to clarify to what extent it provided adequate standards for risk regulation. The review identified major problems. First, the distinction between existing substances, available before 1981, and 'new' substances placed on the market after 1981. By the end of the millennium only 2,700 substances fell into the category of new substances, thus subject to test requirements. The category of 'old' substances, however, contained more than 100,000, only 140 of which had at the time been subject to comprehensive risk assessments carried out by MS authorities on the basis of Council Regulation 793/1993 EEC.[13] Hence, the existing system of risk assessment was identified as being much too slow. Moreover, the existing system only focused on producers, not on downstream users. Consequently, it remained extremely difficult to acquire knowledge about the actual use of the chemical substances, and hence close to impossible to provide scientific evidence of negative impacts throughout the supply chain. The review report was adopted by the Commission in November 1998 and welcomed by the Council in December 1998.[14] In February 1999 a stakeholders' meeting was held with regulators, scientists, industry, consumer and environmental representatives. In June 1999 the Council adopted a set of conclusions for a future strategy, thus acknowledging the need for a new approach to chemicals regulation, and it then called on the Commission to submit a policy document outlining a strategy. The Commission published a White Paper in February 2001 outlining the REACH proposal.[15] An

[12] More specifically, of the amended version of Directive 67/548/EEC of the Council of 27 June 1967 on the approximation of laws, regulations and administrative provisions relating to the classification, packaging and labelling of dangerous substances, Directive 76/769/EEC of the Council of 27 July 1976 relating to restrictions on the marketing and use of certain dangerous substances and preparations, Directive 88/379/EEC of the Council of 7 June 1988 relating to the classification, packaging and labelling of dangerous preparations, revised by Directive 1999/45 EC of the European EP and the Council of 31 May 1999, Regulation (EEC) No 793/1993 of the Council 23 March 1993 on evaluation and control of the risks of existing substances.

[13] Commission White Paper: Strategy for a future Chemicals Policy. COM (2001) 88 final 6.

[14] Commission Working Document SEC (1998) 1986 final.

[15] European Commission: White Paper. Strategy for a future Chemicals Policy. COM (2001) 88 final.

additional stakeholder meeting was held in April 2001. The White Paper provided the basis for a draft proposal which was debated in the Environmental Council in June 2001, leading to a resolution from the EP in November of the same year. Both institutions expressed support for a continuation of the reform process and urged the Commission to strengthen the provisions envisaged for consumer, environment, human and animal protection. Industry largely opposed the proposal.[16] From October 2001 to February 2002 technical working groups with members from the Commission, industry, NGOs and MS authorities carried out detailed studies of the implications of the draft proposal. This was followed by an internet consultation in May–July 2003, which resulted in some 6,400 submissions.[17] In May 2003 early notice was given to WTO members. This was followed up with an impact assessment which estimated the costs of REACH to be between €2.8 and €5.2 billion over a period of 11 to 15 years. The health and environmental benefits were estimated to be €50 billion over a 30-year period.[18] In the meantime the position of the MS changed. From being largely in favour of the proposal, leading MS began to increasingly oppose the initiative. In September 2003 an open letter was sent to the President of the Commission Romano Prodi from Prime Minister Tony Blair, President Jacques Chirac and Chancellor Gerhard Schröder, who, in the light of the Lisbon Strategy, stated that 'a future EC chemicals policy must be designed in such a way as to ensure environmental, health and consumer protection without endangering the international competitiveness of the European chemical industry'.[19] The three Heads of State and Government, in other words, sent a strong signal that the Commission should prioritise economic concerns vis-à-vis environmental, health and consumer concerns, where the realisation of such divergent objectives would be mutually exclusive. Shortly afterwards, the issue was transferred from the Environmental Council, which so far had been the leading Council group, to the newly created Competitiveness Council. A similar attempt to transfer the issue from the EP's Environmental Committee to either the Committee on Industry and Trade or the Legal Affairs Committee failed. In October 2003 the draft REACH regulation

[16] The position of the EC Chemicals industry is available at: http://cms.cefic.be/Templates/shwStory.asp?NID=494&HID=448 , visited 5 July 2009.

[17] For the complete list of submissions see: http://ECropa.EC/enterprise/reach/consultation/public_en.htm, visited 5 July 2009.

[18] European Commission, DG Environment website: http://ec.ECropa.EC/environment/chemicals/background/impact_assessment_intro.htm, visited 5 July 2009.

[19] The letter is available at: http://www.smallbusinessEurope.org/en/upload/File/Issues/REACH/Letter_to_Prodi_from_Blair_Chirac_Schroder.doc.

was adopted by the Commission.[20] The draft regulation contained substantially weaker provisions for consumer, environment, human and animal protection than the White Paper and previous drafts. Moreover, the majority of the suggestions which the Council and EP had made for strengthening the provisions for consumer, environment, human and animal protection following the White Paper had not been incorporated. On the other hand, the general principles for a future chemicals policy as outlined in the White Paper were maintained.[21] The increasingly unfavourable environment, moreover, contributed to a shift in the power balance within the Commission, with DG Environment losing out to the more industry-friendly DG Enterprise. In January 2004 the REACH proposal was notified at the WTO under the TBT agreement.[22] In July 2005 the results of a Strategic Partnership on REACH Testing (SPORT) was published.[23] SPORT was a joint initiative between the Commission, MS and industry aimed at testing the technical aspects of REACH. In November 2005 the first reading took place in the EP, producing a list of 430 provisional amendments.[24] The main changes proposed by the EP were a tougher stand on substitution requirements and a reduction in the information required in order to register a substance. This position was the result of a compromise deal between the Environment Committee and the Committee on Industry and Trade in the EP. The former sought to keep the standards as high as possible and hence negotiated a stronger position in relation to substitution. The latter, on the other hand, sought to lighten the burden on industry and hence negotiated a reduction in the information requirements. The Council adopted its common position in June 2006.[25] Ninety per cent of the amendments proposed by the EP were completely or partially accepted by the Council;[26] however, it proposed a stronger role for MS authorities in the evaluation of substances, and also sought to

[20] Commission Proposal for a Regulation concerning Registration, Evaluation, Authorisation and Restriction of Chemicals (REACH), establishing the European Chemicals Agency and Amending Directive 1999/45/EC, COM(2003)644 of 29 October 2003.

[21] The changes did not only take place because of resistance from the major MS and European industries but also because of fierce criticism from major trading partners, notably the United States.

[22] World Trade Organization, notification G/TBT/N/EEC/52 of 21 January 2004. The EC response is available at European Commission, DG Enterprise website: http://ec.ECropa.EC/enterprise/reach/docs/reach/EC_wto_response_041028.pdf.

[23] The report is available at: http://ec.ECropa.EC/enterprise/reach/docs/trial/sport_report_050704.pdf.

[24] European EP Legislative Resolutions P6_TA(2005)0434 and P6-TA(2005)0435 of 17 November 2005.

[25] Common Positions of the Council of the European Union 7524/06 and 7525/06 of 12 June 2006.

[26] Communication from the Commission to the European EP COM (2006) 375 final 3.

facilitate the requirements for Small and Medium Sized Enterprises (SME). The Commission adopted a favourable opinion on the common position in July 2006.[27] In the second reading the EP proposed 172 amendments. In November 2006 a compromise package was agreed upon between the Council and the EP, strengthening the latter's supervisory role. The EP gained the right to appoint two members to the board of the proposed chemicals agency and the Comitology procedure with scrutiny[28] was incorporated in a number of instances. The Council agreed to a strengthening of the substitution requirements and to a review after six years of a number of outstanding issues. The Council and the EP finally adopted the regulation in December 2006. It entered into force on 1 June 2007.

7.4 THE POLICY OBJECTIVES OF REACH

The version of REACH which was finally adopted is aimed at closing the 'knowledge gap' in relation to chemicals placed on the market before 1981 and to drastically speed up the processes for testing and risk assessment of chemicals in general. In practical terms, REACH serves multiple and partially contradictory purposes as it shall 'ensure a high level of protection of human health and the environment as well as the free movement of substances ... while enhancing competitiveness and innovation'.[29] Inspired by the 1992 Rio Declaration, REACH has 'sustainable development' as an official objective. It foresees that by 2020 'chemicals are produced and used in ways that lead to the minimisation of significant adverse effect on human health and the environment'.[30] Consequently, it is a declared objective of REACH 'to encourage and in certain cases to ensure that substances of high concern are eventually replaced by less dangerous substances or technologies where suitable economically and technically viable alternatives are available'.[31] Some 1,500 substances subject to substitution requirements are already identified in the regulation.[32] The responsibility of assessing the risks and hazards of substances lies with manufacturers and importers. Hence the burden of proof is reversed when compared with the existing regulatory system, where it is the responsibility of the relevant public authorities to provide evidence of potential risks. All actors in the supply chain will, moreover, be obliged to ensure the safety of

[27] *Ibid*.
[28] Decision 1999/468/EC of the Council of 28 June 1999, Art 5a. Decision amended by Decision 2006/512/EC of the Council.
[29] Regulation (EC) No 1907/2006 of the European EP and of the Council, of 18 December 2006, preamble, recital 1.
[30] *Ibid*, preamble, recital 4.
[31] *Ibid*, preamble, recital 12.
[32] European Environmental Law website: http://www.eel.nl/index.asp?sub_categorie=243, visited 30 January 2007.

the substances they handle. Not only producers but also downstream users will therefore be linked within the system. The requirements for safety assessments should be developed by the Commission, 'in close cooperation with industry, MS and other relevant stakeholders'.[33] Innovation will be encouraged through a relaxation of restrictions on chemicals solely used for research and development purposes as well as through lower registration fees for new substances and the requirement to systematically consider the possibility of substitution with less problematic substances.

7.5 THE INSTITUTIONAL FORM OF REACH

REACH establishes a complex institutional system, with a regulatory agency, the European Chemicals Agency, at its centre. It is envisaged that the agency will eventually have around 400 employees,[34] making it the largest EU agency. However, it still follows the overall structure developed for 'quasi-regulatory' agencies in the European context.[35] It is 'established for the purposes of managing and in some cases carrying out the technical, scientific and administrative aspects'[36] of REACH. It consists of a Management Board, an Executive Director, a Secretariat, three committees and a so-called Forum. The Management Board is composed of a member from each MS and a maximum of six representatives appointed by the Commission. Three of these will represent interested parties (for example, industry, traders and consumers) and have no voting rights. In addition the EP will, as mentioned, be able to appoint two independent members.[37] Hence, with the present number of 27 MS the Board will have a maximum of 35 members, 32 with voting rights. The members are nominated by the MS and appointed by the Council. The criteria for selecting members of the board are relevant experience and expertise. The duration of the office is four years, renewable once.[38] The Management Board shall act by a two-thirds majority of all members with the right to vote.[39]

[33] Regulation (EC) No 1907/2006 of the European EP and of the Council, of 18 December 2006, preamble, recital 31.

[34] European Commission, DG Enterprise website: http://ec.ECropa.EC/enterprise/reach/prep_agency_en.htm, visited 1 February 2007.

[35] XA Yatanagas, 'Delegation of Regulatory Authority in the European Union. The Relevance of the American Model of Independent Agencies' (2001) 1 *Jean Monnet Working Papers*.

[36] Regulation (EC) No 1907/2006 of the European EP and of the Council, of 18 December 2006, Art 75(1).

[37] *Ibid*, Art 79(1).

[38] *Ibid*, Art 75(3).

[39] *Ibid*, Art 82.

The Management Board appoints the Executive Director on the basis of a list of candidates proposed by the Commission.[40] He or she will be responsible for the day-to-day management and ensuring timely coordination between the Agency, the Committees and the Forum as well as with other EU institutions. The appointment is for a period of five years, renewable once.

REACH also foresees the establishment of three committees: a Committee for Risk Assessment (CfRA) and a Committee for Socio-Economic Analysis (CfSEA) as well as a Member State Committee (MSC). Each MS may nominate candidates for the CfRA and the CfSEA. The Management Board shall appoint members on the basis of the nominations. Each MS should have a minimum of one member.[41] Members are appointed for three years renewable. Each Committee shall draft a proposal for its own rules of procedure, to be approved by the Management Board.[42] The Committee members will ensure coordination with competent MS authorities, but act in an independent manner and without instructions from their respective authorities. The chairman of each committee will be an employee of the Agency.[43] The committees shall provide MS and the Community institutions with the best possible scientific and technical advice.[44] In forming their opinions the committees shall strive towards reaching consensus. If consensus is not reached, the opinion and grounds for the majority opinion as well as the minority position(s) will be published.[45] The work of the committees will be carried out through the appointment of rapporteurs for each dossier. The rapporteurs shall act in the interest of the Community and provide a declaration of interests in relation to the specific dossier for which they are responsible.[46] MS shall moreover provide a list of relevant experts who can be called upon as members of ad hoc working groups under the different committees. Membership of the committees (and the Forum) shall be made public.[47] All members will annually provide a declaration of commitment and a declaration of interests. On request, these declarations will be accessible to the public.[48] The MSC shall 'aim to reach agreement amongst Member States authorities on specific issues which require a harmonised approach'[49] and assist the Commission in its efforts to implement decisions

[40] *Ibid*, Arts 83 and 84.
[41] *Ibid*, Art 85(1) and (2).
[42] *Ibid*, Art 85(9).
[43] *Ibid*, Art 85(5) (7) and (9).
[44] *Ibid*, Art 77(1).
[45] *Ibid*, Art 85(8).
[46] *Ibid*, Art 87(1).
[47] *Ibid*, Art 88(1).
[48] *Ibid*, Art 88(2).
[49] *Ibid*, preamble, recital 103.

taken on the basis of the recommendations of the CfRA and the CfSEA. Decisions of the agency or the related committees can be contested in front of a Board of appeal.[50] Qualifications for members of the Board of Appeal are determined by the Commission in accordance with the procedure of regulatory committees under Comitology.[51] Any decision of the Board of Appeal (or of the Agency if no right of appeal exists) may be brought before the CFI or the ECJ.[52] Any decision taken by the Agency may be the subject of a complaint to the European Ombudsman.[53]

The Agency budget shall consist of a subsidy from the Community budget and of fees paid in relation to registration and the granting of authorisations. Budget and financial management is subject to the control of the Court of Auditors. The EP and Council will be regularly informed of budgetary developments.[54] The agency is subject to control from the European Anti-Fraud Office (OLAF).[55] The EC regulation guiding public access to documents will apply to the Agency.[56]

The Forum will consist of one member appointed by each MS. The period of appointment is three years, renewable once. Five additional members can be appointed in order to ensure the presence of specific competencies.[57] The Forum will provide a platform 'for Member States to exchange information and to coordinate their activities related to enforcement of chemicals legislation'.[58] The justification for the establishment of the Forum is that 'the currently informal cooperation between Member States ... would benefit from a more formal framework'.[59] The role foreseen for the Forum is, however, also incorporated in a general principle which emphasises 'good cooperation, coordination and exchange of information between the Member States, the Agency and the Commission regarding enforcement'.[60] In addition, the role of the Forum is also supported by an emphasis on the active participation of competent MS authorities since they should, 'because of their closeness to stakeholders in the Member States, play a role in the exchange of information on the risk of substances and on the obligations of natural or legal persons under

[50] *Ibid*, Arts 89–93.
[51] *Ibid*, Art 89(4).
[52] *Ibid*, Art 94.
[53] *Ibid*, Art 118(4).
[54] *Ibid*, Arts 96–97.
[55] *Ibid*, Art 98.
[56] Regulation (EC) No 1049/2001 of the European EP and of the Council of 30 May 2001.
[57] Regulation (EC) No 1907/2006 of the European EP and of the Council, of 18 December 2006, Art 86(1).
[58] *Ibid*, preamble, recital 105.
[59] *Ibid*.
[60] *Ibid*, preamble, recital 120.

chemicals legislation'.[61] The Forum, however, has only an advisory role since implementing measures of a general nature in relation to the regulation should be adopted in accordance with the regulatory procedure with scrutiny under Comitology.[62]

7.6 PROCEDURES

The procedural framework contains four elements which respectively are related to the registration, authorisation, evaluation and restriction of chemical substances falling under the scope of the regulation. Only substances which are available on the market are affected by the regulation. Hence, substances which are only used for R&D purposes are exempted. Producers or importers who handle quantities of less than 1 tonne per year of a specific substance are exempted from the requirements.[63]

7.6.1 Registration

Any producer or importer of articles falling under the regulation shall submit a registration to the Agency, indicating the identity of the producer or importer, quantity of the substances in question, a technical dossier listing the content of the substances as well as a description of the intended use. For all substances subject to registration a safety assessment is required, which shall include an assessment of hazards to human health, physicochemical hazards, environmental hazards as well as an assessment of persistency and bioaccumulative and toxic potential, an exposure assessment and a description of risks.[64] The agency performs a completeness check of the registration and confirms that it is considered to be complete. The Agency will inform the competent authority in the relevant MS, meaning the MS where the producer or importer is established, regarding registration.[65] The registrant may continue to manufacture or import the substance in question if the Agency has not provided any indication to the contrary within three weeks of successful registration.[66]

[61] *Ibid*, preamble, recital 1119.

[62] *Ibid*, preamble, recitals 123 and 124; Council Decision 1999/468/EC of 28 June 1999, Art 5a. Decision amended by Council Decision 2006/512/EC. The Forum is thereby likely to gain the same function within REACH as the Advisory Forum has within EFSA.

[63] Regulation (EC) No 1907/2006 of the European EP and of the Council, of 18 December 2006, Art 7.

[64] *Ibid*, Art 14.

[65] *Ibid*, Art 20(4).

[66] *Ibid*, Art 21.

The registrant remains responsible for updating the registration[67] and is obliged to enquire whether the substance in question has already been registered by another producer or importer.[68] In case of overlap and in order to avoid duplication, potential and previous registrants shall 'make every effort to reach an agreement on the sharing of information requested by the potential registrant'.[69] Should no agreement be reached, the matter may be submitted to an arbitration board. In order to facilitate the process all registrants and potential registrants have access to a substance information exchange forum (SIEF).[70] If testing is required in order to produce the safety assessments a SIEF participant will enquire whether a relevant study is available from other participants. If this is the case the owner of the study will provide proof of the costs. Both parties 'shall make every effort to ensure costs of sharing the information are determined in a fair, transparent and non-discriminatory way'.[71] If no agreement is reached, the costs will be shared. If no study is available, only one study will be carried out and potential registrants share the costs. The claim for participation in a study is enforceable in national courts.[72] Common registration between several producers or importers is expressly allowed and encouraged.

The Agency shall examine all proposals for testing and either (i) require that the registrant(s) carry out the testing; (ii) decide that the test should be modified; (iii) that together with the proposed tests additional tests should be made; or (iv) reject the proposed test. In the latter case the applicant can submit a modified proposal for testing. All tests should be carried out within a deadline specified by the Agency. If several registrants have submitted proposals for the same test they should be given the opportunity to reach agreement on who will carry out the test. If no agreement is reached, the Agency will decide who is to carry out the test.[73]

7.6.2 Evaluation

Evaluations are made for three reasons: (i) in order to consider whether substances which so far have not been included in the list of those falling under regulation should be included in the list; (ii) in order to examine the possibility of de-listing substances falling under the scope of regulation

[67] *Ibid*, Art 22.
[68] *Ibid*, Art 26.
[69] *Ibid*, Art 27(2).
[70] *Ibid*, Art 29.
[71] *Ibid*, Art 30(1).
[72] *Ibid*, Art 30(2) and (3).
[73] *Ibid*, Art 40(3).

because new information about the nature of the substances has become known; (iii) in order to assess what impact of the market availability of specific substances will have.

In co-operation with the MS the Agency will develop criteria for prioritising which substances should be evaluated first. This prioritisation will be decided on a risk-based approach and will be contained in a rolling action plan covering three years. The action plan will be adopted by the Agency on the basis of an opinion from the MSC. The Agency coordinates the evaluation process and identifies the MS that will carry out the evaluation of the substance.[74] MS can express interest in evaluating a specific substance. In case of disagreement among MS concerning who should evaluate a given substance the issue shall be referred to the MSC. If the committee fails to reach a unanimous agreement the Agency shall refer the issue to the Commission, which will decide who the competent authority shall be on the basis of the regulatory Comitology procedure.[75] Evaluations will be carried out within a period of 12 months. In order to ensure a harmonised approach to evaluation, implementing measures shall be adopted where appropriate. The basis for such measures will also be the regulatory Comitology procedure.[76] After evaluation has been carried out by the competent MS authority the Agency will inform other MS and the registrant(s). Registrants shall have the right to comment on the draft decision. Comments from registrants will be circulated to the competent authorities of the remaining MS, who may also propose amendments to the draft decision. The Agency can modify the decision on the basis of such comments, after which the draft decision will be resubmitted to registrant(s) and competent MS authorities for additional comments. If the MSC on the basis of the Agency's (modified) draft decision reaches a unanimous decision the Agency will accept the decision accordingly. If it fails to reach unanimous agreement, the matter will be referred to the Commission, which will make a decision. The regulatory Comitology procedure will provide the basis for adopting such a decision.[77]

7.6.3 Authorisation

The aim of the authorisation procedure is 'to ensure the good functioning of the internal market while assuring that the risks from substances of very high concern are properly controlled and that these substances are progressively replaced by suitable alternative substances or technologies where

[74] *Ibid*, Art 44.
[75] *Ibid*, Art 45(3).
[76] *Ibid*, Art 47(2).
[77] *Ibid*, Art 51(3).

these are economically and technically viable'.[78] Hence all applicants shall analyse the availability of alternatives and consider their risks, and the technical and economic feasibility of substitution. Again a distinction is made between the general authorisation of the inclusion/exclusion of substances on the list of substances regulated by the regulation and specific authorisations concerning the use of particular substances falling under the regulation.

General Authorisations

At least every second year the Agency shall provide a recommendation concerning additional substances to be included in the list of those requiring authorisation or those which should be removed because, as a result of new information, they no longer meet the criteria for inclusion in the list of substances requiring authorisation. All interested parties will have the possibility of commenting on such recommendations. The MS themselves may prepare a dossier and forward it to the Agency. If, after circulation to all interested parties and the remaining MS, no comments have been received, the Agency may include the substance in the draft list. Prior to taking any final decision on inclusion or removal of any substances the Agency will take into account the opinion of the MSC,[79] just as the decision will be subject to the procedures guiding regulatory Comitology procedure with scrutiny.[80] If the MSC fails to reach a unanimous agreement the matter will be referred to the Commission, which will prepare a draft proposal subject to approval under the regulatory Comitology procedure.[81]

Specific Authorisations

Applications for specific authorisations may be made by producers, importers and/or downstream users. The application shall contain the identity of the applicant(s), the description of the substance(s), a request for authorisation indicating the envisaged use of the substance(s), a chemical safety report if not already submitted during registration, an analysis of alternatives including the technical and economical feasibility of such alternatives, and a substitution plan where such alternative exists.[82] The application may include a socio-economic analysis. The Agency acknowledges the receipt of the application and the CfRA and the CfSEA

[78] *Ibid*, Art 55.
[79] *Ibid*, Art 58(1) and (3).
[80] *Ibid*, Art 58(1) and (8).
[81] *Ibid*, Art 59(9).
[82] *Ibid*, Art 62.

will give their draft opinion within 10 months of the date of receipt. The draft opinion of the CfRA will include an assessment of the risk to human health and/or the environment from the use(s) of the substance(s), including the appropriateness and effectiveness of the risk management measures described in the application, as well as a risk assessment of possible alternatives. The CfSEA shall provide an assessment of the socio-economic factors and the availability, suitability and technical feasibility of alternatives. The applicant will have the opportunity of commenting on the draft opinions. After taking these comments into consideration, the draft opinions will be submitted to the Commission, the MS and the applicant. The Commission is responsible for taking a decision. In its decision the Commission will take account of the opinion of the CfRA. Decisions will be taken in accordance with the advisory Comitology procedure.[83]

If an authorisation cannot be granted due to a negative position of the CfRA it may only be granted 'if it is shown that socio-economic benefits outweigh the risk of human health or the environment arising from the use of the substance and if there are no suitable alternative substances or technologies'.[84] However, such a decision can only be made after taking into account the opinions of the CfRA and the CfSEA and after considering the risk posed by the use of the substance, the socio-economic benefits arising from its use, an analysis of alternatives and information available regarding the risks to human health or the environment of any alternative substances or technologies.[85] All authorisations are subject to a time-limited review.

7.6.4 Restrictions

The regulation provides a number of principles for establishing restrictions on specific substances in relation to how they are manufactured, placed on the market and used. The restriction procedure is aimed at introducing new and amending existing restrictions as well as formulating particular restrictions in relation to a specific application.

If the Commission considers that a risk needs to be addressed, should a specific substance that is not adequately controlled be marketed, it shall require the Agency to prepare a dossier on the matter. The Agency itself may prepare a dossier if it considers that risks occurring from a specific substance are not adequately controlled. MS may also propose that the Agency should prepare such a dossier. MS can also request that existing restrictions will be re-examined. The decision to request that an Agency

[83] *Ibid*, Art 64(8).
[84] *Ibid*, Art 60(4).
[85] *Ibid*, Art 60(4).

should prepare a dossier concerning re-examination will be taken by the Commission in accordance with the Comitology procedure for advisory committees.[86] All dossiers concerning restrictions shall be submitted to the CfRA and the CfSEA, which will confirm that the dossier is in conformity with the general provisions concerning possible restrictions in the regulation. At this stage interested parties will have the opportunity to comment on the dossier. If the CfRA and the CfSEA consider the dossier to be in conformity with the general provisions, they will formulate a draft opinion on the proposed restrictions. Interested parties will also have the opportunity to comment on the draft opinion. Taking appropriate comments into account the committees will then adopt an opinion. The dossier and the opinions of the committees will be referred to the Commission, which will adopt a final decision in accordance with the regulatory procedure with scrutiny under Comitology.[87]

7.7 HYBRID GOVERNANCE

The above reconstruction of the institutional structure and procedural infrastructure indicates that REACH builds on four elements, making it a hybrid operating between hierarchy and heterarchy.[88] First, at its centre there is a hierarchical nucleus: it is the outcome of a 'supranational' legislative process subject to co-decision with full involvement of the EP. Moreover, the REACH regulation will enjoy direct effect and supremacy vis-à-vis national law. In addition, the requirements imposed on private actors contain a considerable element of vertical command and control; for example data and testing requirements will be harmonised in detail and hence leave little or no scope for deviations and exceptions. The internal organisation of the secretariat is, moreover, likely to be based on a traditional hierarchical model of bureaucratic organisation. Hence, at first glance REACH is modelled on a classic concept of Kelsian legal hierarchy and Weberian organisational hierarchy.

Secondly, REACH also contains a co-operative element. The regulation only establishes a framework in the form of basic principles and procedures. The fleshing out of detailed standards, criteria and guidelines will be left to the versatile interactions between the Commission, the secretariat, the committees and MS authorities. Actual evaluation of the test results provided by private actors will, moreover, be organised within a complex

[86] *Ibid*, Art 69(5).

[87] *Ibid*, Art 73(2).

[88] For an instructive analysis of the hybridity of REACH see C Hey, K Jacob and A Volkery, 'Better regulation by new governance hybrids? Governance models and the reform of European chemicals policy' (2006) 2 *FFU-report*, Environmental Policy Research Centre, Free University Berlin.

process where the Secretariat will simply play the role of a coordinator and facilitator whereas the actual work will be carried out by competent MS authorities, which might even sub-delegate the tasks nationally. The interaction between the hierarchically organised secretariat and its environment is therefore likely to take place through heterarchical networks, which are legally structured through the establishment of committees and their internal rules of procedures. The social embeddedness of the secretariat is, therefore, likely to depend upon its ability to use the committees as channels which will increase reflexivity as ideally they enable it to receive and submit relevant information from and to its environment. Similarly, competent MS authorities will need to engage actively in the committee processes in order to 'feed in' to the Europeanised regulatory processes and to stabilise their expectations vis-à-vis the societal impact which these processes will have. Hence, the committees are likely to fulfil the role of structural couplings between organisations which were earlier identified as the central function of networks in the European setting.[89] Couplings are intended to offset the structural deficits of the organisations involved and for the Agency in particular these are represented by insufficient resources and its lack of a mandate to carry out the necessary testing and evaluation on its own. The structural deficit for the competent MS authorities lies in their diminishing ability to handle the complexity of risk assessment and risk management in the chemicals sector within an increasingly internationalised social environment. This provides an incitement for sharing the work between MS authorities.

Thirdly, REACH contains an element of obligatory self-regulation as represented by the obligation of private actors to carry out testing and ensure appropriate risk management along the value chain. These requirements are likely to encourage private actors to engage in substantial horizontal co-operation. For example, the co-operation among private actors to submit joint registrations and perform joint assessments is likely to lead to the establishment of a comprehensive network around the SIEF. Such developments might in turn facilitate increased reflexivity and a higher level of involvement of private actors in the larger social realm, since each private actor will be forced to enter into a relationship with other producers and importers characterised by 'co-optition'.[90] Private actors with a long-term strategy will therefore have an incentive for creating a high level of mutual trust among themselves through a stabilisation of their interactions on the basis of well-established norms.

[89] E Kämper and JFK Schmidt, 'Netzwerke als strukturelle Kopplung' in J Weyer (Hrsg), *Soziale Netzwerke. Koncepte und Methoden der Socialwissenschaftlichen Netzwerkforschung* (Oldenburg Verlag, München, 2000) 220.

[90] G Teubner, 'Das Recht hybrider Netzwerke' (2001) 165 *Zeitschrift für das gesamte Handelsrecht und Wirtschaftsrecht* 550, 563.

Fourthly, REACH provides the basis for a strategy of risk communication aimed at the broader public since the Agency will have the role of communicating potential risks not only to MS authorities, industry and traders but also to consumers. The communication of risks is, moreover, likely to demand close coördination between the Agency and competent MS authorities in order to ensure that the risk communication strategy remains coherent.

The hybrid structure means that REACH does not correspond to any of the ideal models of governance advocated throughout the last decade. REACH only establishes a 'quasi-regulatory' agency, which falls short of the requirements that Majone argues should characterise a fully independent regulatory agency.[91] This is the case particularly in relation to the massive decentralisation of the workload which will mainly be carried out by private actors and competent MS authorities, as well as in relation to the actual decisional competencies possessed by the Agency.

In contrast to Majone's vertical agency model the Agency committees will play a strong role in the preparation of draft decisions just as the competence to take final decisions in most cases will remain the prerogative of the Commission on the basis of the Comitology system. But even though Comitology and committees more generally will play a pivotal role within REACH, the structure envisaged does not necessarily follow the theory developed by Joerges and Neyer. Although it is a weak version of a regulatory agency, the Agency is likely to achieve considerable influence since it will play an essential role in the collection and processing of information and in the definition of policy priorities. Hence, the Agency is—over time—likely to develop the features of an autonomous structure with an independent impact on the policy area in question. At first glance, the suggestion made by Sabel and Zeitlin under the heading of DDP concerning a massive expansion of the OMC beyond the scope of its present use and into areas which currently are subject to the CM[92] has not been reflected in the REACH regulation. OMC-inspired instruments are, however, likely to play a certain role in formulating the work of the so-called Forum, which is predicted to become a platform for the exchange of ideas and best practices. This again is likely to provide a basis for the deployment of benchmarking and evaluation tools similar to those which are typically associated with the OMC. In conclusion REACH seems to indicate a move towards a fusion of the three types of governance associated with agencies, Comitology and the OMC, insofar as the REACH system will contain elements from all three.

[91] G Majone (ed), *Regulating Europe* (London, Routledge, 1996).

[92] CF Sabel and J Zeitlin, 'Learning from Difference: The New Architecture of Experimentalist Governance in the European Union' (2006) 18 *La Follette School Working Papers*.

7.8 HYBRID LEGITIMACY

How is REACH being legitimised? Apart from administrative law provisions the REACH system draws on three analytically separate, but in practice partly overlapping, sources of legitimacy, reflecting the hybrid nature of its structure. The first source is democracy, the second is proceduralisation and the third is deliberation. Consequently, legitimacy is neither simply derived from a metaphysical concept of the sovereign people, which provide the foundation for most democratic theory, nor is it merely procedural or purely based on deliberation. In addition, the underlying structural foundation for all three forms is their ability to ensure the autonomy of different social spheres, or systems, while regulating their mutual impact. Hence, the underlying basis for legitimacy during the legislative process as well as in the planned operational form of REACH seems to be the dual ability to maintain and reconcile different functionally differentiated structures through law.

7.8.1 Democracy

At least in its classical liberal form, democracy implies the ability of elected representatives to exercise decision-making power aimed at taking collectively binding decisions, while being subject to the rule of law within a (formal or material) constitutional framework. In this sense the co-decision procedure can be understood as 'quasi-democratic'. 'Quasi-democratic' because the law-making authority only partly lies with the EP due to its sharing of legislative power with the Council and the Commission. On the other hand, the legislative process leading to REACH evolved over an eight-year period within an elaborated constitutional framework, allowing for the intense involvement of MS, EC institutions and private actors. In relation to private actors, it is also noteworthy that the vast majority of the 6,400 submissions which the Commission received during its internet consultation came from industry, trade unions and environmental NGOs, thereby indicating that non-state actors exercised a high level of participation throughout the legislative process.

But even though REACH emerged from a 'quasi-democratic process', the outcome of the process also illustrates that the kind of power which can be exercised through democratic procedures has its limitations. Although often described as a kind of revolution,[93] REACH is instead the result of a long evolutionary development. A considerable part of the substantial changes introduced with REACH simply represents an update

[93] Eg CG Molynecx, 'IV. Chemicals' in *The Yearbook of European Environmental Law, vol 6* (Oxford, Oxford University Press, 2006).

of legislation adopted from the 1960s onwards with the application of new knowledge and increased technological capabilities of testing. Moreover and as previously noted, the principle of prior testing before permitting market availability had already been introduced in 1981, and was, in principle, extended to all products in 1993. In that sense REACH is only—albeit quite drastically—speeding up the realisation of a policy objective which had already been agreed on. In addition, the precautionary principle, which is one of the central principles of REACH, was introduced as a general policy instrument with the ratification of the Maastricht Treaty in 1993[94] and has experienced a rapid expansion of its application since the Commission published a communication on its use in 2000.[95] Since then, the reverse burden of proof, one of the most important elements of REACH, has been considered a generally accepted policy tool in the EU context.[96] REACH is therefore characterised by a considerable path dependency which greatly limited the scope of possible decisions. Instead the quasi-democratic policy process leading to REACH merely formalised and expanded the use of a number of regulatory principles which had already been incrementally introduced. However, it was not only the exercise of power through democratic procedures which faced certain limitations. The policy-making process of REACH illustrates that political power as such is subject to structural limitations insofar as the same limitations which curtailed democracy also curtailed the exercise of brute power politics. For example, although the intervention by the Heads of State and Government of the leading MS considerably increased pressure on the proponents of the proposal, it did not succeed in changing the fundamental principles on which the proposal was founded. Thus not only the role of the democratically elected EP, but also the role of the MS were far more reactive than proactive throughout the process and were merely capable of facilitating or impeding it, but not of introducing fundamental changes to the central principles on which the proposal rested.

Moreover, the main line of conflict seems to have developed along functional lines rather than being a conflict between a supranational dimension, represented by the Commission and the EP, and, on the other hand, an intergovernmental dimension, represented by the MS acting within the Council and the European Council. The proposal was developed by DG Environment and was supported by MS environmental ministers

[94] Art 174 EC. See also V Heyvaert, 'Guidance Without Constraint: Assessing the Impact of the Precautionary Principle on the European Community's Chemicals Policy' in *The Yearbook of European Environmental Law, vol 6* (Oxford, Oxford University Press, 2006).

[95] Commission Communication on the Precautionary Principle COM (2000)1 Final, 2 February 2000.

[96] *Ibid*, 21.

and by the EP Environmental Committee. As noted, the ministers and the MEPs called for stronger safety requirements than originally envisaged by the Commission. The proposal also had strong support from environmental NGOs. Hence, a surprising consensus existed among those involved in the social realm of environmental and health protection irrespective of their institutional affiliation. In other words, as long as the policy process evolved only within the environmental dimension of the EU it was fairly easy to reach agreement. The proposal only faced substantial resistance rather late in the policy-making process when the economic dimension of the EU, represented by industry, the Competitiveness Council, the EP Committee on Industry and Trade and DG Enterprise became aware of the potential impact on the economic sphere. As a policy proposal developed within the environmental dimension of the EU, it is likely that it was 'naturally biased' in the sense that it did not take 'extra-systemic' impacts into account but merely focused on environmental concerns. It is therefore not surprising that successively it was watered down during the latter half of the policy-making process which was mainly focused on minimising the effect on other social spheres, and in this particular case especially the economic sphere. Thus behind the objective of making a collectively binding decision, the substantial function of the process was to ensure coordination and a balance between the environmental and the economic spheres of society, and to regulate their reciprocal impact as regards chemicals. It is precisely this objective that the regulation seeks to achieve through the principle that the highest possible environmental and health standards should be imposed as long as such requirements do not undermine core elements of the economic viability of the chemicals sector.

Since the cleavage between different functionally differentiated spheres was the main area of conflict, the question of which competencies should be transferred to the Community and which should remain in the hands of the MS remained a secondary issue. Instead, the main competency clashes also arose from the differentiation between environmental and economic perspectives. Hence, it was not a clash which followed the logic inherent in the institutional structure of the Community as embodied in the concept of IB, thereby illustrating the problems inherent in the non-functionally differentiated concept of IB. Rather, the clash developed along lines which ran transversally to the IB. In the EP the clash was between the Committee of the Environment and the Committee of Industry and Trade. As already noted, both argued that they should be the leading committee, and the position taken by the EP was nothing other than a compromise between the two Committees. Within the Commission, DG Environment and DG Enterprise clashed continuously on similar accounts. A central question was which Directorate General the Agency should refer to when actually operative. DG Enterprise emerged as the winner of that dogfight. In the

Council the clashes between the Environmental Council and the Competitiveness Council were just as numerous. This triggered the intervention of the European Council. As the buck stopped there the Heads of State and Government were forced to indicate to the Council what the appropriate balance between environmental and economic concerns should be. In this case too the outcome was a carefully developed balance between economic and environmental perspectives.

The outcome of the legislative process was a collectively binding decision. The legitimacy of this decision did not, however, derive from a reference to a metaphysical concept of the sovereign people in the Kantian, Hegelian or Habermasian sense. Rather the legitimacy of the decision was derived from the comprehensive procedural framework of the co-decision procedure.[97] Behind the procedural framework a 'deeper' source of legitimacy was, moreover, derived from the functional differentiation of the policy process. This differentiation allowed the environmental dimension to develop an ideal policy proposal which enjoyed widespread support among those concerned with environmental issues. In the latter half of the process this policy proposal was then adjusted in order to incorporate perspectives derived from the economic sphere in order to minimise the negative impact of the proposal on this same sphere. The political dimension of the EU system was therefore merely acting as an arbitration board between different institutional structures which served as advocates of the economic and environmental spheres of society, thereby confirming the earlier descriptions of the structural transformations of the role of politics in late-modernity. Consequently, the degree of success of the legislative process should be measured by an assessment of the degree of concordance achieved between the perspectives of both societal spheres.

7.8.2 Proceduralisation

The legal infrastructure of REACH provides numerous recourses to administrative law provisions such as participation, transparency and review requirements in order to provide the regulatory framework with certain legitimacy. But behind these legal safeguards functional differentiation plays a crucial role in the way the REACH system operates in practice and in the way its legitimacy is constructed. This is so because the comprehensive procedural infrastructure of REACH is oriented towards upholding functional differentiation and the regulation of the mutual

[97] N Luhmann, *Legitimation durch Verfahren* (Neuwied, Luchterhand, 1978); N Luhmann, *Rechtssoziologie, Band 2* (Berlin, Rowohlt Taschenbuch, 1972) 259; N Luhmann, *Ausdifferenzierung des Rechts, Beiträge zur Rechtssoziologie und Rechtstheorie* (Frankfurt am Main, Suhrkamp Verlag, 1981) 132 *f*.

impact of different functional systems. Essentially, the regulation binds together five different functional systems, namely science, environment, health, and the economic and political systems within a legal frame. The function of the legal system in relation to REACH can therefore be seen as ensuring the stability and operability of a multi-faceted bundle of structural couplings at the same time as asymmetric relations between the systems involved are minimised.[98]

The legal infrastructure for risk assessment is established in the registration and evaluation procedures. The former procedure is largely oriented towards the private sphere, envisaging the conduct of safety assessments by registrants. The latter is mainly oriented towards the public sphere insofar as it regulates the evaluation of substances by competent MS authorities on the basis of the safety assessments provided by registrants. In spite of this distinction both procedures are subsumed under the perspective of science since the objective is to scientifically assess the substances in question. Thus, even though the private/public distinction, which is derived from the classical state/society distinction remains, from an organisational perspective, fairly valid, the risk assessment process is framed through a logic of science which transverses the distinction. Hence, the specific practice, language and modes of argumentation of science, will be applied and act as an overlay to both sides of the private/public distinction.

The authorisation and the restriction procedures are aimed at ensuring appropriate risk management. As noted earlier, general authorisations concerning the inclusion or exclusion of substances falling under the regulation foresee that the MSC will provide a unanimous opinion followed by referral of the final decision to the Commission acting under the Comitology procedure with scrutiny. In the case of disagreement within the MSC, Comitology also has the last say, although the decision will then be taken under the regulatory procedure. In both cases, however, the procedure also permits a transfer of the dossier in question from the realm of science into the political-administrative realm of Comitology.

However, the final decision under the evaluation procedure resides with the MSC and, in the case of dispute, between MS with Comitology. Hence, the procedures permit a transfer of issues from the realm of science and into the 'political administration' of the MSC and Comitology. As regards specific authorisations the procedural chain foresees that the dossiers being prepared within the realm of science are transferred to an analogous but synchronised structure where the CfRA and the CfSEA, in separate but simultaneous processes, will assess the dossiers in question on the basis of

[98] For the concept of asymmetry and its implications see P Kjaer, 'Systems in Context: On the Outcome of the Habermas/Luhmann debate' (2006) *Ancilla Iuris* 66, 75.

their different perspectives, namely the environmental (and health) perspective(s) and the economic perspective. If the outcomes of the analogous processes happen to converge, the issue is clear and is likely to be subject to a rubber stamp decision by the Commission, acting on the basis of the advisory Comitology procedure. In the case of a difference of opinion between the CfRA and CfSEA the Commission can still act, although under very specific limitations. Hence, in the case of divergent opinions the Commission and Comitology will act as a political body entrusted with taking a political decision by balancing the different views. Therefore, in this case too the legal framework is intended to ensure a transfer of dossiers from the realm of science over the intermediary realm of environment and economics to a more politicised sphere.

Concerning the restriction procedure the formal right of initiative resides in the Commission acting under the advisory procedure. Hence, the starting point is the political-administrative realm. The procedure, however, foresees that the CfRA and the CfSEA will confirm that the proposed actions are in conformity with the general provisions before being referred back to the Commission taking a final decision on the regulatory procedure with scrutiny. Hence, the feature common to these different procedures is that they enable a transfer of issues from one societal sphere to another and that the political administration of Comitology has the final word. The question of legitimacy is therefore reduced to an evaluation of the ability of the relevant legal infrastructure to ensure that the perspectives emerging from different societal spheres are in concordance. Or to put it another way: that the legal infrastructure can achieve convergence between the different perspectives of science, environment, health, economics and politics. Taking the complexity of the issues and the multitude of perspectives into consideration, constant convergence is an unlikely outcome. Hence, concordance is only likely to take place momentarily and in relation to specific dossiers. But in addition the idea of convergence will act as a regulatory idea embedded within the regulatory structure, thereby orienting it towards the function of systematically reducing the gap between the different perspectives. Hence, the classic distinction between input and output legitimacy is replaced by an understanding of the process itself as the central source of legitimacy. This therefore addresses an issue which all autonomous structures are faced with, namely the demand for being self-legitimising.

The focus on the process itself also has consequences for the balance between the different dimensions of rationality to which the regulatory structure refers. This is because a process-oriented perspective implies that the strategic dimension of rationality, which often guides the distinction between input and output legitimacy due to its recourse to a concept of affected interests, is complemented by a stronger emphasis on the time dimension. This will probably allow the regulatory structure to continuously increase its reflexivity through new knowledge which again will enable it to revise former positions and thereby produce a structural basis for convergence. In addition, striving for convergence between forms of communication aligned with different functional systems emphasises the importance of the social dimension of rationality. Hence the regulatory framework is directly oriented towards a balancing of the strategic dimension of rationality through an 'uploading' of the social and the time dimensions of rationality.

7.8.3 Deliberation

Deliberation is a disputed concept.[99] Even if a coherent concept of deliberation can be developed, the motives guiding decision making remain unobservable thereby making it impossible to verify claims that 'deliberation has taken place'.[100] In practice most empirical studies of deliberation therefore merely refer to a diluted concept of deliberation in the form of consensus achieved through pragmatic agreements based on common sense. Hence, as indicated above, a concept of convergence between different forms of rationality might be more suitable. The transformation of Habermas' discourse ethics into a discourse theory based on procedural requirements similar to those from which Luhmann derives his concept of legitimacy also confirms this.[101]

Irrespective of the disputed strength of the concept as an analytical tool, it can, however, be argued that the REACH regulation refers more or less consciously to the concept of deliberation, thereby indicating that the regulatory structure describes itself as a consensus-oriented mechanism. This is the case particularly in relation to the way the committees are legally framed. Not only are members obliged not to take any instructions, but the regulation directly stresses the importance of reaching unanimity. In addition, as dissent will include the publication of divergent positions and in most cases also a referral of decisions upstream in the procedural chain, the committees are likely to have a strong incentive to reach agreement. This incentive is further reinforced by the obligation of the committees to provide opinions within specific time limits, thereby putting members under a moderate but constant pressure to reach agreement.

[99] Eg K-H Ladeur, 'Discursive Ethics as Constitutional Theory. Neglecting the Creative Role of Economic Liberties?' (2000) 13 (1) *Ratio Juris* 95.

[100] N Luhmann, '"Was ist der Fall?" und "Was steckt dahinter"? Die zwei Soziologien und die Gesellschaftstheorie' (1993) 22 *Zeitschrift für Soziologie* 345.

[101] P Kjaer, 'Systems in Context: On the Outcome of the Habermas/Luhmann-debate' (2006) *Ancilla Iuris* 66, 75 *f*.

Hence, the legal structure of the committees is such that consensus-oriented norms are likely to become stronger features than would otherwise be the case.

Moreover, in relation to the CfRA and the CfSEA in particular, other features will provide a structural basis which is likely to facilitate agreement. These features are derived from the strong functionally differentiated character of the committees and the heavy reliance on expertise. These two elements are likely to ensure that members will possess a common knowledge base and a shared perspective on how the issues in question should be addressed. Should a shared frame be lacking, the working process itself is likely to create one in that a continued repetition of procedurally framed activities is likely to produce a lifeworld, in the form of a shared and condensed reservoir of knowledge which the participants can draw upon in their problem-solving endeavour.[102]

Although sharing many of the features of the CfRA and the CfSE, the MSC and Comitology will operate in a more complex environment. Members of Comitology committees are likely to operate on mandates, thereby narrowing their manoeuvrability. Both the MSC and Comitology are also likely to be more politicised than the CfRA and the CfSE, because of their function as balancers of different societal dimensions. In some cases at least, this function is likely to imply irreconcilable trade-offs and dilemmas where no optimal solution can be found. When confronted with such paradoxes the solution is likely to be found in the time dimension rather than in the social dimension as such issues are likely to be contained within pragmatic ad hoc solutions or de facto 'non-decisions' which will be subject to review at a later date. Hence, the lower level of functional differentiation is likely to somewhat reduce the potential for reaching agreement within the MSC and the Comitology structures.

7.9 CONTEXTUALISING REACH

Although one should be careful about extrapolating general insights from the specific case of chemicals regulation, this analysis highlights that any model developed to frame the European integration process needs to take the reality and need for functional differentiation into account.[103] The majority of the existing integration theories ignore this element, however, and continue to place themselves somewhere on the intergovernmental/supranational continuum. The case of chemicals policy, which obviously is

[102] *Ibid*, 69.

[103] For a typical example where this is not the case see EO Eriksen and JE Fossum, 'Europe in Transformation. How to Reconstitute Democracy?' (2007) 1 *RECON Online Working Paper*.

not fully representative since it is subject to co-decision and hence represents one of the most 'mature' policy areas in terms of integration, indicates, however, that this distinction, although still relevant, is not the most important. Rather, the focus on functionally differentiated structures running transversally to the intergovernmental/supranational distinction should be increased since the main clashes of rationalities do not seem to emerge from vertical clashes between the MS and Brussels or between stratified social structures, but rather from the continued need to coordinate and balance highly dynamic horizontal processes which are produced within different functionally delineated areas of society. That is also the case within the governing dimension of the EU. Like national parliaments, for example, the EP is characterised by three features: territorial differentiation on the basis of the constituencies and national affiliation of members; the distinction between left and right which traditionally was derived from a stratificatory concept of social class; and through functional differentiation between committees. In contrast to national parliaments the latter feature plays a far stronger—one could argue even the decisive—role in the EP. Any attempt to conceive of the EP as representing a European 'national character' (*Volksgeist*), which potentially will be able to constitute unity in a Hegelian sense, is therefore bound to be even further from reality than it ever was in the national contexts.

8

Constitutionalising Governing and Governance

8.1 INTRODUCTION

HOW CAN THE relationship between the different forms of governance as well as between the governing and the governance dimensions of the EU be constitutionalised? In order to answer this question it is necessary to develop a contextualised concept of constitutionalism, which reflects the specific character of the EU as a hybrid operating between the MS and the wider world. Hence it is necessary to develop a third category of constitutionalism which extends beyond traditional nation-state constitutionalism, at the same time taking into consideration the differences between the EU and truly global GS.

Hence, it is proposed that a coherent concept for the stabilisation of legal conflicts in the European context should be based on a three-dimensional concept of conflict of laws. This concept must be capable of handling horizontal conflicts between territorially delineated states, vertical conflicts between the EU and the MS as well as horizontal conflicts between functionally delineated structures representing different forms of rationality. In relation to the latter dimension, which is concerned specifically with governance, it is moreover suggested that a constitutional principle of functional separation, more extensive than the classic concept of a functional separation of powers, could provide a basis for legal stabilisation of norm production.

8.2 THE TRANSFORMATION OF CONSTITUTIONALISM

Although the MS provide substantial limitations to its level of self-determination, the EU must, as argued in Chapter 2, nonetheless be understood as an autonomous social structure which possesses the freedom to select between various possible operations. This implies that the EU needs to justify its selections. First, this is because all autonomous social structures are faced with a continual demand to ensure their own coherency by reproducing narratives that connect their specific operations with their overall structure. But in addition, autonomous social structures are reflexive and are conscious that they fulfil specific functions towards society as a whole as well as towards other partial social structures. Hence, they are continuously faced with a demand to substantiate their operations towards their environments.

Such justifications are, however, paradoxical in nature, as they are always *self*-justifications. They are internal operations which are based on the structure's own understanding of the expectations emerging within their environments. A common feature of social structures, including a hybrid such as the EU, is therefore that they develop strategies intended to 'cover up' the paradoxical nature of attempts at justification. They internally construct semantic artefacts which they can claim are external in nature. For example, the religious system refers to a concept of God, the economic system to the market, the (democratic) political system to the people and the legal system to systems of (natural) rights. Hence, these systems can claim that their operations merely reflect the will of God, market demand, the will of the people or self-evident universal rights. These metaphors are assigned a foundational quality, but they also serve as mirrors which the respective systems use in order to scrutinise themselves, thereby potentially increasing their level of reflexivity. Hence, these concepts provide the systems with a possibility of internally evaluating and substantiating their operations.

Within the political system such practices are also described by the concept of legitimacy. As indicated, democratic political systems derive their claim for legitimacy through reference to the will of the people, whom the rulers claim to represent. But in addition, the political system has engaged in a specific strategy of 'self-binding' through a carefully developed 'partnership' with the legal system. This strategy goes under the name constitutionalisation. In a narrow sense constitutions serve as structural couplings between the legal and the political systems thereby allowing the former to rely on legislation enacted in the political system as a basis for its rights-based jurisprudence. In the same way, the political system accepts limitations to its autonomy through a legal framing of its activities. The legal framing diminishes the contingent character of political operations, thereby serving as a tool which facilitates a stabilisation of the expectations arising in the environment vis-à-vis the political system. This is central since the continued functioning of social structures is conditioned by generally stable expectations concerning the environment within which they operate. It is exactly this kind of stability which the 'rule of law' ensures for the political system (as well as for other systems) as the central function of law is the stabilisation of normative expectations. The political system can therefore claim legitimacy by referring to the legal framing of its operations as this, in principle, guarantees that its impact on the remaining parts of society is reflected in the selection of its operations.

As previously indicated, constitutionalism was largely oriented towards the relationship between law and politics in the era of classical modernity.[1] The radicalisation of modernity in the latter half of the 20th century has, however, placed the nation states, and thereby the nation-state model of constitutionalism, under increased pressure. As a consequence it is possible to observe two interrelated developments: first, a move towards societal constitutionalism, in that the legal system increasingly engages in couplings that possess a constitutional quality, with social structures falling outside the realm of the political system.[2] Secondly, within the emerging post-modern paradigm of transnational law, it is argued that new types (such as lex mercatoria and lex digitalis) have emerged and that these forms of law operate within a context of 'extreme self-reference'. This arises because the functional synthesis (*Funktionssynthese*) between the legal and political systems, which was made possible in the nation-state realm through structural couplings between the legal and the political systems via constitutions and legislative acts, is not in place at the transnational level. Hence, transnational law is not capable of relying on legislation enacted by the political system to provide external reference points for its jurisprudence. Instead transnational law is forced to rely on itself to a degree which is even more radical than has traditionally been the case at the nation-state level.[3] In contrast to classical international law, new forms of transnational law therefore rely more and more on self-defined principles.[4] The kind of global and regional political-administrative GS identified in Chapter 3 are faced with a similar situation since they increasingly expand their operations without being subject to a formal legal framing. If law is activated at all, this increasingly happens ex post. Scholars who celebrate the intrinsic link between the rule of law and democracy as a key accomplishment of modernity have observed this with some concern.[5] Positive readings of this

[1] As illustrated by Koselleck the limitation of constitutions to the relationship between law and politics is, however, a specifically modern phenomenon. In the Middle Ages constitutions occurred in multiple forms. See R Koselleck, 'Begriffsgeschichtliche Probleme der Verfassungsgeschichtsschreibung' in R Koselleck, *Begriffsgeschichten: Studien zur Semantik und Pragmatik der politischen und Sozialen Sprache* (Frankfurt am Main, Suhrkamp Verlag, 2006).

[2] Eg D Sciulli, *Theory of Societal Constitutionalism: Foundations of a Non-Marxist Critical Theory* (New York, Cambridge University Press, 1992); G Teubner, 'Societal Constitutionalism: Alternatives to State-Centred Constitutional Theory?' in C Joerges, I-J Sand and G Teubner (eds), *Transnational Governance and Constitutionalism* (Oxford, Hart Publishing, 2004).

[3] M Amstutz and V Karavas, 'Rechtsmutation: Zu Genese und Evolution des Rechts im transnationalen Raum' (2006) 8 *Rechtsgeschichte* 14.

[4] For international and transnational economic law see M Panezi, 'Sources of Law in Transition. Re-visiting General Principles of International Law' (2007) *Ancilla Iuris* 66.

[5] J Habermas, 'Die postnationale Konstellation und die Zukunft der Demokratie' in J Habermas, *Die postnationale Konstellation. Politische Essays* (Frankfurt am Main, Suhrkamp Verlag, 1998); J Habermas, *Faktizität und Geltung. Beiträge zur Diskurstheorie des Rechts und demokratischen Rechtsstaats* (Frankfurt am Main, Suhrkamp Verlag, 1992) 167.

development have, on the other hand, emphasised that 'hard' legal norms are merely being replaced or complemented by 'soft' legal norms, acting as functional equivalents to hard norms, at the transnational level.[6] Whichever the interpretation chosen, the emergence of a dense net of transnational structures does, however, imply a break with, or at least a transformation of, traditional concepts of constitutionalism, since the legal framing of non-nation-state political-administrative structures takes a different form compared to the classical modern forms which emerged within the nation-state frame.[7]

8.3 PARTIAL STATEHOOD

When applying the above 'post-modern' perspective to the EU, however, certain 'misfits' are apparent. The EU fulfils Luhmann's minimalist definition of a state,[8] as it consists of a political and a legal system structurally coupled within a constitutional framework. Hence, although imperfect, a functional synthesis between law and politics can actually be observed in the EU context. In addition, the EU's political system is capable of relying on a hierarchically organised bureaucratic machinery of considerable magnitude. The EU is, moreover, structurally coupled to a territory and has (tentatively) developed a concept of citizenship. Within the governing dimension it relies on a distinction between the public and private spheres of society and has adopted traditional state symbols (flag, hymn, etc.). These state-like features are, moreover, reinforced by the understanding that the EU, as we have seen, must be regarded as an autonomous phenomenon as its political system has developed its own policy programmes and, with considerable success, has also been able to ensure implementation of these programmes, just as the EU legal system has established its own legal order and independent sources of authority. If we consider that the 19th and 20th-century nation states, defined by their monopoly on political and legal authority within a given territory, are anomalies which only dominated a relatively short time span of social development[9] it is therefore possible to see nation states as one possible

[6] Eg DM Trubek, P Cottrell and M Nance, '"Hard Law" and EU Integration' in G de Burca and J Scott (eds), *Law and New Governance in the EU and the US* (Oxford, Hart Publishing, 2006).

[7] N Walker, 'Post-Constituent Constitutionalism' in M Loughlin and N Walker (eds), *The Paradox of Constitutionalism* (Oxford, Oxford University Press, 2007).

[8] N Luhmann, *Politik der Gesellschaft* (Frankfurt am Main, Surhkamp Verlag, 2000) 390 *f*.

[9] Eg N MacCormick, 'Beyond the Sovereign State' (1993) 56 (1) *Modern Law Review* 1.

variant among other forms of state, thereby making it possible to argue that the EU also falls within the state category.[10]

Such a view does not, however, sufficiently emphasise the differences between the EU and the nation states. As already pointed out, only a weak distinction can be made between policy programmes and polity structure, and no distinction between government and opposition exists in the EU setting. The EU relies on collective binding decisions but has no means to ensure compliance through negative sanctions and hence no Weberian territorial control exists.[11] Although the distinctions between the political and administrative levels are also blurred at the nation-state level,[12] the EU embodies the perfect dissolution of this distinction through its special form of 'political administration'. This is not only the case within the realm of GS but also within the Commission, where the role that Commissioners play falls between that of a politician and a civil servant, just as the personal cabinets of the Commissioners continue to play a two-fold political and administrative role. Consequently, the EU can also be characterised as a Weberian 'instrument of rule' (*Herrschaftsinstrument*) without a master.[13]

Hence, reaffirming earlier conclusions, the EU must be understood as a hybrid structure oscillating between the form of a state and a transnational governance structure. This is also reflected in its reliance on the basic distinction between governing and governance and its function as a structure mediating in between the nation states and the global realm. Hence the EU consists of a complex bundle of heterogeneous and partly contradictory juridical, political and administrative processes, each producing different forms of rationality on the basis of their respective codes.[14] At the same time, a certain unity is established through their subordination to the integrationist logic embodied in the institutional structure and the concept of IB which runs transverse to the functionally differentiated communication flows.

[10] R Stichweh, 'Dimensionen des Weltstaats im System der Weltpolitik' in M Albert and R Stichweh (Hrsg.), *Weltstaat und Weltstaatlichkeit. Beobachtungen globaler politischer Strukturbildung* (Wiesbaden, VS Verlag, 2007) 26 *ff*.

[11] The EU does not fulfil Pierre Bourdieu's revised Weberian definition of the state either, as he defines the state as the institution which 'successfully claims the monopoly of the legitimate use of physical and *symbolic* violence over a definite territory and over the totality of the corresponding population'; See P Bourdieu, 'Rethinking the State: Genesis and Structure of the Bureaucratic Field' (1994) 12 (1) *Sociological Theory* 1, 3.

[12] HD Jarass, *Politik und Bürokratie als Elemente der Gewaltenteilung* (München, CH Beck'sche Verlagsbuchhandlung, 1975) 125 *ff*.

[13] N Luhmann, 'Europa als Problem der Weltgesellschaft' (1994) 2 *Berliner Debatte* 3, 6.

[14] I-J Sand, 'Understanding the European Union/European Economic Area as Systems of Functionally Different Processes' in P Fitzpatrick and JH Bergeron, *Europe's Other: European Law Between Modernity and Postmodernity* (Aldershot, Ashgate Publishing, 1998).

8.4 PARTIAL CONSTITUTIONALISM

Since Rasmussen pointed out what everyone already knew concerning the 'legal activism' of the ECJ,[15] it has become acceptable to claim in public that the court has been subject to a different kind of rationality than a purely legal one. Rasmussen views this as an unfortunate 'politicisation' of the ECJ. Bearing in mind the earlier reconstruction of the subordination of the EU political policy programme to the logic of integration, one might be able to consider legal activism as reflecting a similar situation whereby the law/non-law (*Recht/Unrecht*) distinction of the Court, acting as an organisation within the realm of the legal system, is also subordinated to the integrationist logic. Such subordination does not imply a complete exclusion of legal rationality, but merely indicates that the operations of the Court are subject to a 'double binary coding'. As has been seen, such limitations can also be understood as a result of 'under-differentiation' leading to an 'over-reduction' of meaning (*Sinn*). Not surprisingly, this form of over-reduction has therefore led to the development of regulatory ideas and normative models concerning the possible transformation of the ECJ, either into a European supreme court[16] or into a court capable of safeguarding its autonomy through increased self-restraint.[17]

However, the EU has also undergone a rapid constitutionalisation process over the last decades.[18] This process collides with the logic of integration. As already indicated, a central function of constitutions is to enable the legal system to observe the system-internal processes of the political system while simultaneously the system-internal processes of the legal system are observed by the political system.[19] Processes of constitutionalisation therefore tend to occur within the context of increased differentiation between law and politics, arising from increases in social complexity.[20] Accordingly, the ongoing constitutionalisation process can be understood as reflecting an increased dissolution of the integration overlay. The tendencies towards dissolution should not, however, necessarily be

[15] H Rasmussen, *On Law and Policy in the European Court of Justice* (Dordrecht, Martinus Nijhoff, 1986); JHH Weiler, 'The Court of Justice on Trial' (1987) 24 *Common Market Law Review* 555.

[16] Eg I Pernice, 'Maastricht, Staat und Demokratie' (1993) 26 *Die Verwaltung* 449; R Dehousse, *The European Court of Justice* (London, Macmillan Press, 1998) 148.

[17] Eg H Rasmussen, *Towards a Normative Theory of Interpretation of Community Law* (Copenhagen, Political Studies Press, 1993).

[18] The narrative of the constitutionalisation process has been written several times. Most notably: C Joerges, 'Das Recht im Prozeβ des Konstitutionalisierung Europas' (2001) 6 *EUI Working Papers*; JHH Weiler, 'The Transformation of Europe' (1991) 100 *Yale Law Journal* 2402; E Stein, 'Lawyers, Judges, and the Making of a Transnational Constitution' (1981) 75 *American Journal of International Law* 1.

[19] N Luhmann, *Politik der Gesellschaft* (Frankfurt am Main, Suhrkamp Verlag) 390 *ff*.

[20] N Luhmann, 'Verfassung als evolutionäre Errungenschaft' (1990) 9 *Rechtshistorisches Journal* 176.

understood as indicating a failure for the EU since its regulatory principle concerning 'an ever closer union' through increased integration implies eventual transformation into some sort of state. In this sense the regulatory principle of statehood through integration implies 'self-dissolution' in that the move towards modern statehood implies that the organic unity established through the IB will be replaced with the kind of purely metaphorical unity that characterises modern states.[21] As indicated earlier, this also explains the ambivalent position of the Commission in relation to the transformation of the concept of IB into a functionally delineated concept of a separation of powers.

The constitutionalisation of the EU is, however, not only characterised by an increased horizontal dissolution of the EU's unity, but also by vertical hierarchisation. The differentiation of increasingly independent dimensions of law and politics is conditioned by a move towards a merger of the EU dimensions of law and politics with their respective counterparts at the nation-state level. This takes place as the EU dimensions form hierarchical peaks in new European-wide subsystems of law and politics, through the legal doctrines concerning 'direct effect' and superiority of Community law. The move towards hierarchisation therefore increasingly blurs the distinction between the EU and the MS legal orders.

On the other hand, the crucial question of competence-competence remains unresolved, just as the interrelated political question of the fundamental nature of the embryonic polity remains largely unanswered. Moreover, the fate of the CT indicates that there are clear limitations to how constitutional the EU can be.[22] Consequently, the EU seems to be oscillating somewhere in between being a separate legal order and engaging in a merger with the national legal orders. Limitations to the EU's evolution arising from the resistance of the political system in the MS form, seem, in other words, to transform the quest for 'complete' statehood into an unattainable mirage even though a certain level of constitutionalisation has been achieved. Instead the EU has entered into a state of 'permanent dissolution', in the sense that it continues to operate on the basis of the regulatory idea of state-building through the dissolution of the unity established by the integration overlay, at the same time as it is faced with structural conditions which make the idea unachievable. The relationship between the EU legal order and the MS legal orders therefore remains fundamentally unresolved.[23]

[21] J Bartelson, *The Critique of the State* (Cambridge, Cambridge University Press, 2001).

[22] MP Maduro, 'The Constitutional Treaty and the Nature of European Constitutionalism: The Tension between Intergovernmentalism and Constitutionalism in the European Union' in DM Curtin, AE Kellermann and S Blockmans (eds), *The EU Constitution: The Best Way Forward?* (The Hague, Asser Press, 2005).

[23] JHH Weiler, *The Constitution of Europe. 'Do the New Clothes Have an Emperor?' and other Essays on European Integration* (Cambridge, Cambridge University Press, 1999) 286.

8.5 HORIZONTAL CONSTITUTIONALISM I

One of the most original attempts to re-conceptualise the relationship between the EU and the MS legal orders is the conflict of laws approach. This approach departs from a paradox in that conflict of laws methodology is oriented towards ensuring unity at the same time as maintaining substantial diversity. It therefore takes the structural conditions characterising the European context into consideration as it departs from the paradoxical 'unity in diversity' which the EU itself describes as its basis.

As argued by Joerges, the response of the EU courts has been the intentional development of 'meta-norms', with the objective of achieving a stabilisation of conflicts between the legal orders which does not imply that national legal orders are broken down. This understanding of EU law is based on a functionalist worldview. Conflicts emerge between MS because of an ever higher level of interdependence between them, thereby creating the functional need for conflict resolution. The key argument promoted by Joerges is, however, normative; increased interdependence means that the MS are increasingly characterised by a democratic deficit since the democratic decisions of the MS ever more frequently have extra-territorial effects. These effects are not reflected in the democratic decisions of those states, since their only point of reference is their own constituency and not those of their neighbours. EU law (and EU integration as such) should therefore be understood as compensatory measures which ensure that the extra-territorial effects of MS actions are taken into account. The European constitutionalisation process should therefore be understood as complementary to nation-state constitutionalism, as its objective is to ensure a reduction in negative externalities arising from the operations of national political systems.

According to Joerges, the development of European 'meta-norms' has provided a legal framework within which regulatory structures such as the 'new approach', mutual recognition of technical standards, the delegation of standardisation activities to private actors, as well as the emergence and expansion of Comitology and agencies have been made possible. It is therefore possible to observe a relationship of mutual increase between the European constitutionalisation process and the emergence of GS. In addition, the incremental build-up of a European legal framework has also served as a frame for the continued expansion of the political dimension of the EU. Hence, it is possible to understand the EU as characterised by a symbiotic relationship between three dimensions: first, the 'semi-hierarchical' legal order; secondly, the political dimension as embodied in the CIS; and thirdly, a hybrid administrative infrastructure as provided for by the GS.[24]

Joerges' version of the conflict of laws approach encapsulates the emergence and purpose of the European project within a highly elegant construction. Moreover, its central strength is that it does not deduct a normative vision for Europe from a purely analytical ideal model concerning how Europe ought to be. Instead it departs from an inductive functional perspective the main focus of which is the pragmatic solution of common problems. It provides a normative justification for the processes of conflict resolution which evolves in Europe on a day-to-day basis. The conflict of laws approach is in touch with reality.

Two problems emerge however: first, the conflict of laws approach does not provide an answer to the question of how the instrumentalisation of EU law as a vehicle of integration can be curbed. As emphasised earlier, increased interdependence, the functional problem from which the conflict of laws approach departs, is to a large extent created through EU integration and the pro-integrationist legal activism of the courts. Hence, the European legal system has itself played a pivotal role by paving the way for the increases in interdependence which—according to Joerges—provide the normative justification for the development of metanorms by the European courts. From this perspective Joerges' conflict of laws approach therefore merely provides a language with which the producers of EU law can engage in a self-justifying exercise of their own achievements.

Hence, if the normative purpose of Joerges' conflict of laws approach should be deemed viable it needs to be complemented by a focus on constitutional safeguards capable of breaking up the integrationist logic and curbing the legal activism of the European courts. As we will shortly see, the vertical relations between, on the one hand Brussels and Luxembourg and, on the other hand the MS, therefore deserve greater attention. In addition, the possibility of strengthening the EU's political dimension through a democratisation of the EU must be addressed since it is the failure of the EU's political dimension to provide the courts with suitable reference points through legislative acts which has made the legal activism of the courts possible.

[24] C Joerges, 'Rethinking European Law's Supremacy: A Plea for a Supranantional Conflict of Laws' (2005) 12 *EUI Working Papers (Law)*; C Joerges, 'Constitutionalism in Postnational Constellations: Contrasting Social Regulation in the EU and in the WTO' in C Joerges and EU Petersmann (eds), *Constitutionalism, Multilevel Trade Governance and Social Regulation* (Oxford, Hart Publishing, 2006) 493 *f*.

Secondly: as pointed out by Chalmers, Joerges' variant of the conflict of laws approach amounts to a re-territorialisation of authority.[25] The main concern of Joerges is the ability of the law to curb the territorially based power of the nation states. This is a relevant objective. But as argued by Chalmers, territorially vested authority is no longer the sole form of authority. The mutation of the EU into a conglomerate compromising a multitude of GS has undercut the claim of territorially based powers to be the only source of authority, since they have increasingly become independent structures operating in an increasingly autonomous manner. Hence, the different dimensions of the European conglomerate to a large extent claim authority through recourse to scientific knowledge and other forms of 'expertise'. The conflict of laws approach promoted by Joerges does not, however, sufficiently address this issue. A central reason for this is that his approach remains based on a traditional variant of the conflict of laws, which focuses on vertical, and especially on horizontal, conflicts between territorially defined entities. But these two forms of conflict are far from the only ones to emerge in a radically functionally differentiated world. As argued earlier, collisions between functionally differentiated structures are increasingly becoming a defining element in world society. Hence, in relation to the EU, operating as a hybrid between world society and the nation states, it is—besides vertical conflicts—possible to observe two forms of horizontal conflicts developing at the same time, namely those between states which Joerges focuses upon, and those between the different functionally differentiated spheres of society.[26] As illustrated in the previous chapter, risk regulation serves as a forceful illustration of the latter, insofar as different forms of rationality, arsing from different functionally differentiated spheres such as the economy, environment and health, tend to collide. A comprehensive constitutional approach, capable of grasping the defining features of the European integration phenomenon, therefore needs to reach beyond Joerges' territorial horizontal approach. His theory needs to be expanded into a three-dimensional structure, as it should be capable of addressing vertical as well as both forms of horizontal (territorial and functionally differentiated) conflicts.

8.6 VERTICAL CONSTITUTIONALISM

As already discussed, the question of how the instrumentalisation of EU law can be curbed leads directly to the question of how the balance

[25] D Chalmers, 'Deliberative Supranationalism and the Reterritorialization of Authority' in C Joerges, 'Rethinking European Law's Supremacy' (2005) 12 *EUI Working Paper Law*.

[26] That is of course also the case within nation states and at the transnational level. 'Double-horizonatlity' is, however, a particularly strong feature of the EU.

between politics and law can be reconfigured in the EU context to ensure that the operations of the legal dimension converge with those of the political dimension. Until now the central impetus for increased integration has come from the Heads of State and Government operating within the realm of the European Council. At the same time—once the Commission has prepared the ground—the Council has played the main role in the day-to-day making of integrative decisions. It is, however, exactly this form of policy making which has proved inadequate when it comes to the development of constitutional principles and legislative acts capable of providing suitable reference points for the European courts. The reliance on power sharing means that it is immensely difficult for the EU to produce coherent legal texts since sharing power between multiple institutions with the ability to block progress means that the outcome of legislative processes typically represents the lowest denominator. Dictated by the need to make political compromises, the result is that insufficient solutions are provided for pressing functional problems. In addition, systemic deficits occur because power sharing tends to produce legislation characterised by a mismatch of contradictory objectives and deliberately vague formulations. In other words, the EU's political dimension systematically produces suboptimal outcomes thereby creating decisional vacuums, forcing the courts to define the actual scope and intentions of community legislation.[27] Hence, it is the deficiency of the EU's political dimension in the production of coherent legislative texts which has prevented the emergence of an optimal functional synthesis between law and politics. As a result the courts are able to engage in legal activism based on their pro-integrationist bias.

The standard solution suggested for overcoming this problem has been increased politicisation. In general increased politicisation is equalled with increased democratisation.[28] The question of how or to what extent the EU can be democratised must, however, begin with an analysis of the structural conditions which must be in place in order for democratic structures to emerge and function. Democracy can be understood as a particular form through which the political system observes its environment through reference to a collective in the form of the people. This reference allows the political system to define the section of its environment which it deems relevant when taking account of its continual selection of operations. In addition, democracy can be understood as a specific mode of legally

[27] A typical example is the recently adopted service directive, which essentially leaves it to the courts to define the scope of directives. See Directive 2006/123/EC of the European Parliament and of the Council of 12 December 2006 on services in the internal market.

[28] Eg EO Eriksen and JE Fossum, 'Europe at a Crossroads: Government or Transnational Governance?' in C Joerges, I-J Sand and G Teubner (eds), *Transnational Governance and Constitutionalism* (Oxford, Hart Publishing, 2004).

regulated collective decision making, characterised by a differentiation of roles between government and opposition, which relies on the existence of a hierarchically organised and legally framed bureaucratic structure capable of implementing such collective decisions through the (potential) invoking of negative sanctions.[29]

As already seen in relation to the REACH policy process, the EU only partially shares these characteristics of democracy and hence remains a 'quasi-democracy'. The status as a 'quasi-democracy' is being further reinforced by the absence of a singular European people (*Staatsvolk*). A solution has emerged with the concept of 'multiple demoi'.[30] Such conceptual 'arm-twisting' will, however, not solve the real problem, namely that the concept of the people is too general to serve as a point of reference for the kind of hyper-complex decision making which the EU undertakes. In addition, decisions are only partly taken within a developed constitutional framework because GS such as the OMC fall outside the CM and the logic guiding the IB. In parliamentary democracies the locus of power, at least formally, resides in an elected assembly operating on the basis of the distinction between government and opposition. Despite the rise of the EP, however, this is not the case in relation to the EU, where no formal locus of sovereignty exists. The EU possesses an instrument of rule in the form of the Commission bureaucracy. But this instrument is only a partial source of control since implementation and the ability to introduce negative sanctions rests mainly with the MS, which in most cases still possess the monopoly on legitimate deployment of sanctions within their territories.

Of all the deficits listed it is probably the government/opposition issue that receives most attention within academic discussions as well as in the broader public. Yet this issue is the easiest to solve. In fact the progressive refinement and expansion of the co-decision procedure and the strengthening of the EP might gradually lead to the emergence of a parliamentary structure resembling the nation-state form of democracy. The more fundamental problem lies in the reach of democracy. As noted, democratic decision making remains conditioned by the existence of legal as well as organisational hierarchies, since meaningful decision making is conditioned by the ability to ensure implementation and the possible deployment of negative sanctions. In other words: democracy remains a 'parasite' on power[31] because it is conditioned by the existence of an instrument of rule

[29] N Luhmann, 'Die Zukunft der Demokratie' in N Luhmann, *Soziologische Aufklärung, Band 4. Beiträge Zur Funktionalen Differenzierung der Gesellschaft* (Opladen, Westdeutscher Verlag, 1994) 127.

[30] JHH Weiler, 'Does Europe Need a Constitution? Reflections on Demos, Telos and the German Maastricht Decision' (1995) 1 *European Law Journal* 219.

[31] N Luhmann, *Die Politik der Gesellschaft* (Frankfurt am Main, Suhrkamp Verlag, 2000) 357.

and by a monopoly of power through which democratically made decisions can be channelled.[32] Democracy is therefore intrinsically linked to the existence of strong vertical political and legal control and demand structures on the basis of a distinction between the rulers and the ruled. This structural limitation explains why 'radical democracy' (*Basisdemokratie*), encompassing society as whole, has never been able to manifest itself. Democracy remains a limited concept which is unable to manifest itself beyond the boundaries of the hierarchic order or the political system.

The insight that democracy is impossible beyond the realm of hierarchy has profound implications for the possibility of achieving a democratisation of the EU, because it remains a structure which partly is based on governing and partly on governance. As illustrated earlier, these two dimensions are bound together through a relationship of mutual increase. This means that the EU is an expanding universe, in that the governing and governance dimensions both expand at the same time. A continuous move towards democratisation of the governing dimension through the progressive strengthening of the co-decision procedure and the EP can therefore be observed together with an expansion of the governance dimension. A governance dimension which is not an undemocratic structure which potentially can be subject of democratisation. Rather it is an a-democratic structure which is beyond the reach of democracy. Hence, calls for a 'complete' democratisation of the EU through a transfer of the basic features of nation-state democracy to the EU cannot be realised since only the governing dimension of the EU can be subject to democratisation.

Alternatively, the attempt to grasp ongoing developments within the EU must be based on a dual approach. A pincer movement (*Zangenbewegung*) is required which on the one hand explores the viability and consequences of increased democratisation of the governing dimension, while on the other hand alternative concepts are developed to frame the governance dimension. From a constitutionalisation perspective, the key issue is therefore how law can contribute to the double-sided task of facilitating and curbing the exercise of power within the two dimensions at the same time as maintaining the carefully developed balance between the two dimensions.

Regarding the governing dimension, we once again need to return to the diagnosis provided in Chapter 3, namely that the central problem of this dimension is reliance on the concept of IB. The real problem in relation to the IB is not 'under-democratisation' but rather 'under-differentiation'.

[32] Hence, it is no coincidence that, in Europe, democracy first emerged after the creation of the territorial states and that it simply took the form of an exchange of the already existing sovereignty of the prince with the sovereignty of the people. See N Elias, *Über den Prozeß der Zivilisation, Band 2* (Frankfurt am Main, Suhrkamp Verlag [1938] 1976).

This diagnosis also contains a possible answer to the problem of developing an adequate political 'partner' for the legal system. That is because the tentative move towards transforming the IB into a functionally differentiated structure resembling the classical modern differentiation between the legislative, the executive and the juridical branches advocated by Sieyès and Kant would potentially rationalise the system by granting specific institutions a monopoly on specific functions. This would undermine the kind of legislative blocking-capability which tends to lead to community legislation characterised by a patchwork of contradictory objectives. Simultaneously, functional differentiation would ensure effective limitations on the exercise of power because specific institutions would be confined to the exercise of specific functions thereby making it possible to clearly identify the institution possessing the ultimate responsibility. A stronger reliance on functional separation is therefore likely to improve the flexibility of the system and hence increase the EU's ability to react to changes in its environment through the incorporation of new knowledge without relinquishing the 'rule of law'.

8.7 HORIZONTAL CONSTITUTIONALISM II

For the governance dimension the task is somewhat more complicated. The key issue is to develop a concept of constitutionalisation which ensures the stabilisation of GS without damaging the flexibility of these structures, while maintaining the balance between the governing and governance dimensions. Hence, it is necessary to develop a concept which binds the OMC, Comitology and agencies within a coherent legal structure at the same time as the functional demand for integration is taken seriously. Two issues are therefore at stake: (i) the positioning of the three forms of governance in relation to each other and (ii) the internal organisation of the three forms of governance.

In relation to the first problem the proponents of DDP have called for a constitutionalisation of the OMC.[33] Viewed from a traditional perspective on constitutionalism this objective proceeds from an insoluble contradiction, in that purely political processes which operate outside the realm of law cannot be constitutionalised. From this perspective constitutionalisation implies a legal framing of a social structure which facilitates the exercise of power at the same time as the versatility of the power structures are being reduced on the basis of a reference to a people which confers restricted authoritative power to political structures for a limited period of time. In the case of the EU, however, it is the MS who confer power to the

[33] J Zeitlin, 'Social Europe and Experimentalist Governance: Towards a New Constitutional Compromise?' (2005) 4 *European Governance Papers (EUROGOV)*.

Union. In addition, in a strictly legal sense, the OMC does not imply that power is conferred on the EU: one of the most widely acclaimed aims of the OMC is precisely to avoid further increases in the legal competencies of the EU. Instead it is seen as a 'pure' political process aimed at achieving results through 'experimentation'. Hence, OMC processes are directly aimed at increasing the versatility of EU policy making by surpassing legal constraints. The OMC therefore implies a break with the bonds between law and politics which have traditionally been celebrated as one of the most fundamental achievements of modernity and which were directly aimed at ensuring a balance between versatility and stability. As the OMC represents an attempt to remove the law's 'irritation' of the policy-making process, it is not surprising that its emergence has been greeted, mainly by the political scientists, as a welcome innovation. Nor is it surprising that legal scholars have been much more reserved.

Despite the unease of lawyers the OMC will not go away. As argued in Chapters 5 and 6 the OMC fulfils a specific 'pre-integrative' function within the realm of the European integration process. Moreover this function is not new. Instead the OMC merely professionalises and formalises the kind of pre-integrative mutual observation between MS which has existed ever since the Community was established.[34] From a functional perspective, the OMC is therefore neither a vehicle of deliberation nor merely an intrusive instrument. Such unhelpful dichotomies can be circumvented by focusing on the usefulness of the OMC, as long as it remains strictly a preliminary tool, applied within policy areas where legal integration, conferring legal competencies to the EU, has not taken place. Policy areas that operate on the basis of relatively unrestrained forms of political rationality because relevant juridical frames have not yet been established.

A constructive approach to the OMC would therefore be to regard it as a necessary first encounter in the integration process within a given policy area. Rather than calling for its abolition a positive first step would therefore be to negatively delineate its areas of deployment through legal means, thus ensuring that 'colonisation' of more mature policy areas is avoided. A constitutional containment of the non-legal character of the OMC would establish firewalls between 'pre-integrationist', and therefore 'pre-legal', and inherently political operations and policy areas where power politics has already been successfully restrained via legal instruments. Such restraints could be achieved if the treaty basis of the EU limited the deployment of OMC processes to policy areas where the Union possesses complementary (or supportive), as opposed to shared or exclusive competencies. This would not only serve as a safeguard against

[34] And in fact ever since a system of European states emerged in the 17th century. See N Elias, *Die höfische Gesellschaft* (Frankfurt am Main, Suhrkamp Verlag, [1969] 2002).

colonising tendencies but would also ensure that the current tendency towards the application of OMC processes in policy areas where the EU does not have any competencies at all is avoided.[35] Such a safeguard would therefore increase the probability that any expansion of the OMC is based on a conscious political decision to grant the EU the possibility of initiating such processes.

A safeguard of this kind would of course merely amount to a negative limitation of the OMC and not to a substantial juridification of the method. But as illustrated in Chapter 5 the kind of power produced within the OMC processes is inherently difficult to curb through the deployment of legal instruments because of its fluid and non-institutionalised nature. The kind of power produced is therefore difficult to frame through constitutional measures because constitutional language remains tied to an 'old-European' institutionalist perspective. As a consequence, moves towards constitutionalisation remain dependent on the existence of formalised institutions. A negative constitutional limitation would, however, limit the damage which the OMC already inflicts on fundamental elements of the European legal order such as the principle of IB. More generally, such a safeguard would ensure that the balance between law and politics and thus the balance between contingency and stability in the EU is maintained.

The concept of the regulatory state contrasts with that of the OMC across virtually all dimensions. As Majone convincingly argues, for structural reasons there are specific societal functions which are not suitable for politisation (for example, central banking, competition policy and some forms of risk regulation). Indeed, independent regulatory institutions with discretionary power are today a common feature of most, if not all, mature democracies. Given that such functions already have been transferred to the EU system, a case can therefore be made for the establishment of truly independent regulatory agencies within narrowly defined policy areas.

As already noted, many agencies have already been established. However, the majority are not concerned with regulatory issues as such but instead with, for example, monitoring and dissemination. Currently there are few indications that any of these agencies will develop into regulatory agencies with fully fledged discretionary competencies in the foreseeable future. As previously argued, a central reason for the failure of Majone's policy proposal is that the Community itself only possesses exclusive competencies in few and very narrowly defined policy areas. Hence, the range of policy areas where delegation of exclusive competencies from the Community to agencies is possible remains very limited. Yet, as the unexpected emergence and evolution of Comitology and OMC illustrates,

[35] Eg and as mentioned earlier, the OMC processes in R&D and the information society operate without a specific legal basis.

the future remains unknown. One possible way of avoiding the emergence of European agencies with full discretionary powers—where this lacks functional justification—is therefore to introduce a constitutional safeguard stressing that a complete transfer of discretionary competencies to regulatory agencies can only occur within policy areas under exclusive Community competence. Any move towards the establishment of full-blown regulatory agencies would therefore be conditioned by the previous consent of all MS as well as the EP to grant the Community exclusive powers in the relevant policy area.

In between the OMC and the concept of the regulatory state, Comitology retains vibrancy. Comitology is strongest in areas of specific and complex regulation, where detailed harmonisation is needed. But even if Comitology is an adequate frame for producing harmonisation, its uncontrolled spread across policy areas since the 1960s embodies integration by stealth. To counter this development, a constitutional safeguard could be introduced limiting the deployment of Comitology structures to policy areas falling under the CM and which are characterised by shared competencies. Such a limitation would moreover reflect the nature of Comitology as a partly MS-dominated and partly Commission-dominated realm.

A division of labour between the OMC, Comitology and agencies along the lines outlined above has the advantage that it is functionally based since it reflects the distinction, identified in Chapter 5, between the specific pre-integrative, integrative and post-integrative functions which are reflected in the three forms of governance.

The move towards a clear division of labour between the three modes of governance could, moreover, be complemented by the adoption of a suggestion tabled several times by the Czech Republic during the two last rounds of treaty negotiations. The Czech Republic suggested that the ability of the European Council, acting under unanimity, to transfer policy areas from the category of supportive competencies to the category of shared or exclusive competencies or shared competencies to the category of exclusive competencies without a treaty amendment should be a two-way street. In the CT as well as the LRT, this mechanism has, however, been developed as a one-way street; while it is possible for the Union to increase its competencies, devolution from the Union to the MS remains blocked. The functional need for integration, however, remains a contingent phenomenon insofar as it reflects the general level of societal interdependence, which in turn is dependent on, for example, economic and technological developments. The need for European meta-norms, as well as the density of such norms, therefore changes over time because the nature of the specific policy areas is constantly changing. This creates functional needs for the adaptation of policies and the institutional structures which policy making relies on through evolution or devolution of competencies. The ongoing evolution of the EU's institutional and legal structures does not, however, reflect the perception that a Union characterised by adaptability rather than uniformity would be a far more viable construction. Instead of pursuing a constitutionalisation of the de facto existing change-constitution (*Wandelverfassung*), the EU remains committed to the continual reinforcement of the integrationist strait-jacket on the basis of the concept of an 'ever closer Union' in spite of the fact that the turn to governance made this objective unviable a long time ago.

As regards the internal organisation, it is important to keep the societal function of GS in mind. GS are structural couplings which serve as the form through which the EU ensures its embeddedness in society. Whereas the EU's governing dimension can be understood in the narrow sense as an (embryonic) state because it consists of a political and a legal system coupled within a constitutional framework, a broad perspective including both the governing and governance dimensions requires an understanding of the EU as a social conglomerate. This is necessary because the governance dimension, in contrast to the governing dimension, horizontally binds together a multiplicity of functional systems and hence a multiplicity of forms of rationality. Different forms of rationality, such as economic, scientific and ecological, are of course also present within the vertical governing dimension but here they remain subordinate to and framed by legal, political and bureaucratic forms of rationality. In contrast, the governance dimension is characterised by horizontal (*nebengeordnete*) forms of coordination of different kinds of rationality. Hence, GS must be understood as regimes characterised by multi-rationality which act as interfaces between different functional systems.[36] This is also expressed in the dissolution of the public/private distinction within the governance dimension. Governance extends beyond public structures to include, for example, the economic system, the scientific system as well as ecological forms of communication. This is because the EU's political and bureaucratic structures are dependent on the kind of knowledge which can be derived from other systems and because the EU itself is faced with a need to stabilise its relations with its environment. But GS are more than merely supportive measures for the governing dimension since they also embody a systematic attempt to directly stabilise relations between the non-legal and non-political spheres of society and to achieve the kind of coordination (*Abstimmung*) between functionally differentiated spheres such as

[36] The focus on multi-rationality means that this concept of regimes differs from the one presented by Fischer-Lescano and Teubner. See A Fischer-Lescano and G Teubner, 'Fragmentierung des Weltrechts: Vernetzung globaler Regimes statt etatistischer Rechtseinheit' in M Albert and R Stichweh (Hrsg.), *Weltstaat und Weltstaatlichkeit. Beobachtungen globaler politischer Strukturbildung* (Wiesbaden, Vs Verlag, 2007).

economy, health and ecology, which is the primary societal contribution (*Leistung*) of politics in a radicalised modernity.

When compared with the period of classical modernity GS can, in other words, be understood as functional equivalents to corporatist structures. Whereas the diminishing phenomenon of corporatism relied on the distinction between employers and employees and hence indirectly on the stratified class structure of the industrial society, the emergence of GS are, on the other hand, a consequence of the move away from stratificatory and territorial forms of differentiation towards the ever-increasing relevance of functional differentiation. With the functional equivalence of corporatism and governance in mind it is not surprising that the demands for a democratisation of European GS resembles the calls for a democratisation of the corporatist system through association democracy (*Verbandsdemokratie*) which emerged during the period of classical modernity.[37] Such an objective was only possible, however, because corporatist organisations are hierarchically ordered entities. They are 'mini-states', which have copied the basic features of the hierarchical model of organisation characterising state bureaucracies.[38] In addition, corporatism only brings together two forms of rationality—the political and the economic—within the framework of economic constitutions. In contrast, GS are characterised by strong horizontal features and far more complex couplings of a whole range of rationalities, thereby making a transfer of the ideals of corporatist democracy to the context of GS unfeasible.

As GS must be understood as highly dynamic autonomous structures, a 'state-centred' perspective only focusing on the governing dimension remains inadequate. Hence, achievement of a classic separation of functions within the governance dimension is not sufficient. Instead of the limited focus on the intersection between legal and political rationalities within the traditional doctrine of a separation of powers, it is necessary to develop a special variant. This would be directly oriented towards the separation of functions within the broader range of horizontal societal settings that are characterised by a multiplicity of forms of rationality. The principle of functional separation could, in other words, be transformed into a constitutional principle which should be applied to regulatory structures as such. Hence, not only the governing dimension but also horizontal intermediate structures operating in between the public and the

[37] For an analysis of the possibilities see G Teubner, *Organisationsdemokratie und Verbandsverfassung: Rechtsmodelle für politisch relevante Verbände. Tübinger Rechtswissenschaftliche Abhandlungen, Band 47* (Tübingen, Mohr Siebeck, 1978).

[38] PF Kjaer, 'Post-Hegelian Networks: Comments on the Chapter by Simon Deakin' in M Amstutz and G Teubner (eds), *Networks: Legal Issues of Multilateral Co-operation* (Oxford, Hart Publishing, 2009).

private spheres should be subject to the constitutional principle of functional separation. Within risk regulation a move in this direction has already been made through the introduction of the distinction between risk assessment, risk evaluation and risk management. However, a far more incisive move towards institutional separation is needed and should reflect the reproduction of different forms of rationality within the functionally differentiated spheres of society. As has been demonstrated, the institutional structure of REACH follows this logic exactly, through the introduction of simultaneous but separate evaluation processes within the committee representing the environmental and health perspectives and the committee for socio-economic analysis. Within REACH, functional separation is, moreover, combined with a central complexity-reducing mechanism that provides a solution to the problem of political overload. This mechanism reduces the problems which are of political relevance to those where real conflicts between functionally different spheres occur and moves the dossiers where convergence has been achieved to the background, thereby allowing the political system to deal only with cases of major importance.

The OMC process on R&D analysed in Chapter 5 serves to illustrate what functional separation can contribute. As noted, the OMC on R&D is characterised by a bias in rationality since the process is framed by economic rather than scientific rationality. It is precisely to avoid such asymmetries that functional separation is needed. Hence, extending the earlier call for a purely negative delimitation of the OMC through law, one might consider whether functional separation allowing for the separate but simultaneous processing of different rationalities can be introduced within the OMC. In the specific example of the OMC within R&D a 'duplication' of the processes could be introduced, as benchmarking and other evaluation exercises could be carried out by two separate structures. Respectively these structures would provide evaluations from a socio-economic and a scientific perspective remaining at the same time linked within a procedural framework which ensures coherency. Ideally this would provide a basis for informed political decision making as it would allow the political system to make decisions reflecting economic as well as scientific perspectives, thereby enabling it to fulfil the function of ensuring a balance between rationalities. From this perspective, the merger of the three council configurations for internal market, industry and research into a single competitiveness configuration which was undertaken to facilitate the OMC process in R&D was a move in the wrong direction. Indeed, the merger that took place clearly illustrates the de-differentiation consequences of the OMC in its present form and the dangers that lie in deformalised forms of governance as well as the value of a formal legal framing of such processes.

8.8 THE GOVERNING OF GOVERNANCE

So far we have dealt with the three forms of governance as somewhat separate entities. But as pointed out by Sabel and Zeitlin,[39] areas such as electricity regulation, drug authorisation and occupational health and safety have all been reformed in recent years through the introduction of models combining traditional legal instruments, such as directives, with network models relying on agencies, Comitology and OMC-inspired methods. Hence, the movement towards an integrated model binding the three forms of governance together, which also was observed in the case of REACH, seems to be a general trend within mature policy areas. In other words in many policy areas we are not seeing a move towards a step-by-step build-up whereby policy processes start out as OMC processes, then turn into Comitology processes, which finally lead to the establishment of full-blown regulatory agencies within completely harmonised policy areas. Rather the unexpected evolutionary turn of the EU away from the 'ever-closer Union' and towards governance means that mature policy areas tend to mutate into hybrids which rely on all three forms of GS. What we are seeing is a move towards the emergence of three-tier governance complexes, consisting of administrative (as opposed to truly regulatory) agencies, occupied with information gathering and network coordination, combined with information-evaluating committees and OMC-style benchmarking forums, which provide a basis for decision making within the political-administrative realm of Comitology. Although the structures differ markedly from policy area to policy area, Comitology remains, in other words, a central forum of contestation within most mature policy areas; it is here that clashes of rationality are addressed through decisions possessing a distinctly political character. In many cases contestations can be transferred to the Governing dimension through the intervention of the Council and (after the 2006 reform) the EP.

The movement towards a hybridisation of governance indicates the ability of the governing dimension to provide an overall framing of the GS. Such a framing should not be seen simply as the substitution of GS with hierarchical governing mechanisms. Rather the ongoing process contains the possibility of moving towards increased reliance on framework laws which retain legal ground in the form of legislative procedures and access to juridical review at the same time as safeguarding the flexibility of the GS. The move towards more flexible framework legislation is therefore likely to reduce the trade-offs between centralisation and decentralisation and between harmonisation and flexibility.

[39] CF Sabel and J Zeitlin, 'Learning from Difference: The New Architecture of Experimentalist Governance in the European Union' (2006) 18 *La Follette School Working Papers*.

The Commission has, moreover, presented a draft Inter-institutional Agreement on an operating framework for the European agencies.[40] The proposal, which has received strong support from the EP but so far failed to overcome MS opposition, is aimed at adopting a horizontal approach to future European agencies. It seeks to ensure coherency through the establishment of minimum core principles concerning the creation, operation and control of agencies. The proposal draws upon the entire list of governance concepts such as effectiveness, accountability and participation. It provides a formal definition of agencies,[41] determines their legal basis, the procedure for deciding their physical location, their tasks and organisational structure as well as the control mechanisms which should be in place. Compared to the current situation, adoption of the agreement would represent a considerable step forward. When seen in conjunction with the 2006 Comitology decision analysed in Chapter 3, which increased the EP's influence for example, considerable steps towards a constitutionalisation of GS can therefore be observed. However, as already pointed out, the move towards a fusion of the three forms of governance makes such partial approaches insufficient. What is needed instead is a basic law of governance which merges the Comitology decision, the draft agreement on agencies and a framework for the OMC processes, into a single coherent legal framework which has the principle of functional separation as its core principle. Such a basic law would establish a procedural framework aimed at achieving convergence between different forms of rationality and ensuring that cases involving divergent perspectives and possessing a principal character are transferred into the political realm in order to make such cases the subject of political contestation and decision making.

[40] Commission of the European Communities: Draft Interinstitutional Agreement on the operating framework for the European regulatory agencies. COM/2005/0059 Final.

[41] The definition is as follows: 'A European regulatory agency may therefore be defined as an independent legal entity created by the legislator in order to help regulate a particular sector at European level and help implement a particular Community policy. By performing its tasks, it helps to improve the way in which the rules are implemented and applied throughout the EU. It thus plays an active role in exercising executive powers at Community level'. See COM/2005/0059 Final, 3.

9

Conclusion

THE POINT OF departure was the observation that the intergovernmental/supranational distinction no longer provides an adequate basis for understanding the central characteristics of the European integration process and the EU. As an alternative it was suggested that the EU must be understood as a hybrid consisting, on the one hand, of governing structures characterised by legal and organisational hierarchy—Commission, Council and the EP—and, on the other hand, governance structures (GS) characterised by legal and organisational heterarchy. Hence, it is argued that an adequate paradigm of EU research must be based on a distinction between governing and governance. This distinction was also considered a suitable starting point from which an analysis of the *structural* conditions necessary to achieve safeguards for democracy and the rule of law in the EU context must depart.

Against this background the emergence and function of three forms of GS—OMC, Comitology and agencies—within the context of the European integration process were reconstructed, with the objective of assessing how the relationship between governing and governance structures can be conceptualised. It was argued that the emergence of the EU represents a move away from the territorial forms of differentiation characterising the nation states and towards an increased reliance on functional differentiation. It was argued that an intrinsic link exists between this move and the hybrid structure of the EU.

On this basis the concrete logic guiding the emergence of GS was reconstructed. It was suggested that internally the EU is an 'under-differentiated' phenomenon in that it is based on 'power sharing' rather than on a functional differentiation between branches of power. The consequence is 'decisional overload' in the sense that the EU suffers from a discrepancy between decision-making capacities and the ability to make and implement decisions, thereby creating a need for 'decisional outsourcing' to GS.

The network form plays a central role within GS. Accordingly, a contextualised concept of networks suitable for describing developments in the European context has been developed. It was argued that networks serve as structural couplings between organisations. These structural couplings have emerged in order to allow the EU institutions as well as MS administrations and private actors to compensate for their own structural deficiencies by relying on meaning (*Sinn*) components produced within other organisations. Within mature policy areas a move towards the emergence of hybrids combining a whole range of hierarchical and heterarchical elements are, moreover, observed. Hybrids of this kind reflect the generally hybrid nature of the EU.

This was followed by an ideal type analysis of the forms of power which the three modes of governance produce. The analysis found that the advocates of the three forms refer to power as a way of producing control (agencies), consensus (Comitology) and 'conduct of conduct' (OMC). These three forms are seen as reflecting the function which the three forms of governance fulfils within the larger context of the integration process since respectively they are oriented towards producing steering, harmonisation and convergence. Each of the three forms of governance is particularly prevalent within different cycles of policy development, thereby allowing for the introduction of an analytical distinction between 'pre-integrative', 'integrative' and 'post-integrative' phases of policy making.

The theoretical reflections were followed by a case study exploring the operational mode of the OMC within the policy area of R&D. It was found that the function of the OMC within this area is 'entrepreneurial discourse construction', since the OMC process is oriented towards the creation of a 'common basis' thereby increasing the probability of success for later integrative initiatives. The asymmetric relation between economic and scientific rationality within the OMC in R&D was, moreover, identified as the central problem of the process.

In an additional case study analysing the regulatory structure for the European chemicals market (REACH) it was argued that the REACH model of market regulation points in the direction of the establishment of an 'integrated model' of governance, combining elements of the three forms of governance structures in a coherent manner. It was also argued that the REACH model might be conceived of as a possible role model for the EU's governance dimension because it not only reflects the hybrid character of the union but also the increased societal reliance on functional differentiation relative to territorial and stratificatory forms of differentiation. This is especially the case since the REACH model is directly oriented towards securing a symmetric stabilisation of different forms of rationality through convergence.

Finally, a conflict of laws perspective was introduced with the aim of outlining a constitutional framework for a Union which is partly characterised by governing and partly by governance. It is stressed that existing conflict of laws approaches either remain tied to a traditionalist view where conflicts essentially are reduced to those between territorial entities (states), or instead reflect a radical post-modern view which is only suitable for a limited number of extremely globalised and functionally differentiated structures. Alternatively, a middle position is developed which is suitable for the EU. Hence, a coherent three-dimensional conflict of laws model, which integrates the handling of horizontal conflicts between states, vertical conflicts between the EU and the MS, as well as horizontal conflicts between functionally differentiated spheres of society, was developed. The latter dimension is, moreover, considered as an element which can partially act as a functional equivalent to democracy. Democracy remains a limited concept insofar as viable democratic structures are conditioned by legal and organisational hierarchy. Hence, the EU can only become a partial democracy, as only the governing dimension can be subject to democratisation. Consequently, functional equivalents to democracy must be developed in relation to the governance dimension, through the activation of legal instruments.

Bibliography

Books

ARMSTRONG, KA and BULMER, SJ, *The Governance of the Single European Market* (Manchester, Manchester University Press, 1998).

BACH, M, *Die Bürokratisierung Europas. Verwaltungseliten, Experten und politische Legitimation in Europa* (Frankfurt am Main, Campus Verlag, 1999).

BAIER, H, *Soziologie als Aufklärung, oder die Vertreibung der Transzendenz aus der Gesellschaft* (Konstanz, UVK Universitätsverlag Konstanz, 1998).

BARNETT, S (ed), *Hegel After Derrida* (London, Routledge, 1998).

BARTELSON, J, *The Critique of the State* (Cambridge, Cambridge University Press, 2001).

BAUDRILLARD, J, *America* (London, Sage Publications, 2000).

BECK, U, *Risikogesellschaft. Auf dem Weg in eine andere Moderne* (Frankfurt am Main, Suhrkamp Verlag, 1986).

——, *Die Feindlose Demokratie* (Stuttgart, Reclam, 1995).

CASTELLS, M, *The Information Age: Economy, Society and Culture. Volume 1. The Rise of the Network Society* (Blackwell, Oxford, 1999).

CHRISTIANSEN, T and PIATTONI S (eds), *Informal Governance in the European Union* (Cheltenham, Edward Elgar, 2004).

CLAM J, *Droit et société chez Niklas Luhmann* (Paris, Presses Universitaires de France, 1997).

DEHOUSSE, R, *The European Court of Justice* (London, Macmillan Press, 1998).

DURKHEIM, E, *De la division du travail social* (Paris, Presses universitaires de France, [1893] 1973).

ELIAS, N, *Über den Prozeß der Zivilisation, Band 2* (Frankfurt am Main, Suhrkamp Verlag, [1938] 1976).

——, *Die höfische Gesellschaft* (Frankfurt am Main, Suhrkamp Verlag, [1969] 2002).

GEHRING, T, *Die Europäische Union als komplexe internationale Organisation: wie durch Kommunikation und Entscheidung soziale Ordnung entsteht* (Baden-Baden, Nomos Verlag, 2002).

GRABHER, G (ed), *The Embedded Firm* (London, Routledge, 1993).

GWYN, WB, *The Meaning of the Separation of Powers* (The Hague, Martinus Nijhoff, 1965).

HAAS, EB, *The Uniting of Europe: Political, Social and Economic Forces 1950–1957* (Palo Alto, Stanford University Press, 1958).

HABERMAS, J, *Theorie des kommunikativen Handelns, Band 1: Handlungsrationalität und gesellschaftliche Rationalisierung* (Frankfurt am Main, Suhrkamp Verlag, 1981).

——, *Theorie des kommunikativen Handelns, Band 2: Zur Kritik der funktionalistischen Vernunft* (Frankfurt am Main, Suhrkamp Verlag, 1981).

——, *Der philosophische Diskurs der Moderne: Zwölf Vorlesungen* (Frankfurt am Main, Suhrkamp Verlag, 1985).
——, *Die Moderne, ein unvollendetes Projekt. Philosophisch-politische Aufsätze 1977–1990* (Leipzig, Reclam, 1990).
——, *Faktizität und Geltung. Beiträge zur Diskurstheorie des Rechts und des demokratischen Rechtsstaats* (Frankfurt am Main, Suhrkamp Verlag, 1992).
HARSTE, G, *Modernitet og Organisation* (København, Forlaget politisk Revy, 1997).
HEGEL, GWF, *Grundlinien der Philosophie des Rechts. Oder Naturrecht und Staatswissenschaft im Grundrisse* (Frankfurt am Main, Suhrkamp Verlag, [1821] 1976).
HIX, S, *The Political System of the European Union* (Basingstoke, Macmillan, 1999).
JACHTENFUCHS, M and KNODT, M (Hrsg.), *Regieren in internationalen Institutionen* (Opladen, Leske + Budrich, 2002).
JARASS, HD, *Politik und Bürokratie als Elemente der Gewaltenteilung* (München, CH Beck'sche Verlagsbuchhandlung, 1975).
KANTOROWICZ, E, *The King's Two Bodies. A Study in Mediaeval Political Theology* (Princeton, Princeton University Press, [1957] 1997).
KARSTEN, A and THIESEN, H VON (Hrsg.), *Nützliche Netzwerke und korrupte Seilschaften* (Göttingen, Vandenhoeck & Ruprect, 2006).
KNIGHT, MM, *Economic History of Europe. To the End of the Middle Ages* (London, George Allen & Unwin, 1928).
KUHN, TS, *The Structure of Scientific Revolutions* (Chicago, Chicago University Press, [1962] 1996).
LADEUR, K-H, *Postmoderne Rechtstheorie – Selbstreferenz – Selbstorganisation – Prozeduralisierung* (Berlin, Duncker & Humblot, 1995).
——, *Negative Freiheitsrechte und gesellschaftliche Selbstorganisation. Zur Erzeugung von Sozialkapital durch gesellschaftliche Institutionen* (Tübingen, Mohr Siebeck, 2000).
LANDFRIED, C, *Das politische Europa. Differenz als Potential der Europäischen Union*, 2 überarbeitete und erweiterte Auflage (Baden-Baden, Nomos Verlag, 2005).
LATOUCHE, R, *Les origines de l'eéconomie occidentale, IVe–XIe sieècle* (Paris, A Michel, 1956).
LINDBERG, LN, *The Political Dynamics of European Economic Integration* (Palo Alto, Stanford University Press, 1963).
LOCKE, J, *Two Treatises of Government* (Cambridge, Cambridge University Press, [1690] 1967).
LUHMANN, N, *Zweckbegriff und Systemrationalität. Über die Funktion von Zwecken in Sozialen Systemen* (Frankfurt am Main, Suhrkamp Verlag, 1968).
——, *Legitimation durch Verfahren* (Berlin, Neuwied, 1969).
——, *Rechtssoziologie, Band 2* (Berlin, Rowohlt Taschenbuch, 1972).
——, *Ausdifferenzierung des Rechts. Beiträge zur Rechtssoziologie und Rechtstheorie* (Frankfurt am Main, Suhrkamp Verlag, 1981).
——, *Rechtssoziologie* (Opladen, Westdeutscher Verlag, [1972] 1983).
——, *Soziale Systeme. Grundriß einer allgemeinen Theorie* (Frankfurt am Main, Suhrkamp Verlag, 1984).

——, *Ökologische Kommunikation: Kann die moderne Gesellschaft sich auf ökologische Gefährdungen einstellen?* (Opladen, Westdeutscher Verlag, 1986).
——, *Die Wirtschaft der Gesellschaft* (Frankfurt am Main, Suhrkamp Verlag, 1988).
——, *Soziologie des Risikos* (Berlin, de Gruyter, 1991).
——, *Das Recht der Gesellschaft* (Frankfurt am Main, Suhrkamp Verlag, 1993).
——, *Die Gesellschaft der Gesellschaft* (Frankfurt am Main, Suhrkamp Verlag, 1997).
——, *Die Politik der Gesellschaft* (Frankfurt am Main, Suhrkamp Verlag, 2000).
LUKES, S, *Power: A Radical View* (Hampshire, Palgrave, 1974).
LYOTARD, JF, *La condition postmoderne: rapport sur le savoir* (Paris, Minuit, 1979).
MAJONE, G, *Regulating Europe* (London, Routledge, 1996).
——, *Dilemmas of European integration: the ambiguities and pitfalls of integration by stealth* (Oxford, Oxford University Press, 2005).
MAUS, I, *Zur Aufklärung der Demokratietheorie. Rechts- und demokratietheoretische Überlegungen im Anschluß an Kant* (Frankfurt am Main, Suhrkamp Verlag, 1994).
MILWARD, AS, *The European Rescue of the Nation-State* (Oxford, Routledge, 2000).
MONTESQUIEU, CL DE SECONDAT, *De l'Esprit des lois* (Paris, Gallimard, [1748] 1995).
MORAWCSIK, A, *The Choice for Europe. Social Purpose and State Power from Messina to Maastricht* (Ithaca, Cornell University Press, 1998).
PALAYRET, JM, WALLACE, H and WINAND, P (eds), *Visions, Votes and Vetoes: Reassessing the Luxembourg Compromise 40 Years On* (Brussels, Peter Lang, 2006).
PARSONS, T, *The System of Modern Societies* (Englewood Cliffs, Prentice-Hall, 1971).
PIORE, MJ and SABEL, C, *The Second Industrial Divide: Possibilities for Prosperity* (New York, Basic Books, 1984).
POCOCK, JGA, *The Ancient Constitution and the Feudal Law: A Study of English Historical Thought in the Seventeenth Century* (Cambridge, Cambridge University Press, [1957] 1987).
POLANYI, K, *The Great Transformation: The Political and Economic Origins of Our Time* (Boston, Beacon Press, [1944] 2001).
RASMUSSEN, H, *On law and policy in the European Court of Justice: A comparative study in judicial policymaking* (Dordrecht, Kluwer, 1986).
——, *Towards a Normative Theory of Interpretation of Community Law* (Copenhagen, Political Studies Press, 1993).
RIEKMANN, SP, *Die kommissarische Neuordnung Europas. Das Dispositiv der Integration* (Wien, Springer Verlag, 1998).
RIKLIN, A, *Machtteilung – Geschichte der Mischverfassung* (Darmstadt, Wissenschaftliche Buchgesellschaft, 2005).
RODRIGUES, MJ, *European Policies for a Knowledge Economy* (Cheltenham, Edward Elgar, 2003).
ROSA, H, *Bechleunigung. Die Veränderung der Zeitstrukturen in der Moderne* (Frankfurt am Main, Suhrkamp Verlag, 2005).

ROSTOCK, M, *Die Lehre von der Gewaltenteilung in der politischen Theorie von John Locke* (Meisenheim, Anton Hain, 1974).

SCHELSKY, H, *Die Soziologen und das Recht. Abhandlungen und Vorträge zur Soziologie von Recht, Institution und Planung* (Opladen, Westdeutscher Verlag, 1980).

SCHEPEL, H, *The Constitution of Private Governance: Product Standards in the regulation of integrating markets* (Oxford, Hart Publishing, 2004).

SCHEUERMAN, W. E.: *Liberal Democracy and the Social Acceleration of Time* (Baltimore, Johns Hopkins University Press, 2004).

SCHMITT, C, *Der Nomos der Erde. Im Völkerrecht des Jus Publicum Europaeum*, (Berlin, Duncker & Humblot, 1950).

SCHUPPERT, GF, PERNICE, I and HALTERN, U (Hrsg.), *Europawissenschaft* (Baden-Baden, Nomos, 2005).

SCIULLI, D, *Theory of Societal Constitutionalism: Foundations of a Non-Marxist Critical Theory* (New York, Cambridge University Press, 1992).

SMISMANS, S, *Law, Legitimacy and European Governance. Functional Participation in Social Regulation* (Oxford, Oxford University Press, 2004).

STÄHELI, U, *Poststrukturalistische Soziologien* (Bielefeld, Transcript Verlag, 2003).

STICHWEH, R, *Die Weltgesellschaft. Soziologische Analysen* (Frankfurt am Main, Suhrkamp Verlag, 2000).

——, *Inklusion und Exklusion. Studien zur Gesellschaftstheorie* (Bielefeld, Transcript Verlag, 2005).

TEUBNER, G, *Organisationsdemokratie und Verbandsverfassung: Rechtsmodelle für politisch relevante Verbände. Tübinger Rechtswissenschaftliche Abhandlungen, Band 47* (Tübingen, Mohr Siebeck, 1978).

—— (ed), *Global Law without a State* (Aldershot, Dartmouth, 1997).

——, *Netzwerk als Vertragsverbund. Virtuelle Unternehmen, Franchising, Just-in-time in Sozialwissenschaftlicher und juristischer Sicht* (Baden-Baden, Nomos Verlag, 2004).

TÖLLER, AE, KOMITOLOGIE. *Theoretische Bedeutung und praktische Funktionsweise von Durchführungsausschüssen der Europäischen Union am Beispiel der Umweltpolitik* (Opladen, Leske + Budrich, 2002).

VERHOFSTADT, G, *Les Etats-unis d'Europe* (Bruxelles, Luc Pire, 2006).

VILE, MJC, *Constitutionalism and the Separation of Powers* (Oxford, Clarendon Press, 1967).

VIRILIO, P, *Vitesse et Politique: essai de dromologie* (Paris, éd. Galilée, 1977).

WEBER, M, *Wirtschaftsgeschichte* (Leipzig, Duncker & Humblot, 1923).

WEBER, M, *Wirtschaft und Gesellschaft, 2 vols* (Tübingen, JCB Mohr, 1925).

WEILER, JHH, *The Constitution of Europe. 'Do the New Clothes Have an Emperor?' and Other Essays on European Integration* (Cambridge, Cambridge University Press, 1999).

WILKE, H, *Global Governance* (Bielefeld, Transcript Verlag, 2006).

ZEITLIN, J and POCHET, P (eds), *The Open Method of Co-ordination in Action: the European employment and social inclusion strategies* (Bruxelles, Presses Interuniversitaires Européennes, 2005).

Academic literature Articles

ABROMEIT, H, 'Jenseits des "*sui generis*"' in C Landfried (Hrsg.), *Politik in einer entgrenzten Welt. Beiträge zum 21. Kongreß der Deutschen Vereinigung für Politische Wissenschaft* (Köln, Verlag Wissenschaft und Politik, 2001) 91–96.

ALBERT, M, 'Governance and democracy in European systems: on systems theory and European integration' (2002) 28 *Review of International Studies* 293–309.

AMSTUTZ, M, 'In Between Worlds: Marleasing and the Emergence of Interlegality in Legal Reasoning' (2006) 12 (6) *European Law Journal* 766–84,.

—— and Karavas, V, 'Rechtsmutation: Zu Genese und Evolution des Rechts im transnationalen Raum' (2006) 8 *Rechtsgeschichte*, 14–32.

ANDERSEN, TM and HERBERTSSON, TT, 'Measuring Globalization', 2003 *IZA Discussion Papers* 817.

ANDRÉ, M, 'L'espace européen de la recherche: histoire d'une idée' (2006) 12 (2) *Revue d'Histoire de l'Integration Européenne* 131–50.

BACH, M, 'Transnationale Integration und institutionelle Differenzierung' (1993) 14 (2) *Zeitschrift für Rechtssoziologie* 223–42.

BAECKER, D, 'Why Systems?' (2001) 18 (1) *Theory, Culture & Society* 59–74.

BANCHOFF, T, 'Institutions, Inertia and European Union Research Policy' (2002) 40 (1) *Journal of Common Market Studies* 1–21.

——, 'The Politics of the European Research Area' 2002 *ACES Working Paper* 3.

BENZ, A, 'Einleitung: Governance – Modebegriff oder nützliches sozialwissenschaftliches Konzept?' in Benz, A (Hrsg.), *Governance – Regieren in Komplexen Regelsystemen. Eine Einführung* (Wiesbaden, VS Verlag für Sozialwissenschaften, 2004) 11–28.

BORCH, C, 'Systemic Power. Luhmann, Foucault and Analytics of Power' (2005) 48 (2) *Acta Sociologica* 155–67.

BORRÁS, S and GREVE, B, 'Concluding Remarks: New Method or Just Cheap Talk?' (2004) 11 (2) *Journal of European Public Policy* 329–36.

—— and Jacobsson, K, 'The open method of co-ordination and new governance patterns in the EU' (2004) 11 (2) *Journal of European Public Policy* 185–208.

BOURDIEU, P, 'Rethinking the State: Genesis and Structure of the Bureaucratic Field' (1994) 12 (1) *Sociological Theory* 1–18.

BOUSSUAT, G, 'Les coopérations européennes pour la researche scientifique et technique' (2006) 12 (2) *Revue d'Histoire de l'Integration Européenne* 5–10.

BOUWEN, P, 'A Theoretical and Empirical Study of Corporate Lobbying in the European Parliament' (2003) 7 (11) *European Integration online Papers* (EIoP).

BRODOCZ, A, 'Strukturelle Kopplung durch Verbände' (1996) 2 *Soziale Systeme. Zeitschrift für Systemtheorie* 361–87.

BÜCKER, A and SCHLACKE, S, 'Die Entstehung einer politischen Verwaltung durch EG-Ausschüsse – Rechtstatsachen und Rechtsentwicklungen' in Falke, J and Joerges, C (Hrsg.), *Das Ausschußwesen der Europäischen Union. Die Praxis der Risikoregulierung im Binnenmarkt und ihre rechtliche Verfassung* (Baden-Baden, Nomos Verlag, 2000) 161–256.

CAPORASO, JA, 'The European Union and Forms of State: Westphalian, Regulatory or Post-Modern' (1996) 1 (34) *Journal of Common Market Studies* 29–52.

CHALMERS, D, 'Accounting for Europe' (1999) 19 *Oxford Journal of Legal Studies* 517–39.

——, 'Deliberative Supranationalism and the Reterritorialization of Authority' in C Joerges, 'Rethinking European Law's Supremacy' 2005 *EUI Working Paper Law* 12, 29–44.

—— and Lodge, M, 'The Open Method of Co-ordination and the European Welfare State' 2003 *ESRC Discussion Paper* 11.

COHEN, J and SABEL, C, 'Directly-Deliberative Polyarchy' (1997) 3 (4) *European Law Journal* 313–42.

—— and ——, 'Sovereignty and Solidarity: EU and US' in Zeitlin, J and Trubek, DM, *Governing Work and Welfare in a New Economy. European and American Experiments* (Oxford, Oxford University Press, 2003) 345–75.

COOMBES, D, *Politics and Bureaucracy in the European Community. A Portrait of the Commission of the EEC* (London, George Allen and Unwin, 1970).

CRAIG, P, 'The Nature of the Community: Integration, Democracy and Legitimacy' in Craig, P and de Burca, G, *The Evolution of EU Law* (Oxford, Oxford University Press, 1999) 1–54.

DAHL, R, 'The Concept of Power' in Scott, J (ed), *Power. Critical Concepts* (London, Routledge, 1994), 288–309.

DEAKIN, S, 'The return of the guild? Network relations in historical perspective' in Teubner, G and Amstutz, M (eds), *Networks: Legal Issues of Multilateral Co-operation* (Oxford, Hart Publishing, 2009) 53–73.

DE ELERA, A, 'The European Research Area: On the Way Towards a European Scientific Community?' (2006) 12 (5) *European Law Journal* 559–74.

DEHOUSSE, R, 'Misfits: EU Law and the Transformation of European Governance' (2002) *Jean Monnet Working Paper* 2.

——, 'Misfits: EU Law and the Transformation of European Governance' in Joerges, C and Dehousse, R (eds), *Good Governance in Europe's Integrated Market* (Oxford, Oxford University Press, 2002) 216–24.

DE LA PORTE, C, 'Is the Open Method of Co-ordination Appropriate for Organising Activities at the European Level in Sensitive Policy Areas?' (2002) 8 (1) *European Law Journal* 38–58.

DEMMKE, C, Eberharter, E, Schaefer, GF and Türk, A, 'The History of Comitology', in Pedler, RH and Schaefer, GF (eds), *Shaping European Law and Policy. The Role of Committees and Comitology in the Political Process* (Maastricht, European Institute of Public Administration, 1996) 61–82.

DE WITTE, B, 'Direct Effect, Supremacy, and the Nature of the Legal Order' in Craig, P and de Burca, G (eds), *The Evolution of EU Law* (Oxford, Oxford University Press, 1999) 177–213.

EBERLEIN, B, 'Formal and Informal Governance in Single Market Regulation' in Christiansen, T and Piattoni, S (eds), *Informal Governance in the EU*, (Cheltenham, Edward Elgar, 2004) 150–72.

ERIKSEN, EO and FOSSUM, JE, 'Europe at a Crossroads: Government or Transnational Governance?' in Joerges, C, Sand, I-J and Teubner, G (eds), *Transnational Governance and Constitutionalism* (Oxford, Hart Publishing, 2004) 115–46.

—— and ——, 'Europe in Transformation. How to Reconstitute Democracy?' 2007 *RECON Online Working Paper* 1.

FALKE, J, 'Komitologie – Entwicklung, Rechtsgrundlagen und erste empirische Annährung' in Joerges, C and Falke, J (Hrsg.), *Das Ausschußwesen der Europäischen Union. Praxis der Risikoregulierung im Binnenmarkt und ihre rechtliche Verfassung* (Baden-Baden, Nomos Verlag, 2000) 43–159.

FENSKE, H, 'Gewaltenteilung' in Brunner, O, Conze, W, Koselleck, R (Hrsg.), *Geschichtliche Grundbegriffe. Historisches Lexikon zur politisch-sozialen Sprache in Deutschland*, Band 2 (Stuttgart, Klett-Cotta Verlag, 1975) 923–58.

FISCHER, J, *Vom Staatenverbund zur Föderation – Gedanken über die Finalität der europäischen Integration*, speech at the *Humboldt-Universität zu Berlin*, 12 May 2000.

FISCHER-LESCANO, A, 'Themis Sapiens. Comments on Inger-Johanne Sand' in Joerges, C, Sand, I-J and Teubner, G (eds), *Transnational Governance and Constitutionalism* (Oxford, Hart Publishing, 2004) 67–80.

—— and Teubner, G, 'Regime-Collisions: The Vain Search for Legal Unity in the Fragmentation of Global Law' (2004) 25 (4) *Michigan Journal of International Law* 999–1046.

—— and ——, 'Fragmentierung des Weltrechts: Vernetzung globaler Regimes statt etatistischer Rechtseinheit' in Albert, M and Stichweh, R (Hrsg.), *Weltstaat und Weltstaatlichkeit. Beobachtungen globaler politischer Strukturbildung* (Wiesbaden, Vs Verlag, 2007) 37–61.

FOLLESDAL, A and HIX, S, 'Why there is a Democratic Deficit in the EU: A Response to Majone and Moravcsik' (2005) 44 (3) *Journal of Common Market Studies* 533– 62.

FOUCAULT, M, 'The Subject and Power' in Dreyfus, HL and Rabinow, P (eds), *Michel Foucault: Beyond Structuralism and Hermeneutics* (Chicago, University of Chicago Press, 1982) 208–26.

GÖHLER, G, 'Constitution and Use of Power' in Goverde, H, Cerny, PG, Haugaard, M and Lentner H (eds), *Power in Contemporary Politics. Theories, Practices, Globalizations* (London, Sage Publications, 2000) 41–58.

GOLUB, J, 'In the Shadow of the Vote? Decision-making Efficiency in the European Community 1974–1995' 1997 *MPIfG Working Papers* 3.

GORNITZKA, Å, 'Coordinating policies for a "Europe of Knowledge". Emerging practices of the "Open Method of Coordination" in education and research' 2005 *Arena Working Paper* 16, Oslo.

HABERMAS, J, 'Hannah Arendt's Communications Concept of Power' (1977) 44 (1) *Social Research* 3–24.

——, 'Further Reflections on the Public Sphere' in Calhoun, C (ed), *Habermas and the Public Sphere* (Cambridge, MIT Press, 1992).

——, 'Die postnationale Konstellation und die Zukunft der Demokratie' in Habermas, J, *Die postnationale Konstellation. Politische Essays* (Frankfurt am Main, Suhrkamp Verlag, 1998) 91–169.

——, 'Aus Katastrophen Lernen? Ein Zeitdiagnostischer Rückblick auf das kurze 20. Jahrhundert' in *Die postnationale Konstellation. Politische Essays* (Frankfurt am Main, Suhrkamp Verlag, 1998) 65–90.

——, 'Euroskepsis, Matkteuropa oder Europa der (Welt-)Bürger' in Preuß, UK and Maak, T (Hrsg.), *Die Wirtschaft in der Gesellschaft* (Bern, Paul Haupt Verlag, 2000) 151–72.

——, 'Why Europe Needs A Constitution' (2001) 11 *New Left Review* 5–26.

HAIBACH, G, 'Comitology after Amsterdam: A Comparative Analysis of the Delegation of Legislative Powers' (1997) 3 *EIPASCOPE* 1–7.

——, 'Separation and Delegation of Legislative Powers: A Comparative Analysis' in Andenas, M, and Türk, A, (eds), *Delegated Legislation and the Role of Committees in the EC* (The Hague, Kluwer, 2000) 53–66.

——, 'The History of Comitology' in Andenas, M and Türk, A (eds), *Delegated Legislation and the Role of Committees in the EC* (The Hague, Kluwer, 2000) 185–215.

HALTERN, U, 'Internationales Verfassungsrecht? Anmerkungen zu einer kopernikanischen Wende' (2003) 128 *Archiv des öffentlichen Rechts* 511–57.

HEGEL, GWF, 'Die Verfassung Deutschlands' in Hegel, GWF, *Gesammelte Werke, Band 1* (Frankfurt am Main, Suhrkamp Verlag, [1800–02] 1971) 451–610.

HEIDER, F, 'Ding und Medium' (1926) I *Symposium* 109–57.

HÉRITIER, A, 'New Modes of Governance in Europe: Policy-Making without Legislating?' in Héritier, A (ed), *Common Goods: Reinventing European and International Governance* (Lanham, Rowman and Littlefield, 2002) 185–206.

HEY, C, Jacob, K and Volkery, A, 'Better regulation by new governance hybrids? Governance models and the reform of European chemicals policy' 2006 *FFU-report* 2, Environmental Policy Research Centre, Free University Berlin.

HEYVAERT, A, 'Guidance Without Constraint: Assessing the Impact of the Precautionary Principle on the European Community's Chemicals Policy', *The Yearbook of European Environmental Law* 6 (Oxford, Oxford University Press, 2006) 27–60.

HINTZE, O, 'Der Commissarius und seine Bedeutung in der allgemeinen Verwaltungsgeschichte. Eine vergleichende Studie' in Hintze, O, *Beamtentum und Bürokratie* (Göttingen, Vandenhoeck and Ruprecht, [1910] 1981) 78–112.

HOFMANN, HCH and TÜRK, A, 'The Development of Integrated Administration in the EU and its Consequences' (2007) 13 (2) *European Law Journal* 253–71.

HUTTER, M and TEUBNER, G, 'The Parasitic Role of Hybrids' (1993) 149 (4) *Journal of Institutional and Theoretical Economics* 706–15.

JACOBSSON, K, 'Soft Regulation and the Subtle Transformation of States: The Case of EU Employment Policy' (2004) 14 (4) *Journal of European Public Policy* 355–70.

JOERGES, C, 'The Market without the State? The "Economic Constitution" of the European Community and the Rebirth of Regulatory Politics' (1997) 1 (19) *European Integration online Papers (EIoP).*

——, 'States Without a Market? Comments on the German Constitutional Court's Maastricht Judgment and a Plea for Interdisciplinary Discourses' (1997) 1 (20) *European Integration online Papers (EIoP).*

——, 'Die Europäische "Komitologie": Kafkaeske Bürokratie oder Beispiel "deliberativen Regierens"' in Joerges, C and Falke, J (Hrsg.), *Das Ausschußwesen der Europäischen Union. Praxis der Risikoregulierung im Binnenmarkt und ihre rechtliche Verfassung* (Baden-Baden, Nomos Verlag, 2000) 17–42.

——, Constitutionalism in Postnational Constellations: Contrasting Social Regulation in the EU and in the WTO in Joerges, C and Petersmann, EU (eds), *Constitutionalism, Multilevel Trade Governance and Social Regulation* (Oxford, Hart Publishing, 2006) 491–527.

——, 'Das Recht im Prozeβ des Konstitutionalisierung Europas' 2001 *EUI Working Papers* 6.

——, 'Deliberative Supranationalism – Two Defences' (2002) 8 (1) *European Law Journal*, 133–51.

——, 'Integration through de-legalisation? An irritated heckler' 2003 *European Governance Papers* (EUROGOV) 7.

——, 'Rethinking European Law's Supremacy: A Plea for a Supranantional Conflict of Laws' 2005 *EUI Working Papers (Law)* 12.

——, 'Integration durch Entrechtlichung? Ein Zwischenruf' 2007 *ZERP-Diskussionspapier* 1.

—— and Neyer, J, 'From Intergovernmental Bargaining to Deliberative Political Processes: The Constitutionalisation of Comitology' (1997) 3 (3) *European Law Journal* 273–99.

—— and Neyer, J, 'Transforming Strategic interaction into deliberative problem-solving: European comitology in the foodstuffs sector' (1997) 4 (4) *Journal of European Public Policy* 609–25.

—— and Zürn, M (eds), *Law and Governance in Postnational Europe. Compliance Beyond the Nation-State* (Cambridge, Cambridge University Press, 2005).

KAISER, R and PRANGE, H, 'A New Concept of Deepening European Integration? The European Research Area and the Emerging Role of Policy Coordination in a Multi-level Governance System' (2005) 3 (3) *Comparative European Politics* 289–306.

KÄMPER, AE and SCHMIDT, JFK, 'Netzwerke als strukturelle Kopplung. Systemtheoretische Überlegungen zum Netzwerkbegriff' in Weyer, J (Hrsg.), *Soziale Netzwerke – Konzepte und Methoden der sozialwissenschaftlichen Nertzwerkforschung* (München, Oldenbourg Verlag, 2000) 211–35.

KANT, I, 'Zum Ewigen Frieden' in Buchenau, A, Cassirer, E and Kellerman, B, *Immanuel Kants Werke, Schriften von 1790–1796* (Berlin, Bruno Cassirer, [1795] 1914) 425–76.

——, *Die Metaphysik der Sitten* (Stuttgart, Reclam, [1797] 1990).

KASSIM, H, 'Air transport' in Kassim, H and Anand, M (eds), *The European Union and National Industrial Policy* (Oxford, Routledge, 1996) 106–31.

KJAER, P, 'Systems in Context. On the Outcome of the Habermas/Luhmann Debate' (2006) *Ancilla Iuris* 66–77.

——, 'Rationality within REACH? On Functional Differentiation as the Structural Foundation of Legitimacy in European Chemicals Regulation' 2007 *EUI Working Papers (Law)* 18.

——, 'The Societal Function of European Integration in the Context of World Society' (2007) 13 (1/2) *Soziale Systeme. Zeitschrift für Soziologische Theorie* 367–78.

——, 'Three Forms of Governance and Three Forms of Power' in Erik O. Eriksen/Christian Joerges/Florian Rödl (eds), *Law, Democracy and Solidarity in a Post-national Union* (Routledge, Oxford, 2008) 23–43.

——, 'Post-Hegelian Networks: Comments on the Chapter by Simon Deakin' in Marc Amstutz/Gunther Teubner (eds), *Networks: Legal Issues of Multilateral Co-operation* (Hart Publishing, Oxford, 2009) 75–85.

——, 'Formalisation or De-formalisation through Governance?' in Nickel, R (ed), *Conflict of Laws and Laws of Conflict in Europe and Beyond – Patterns of Supranational and Transnational Juridification* (Oslo, ARENA Report Series, 01, 2009) 243 -257.

KLIMOWSKY, E, 'Die englische Gewaltenteilungslehre bis zu Montesquieu' (1927) 22 *Archiv für Rechts- und Wirtschaftsphilosophie*.

KOHLER-KOCH, B, 'The Evolution and Transformation of European Governance', in Kohler-Koch, B and Eiing, R (eds), *The Transformation of Governance in the European Union* (London, Routledge, 1999) 14–35.

——, 'European governance and system integration' 2005 *European Governance Papers (EUROGOV)* 1.

KOOPMANS, T, 'The Birth of European Law at the Crossroads of Legal Traditions',(1999) 39 (3) *American Journal of Comparative Law* 493–507.

KOSELLECK, R, 'Begriffsgeschichtliche Probleme der Verfassungsgeschichtsschreibung' in Koselleck, R, *Begriffsgeschichten: Studien zur Semantik und Pragmatik der politischen und Sozialen Sprache* (Frankfurt am Main, Suhrkamp Verlag, 2006) 365–82.

KRAPOHL, S, 'Credible Commitment in Non-Independent Regulatory Agencies: A Comparative Analysis of the European Agencies for Pharmaceuticals and Foodstuffs' (2004) 10 (5) *European Law Journal* 518–38.

—— and Zurek, K, 'The Perils of Committee Governance: Intergovernmental Bargaining during the BSE Scandal in the European Union' (2006) 10 (2) *European Integration Online Papers* (EioP).

KRÖGER, S, 'When learning hits politics or: Social policy coordination left to the administrations and the NGOs?' (2006) 3 *European Integration Online Papers* (EioP).

LADEUR, K-H, 'Towards a Legal Theory of Supranationality – The Viability of the Network Concept' (1997) 3 (1) *European Law Journal* 33–54.

——, 'Discursive Ethics as Constitutional Theory. Neglecting the Creative Role of Economic Liberties?' (2000) 13 (1) *Ratio Juris* 95–116.

——, 'Regulierte Selbstregulierung als Steuerungskonzept des Gewährleistungsstaates' (2001) 4 *Die Verwaltung* 59–77.

——, '"Deliberative Demokratie" und "Dritter Weg" – eine neue Sackgasse? Transformation des "alten" Sozialstaats in den "aktivierende" Staat?' (2002) 41 *Der Staat* 3–27.

——, 'The Changing Role of the Private in Public Governance – The Erosion of Hierarchy and the Rise of a New Administrative Law of Cooperation. A Comparative Approach' 2002 *EUI Working Papers Law* 9.

LEGRAND, P, 'The Impossibility of Legal Transplants' (1994) 4 *Maastricht Journal of Comparative Law* 111–24.

LENAERTS, K, 'Some Reflections on the Separation of Powers in the European Community' (1990) 28 *Common Market Law Review* 11–35.

—— and Verhoeven, A, 'Institutional Balance as a Guarantee for Democracy in EU Governance' in Joerges, C and Dehousse, R (eds), *Good Governance in Europe's Integrated Market* (Oxford, Oxford University Press, 2002) 35–88.

LEVI-FAUR, D, 'On the "Net Impact" of Europeanization. The EU's telecoms and electricity regimes between the global and the national' 2002 (6) 7 *European Integration online Papers (EIoP).*

LUHMANN, N, 'Die Funktionsbegriff in der Verwaltungswissenschaft' (1958) 49 *Verwaltungsarchiv. Zeitschrift für Verwaltungslehre, Verwaltungsrecht und Verwaltungspolitik* 97–105.

——, 'Lob der Routine' (1964) *Verwaltungsarchiv* 1–33, 55.

——, 'Die Knappheit der Zeit und die Vordringlichkeit des Befristeten' in Luhmann, N, *Politische Planung* (Opladen, Westdeutscher Verlag, 1971) 143–64.

——, 'Sinn als Grundbegriff der Soziologie' in Habermas, J and Luhmann, N, *Theorie der Gesellschaft oder Sozialtechnologie* (Frankfurt am Main, Suhrkamp Verlag, 1971) 25–100.

——, 'Die Weltgesellschaft' in Luhmann, N, *Soziologische Aufklärung Band 2* (Opladen, Westdeutscher Verlag, 1975) 51–71.

——, 'The Future Cannot Begin: Temporal Structures in Modern Society' (1976) 1 (43) *Social Research* 130–52.

——, 'Wohlfahrtsstaat zwischen Evolution und Rationalität' in Koslowski, P u. a. (Hrsg.), *Chancen und Grenzen des Sozialstaats* (Tübingen, Mohr Siebeck, 1983) 26–40.

——, 'Die Lebenswelt – nach Rücksprache mit Phänomenologen' (1986) 72 (2) *Archiv für Rechts- und Sozialphilosophie* 176–94.

——, 'Familiarity, Confidence, Trust: Problems and Alternatives' in Gambetta, D (ed), *Trust: Making and Breaking Cooperative Relations* (New York, Basil Blackwell Ltd, 1988) 94–107.

——, 'Theorie der Politischen Opposition' (1989) 36 (1) *Zeitschrift für Politik*, 13–26.

——, 'Verfassung als evolutionäre Errungenschaft' (1990) 9 *Rechtshistorisches Journal* 176–220.

——, '"Was ist der Fall?" und "Was steckt dahinter"? Die zwei Soziologien und die Gesellschaftstheorie' (1993) 22 *Zeitschrift für Soziologie* 245–60.

——, 'Die Zukunft der Demokratie' in Luhmann, N, *Soziologische Aufklärung, Band 4, Beiträge Zur Funktionalen Differenzierung der Gesellschaft* (Opladen, Westdeutscher Verlag, 1994) 126–32.

——, 'Europa als Problem der Weltgesellschaft' (1994) 2 *Berliner Debatte* 3–7.

——, 'Inklusion und Exklusion', in Luhmann, N, *Soziologische Aufklärung Band 6* (Opladen, Westdeutscher Verlag, 1995) 237–64.

MACCORMICK, N, 'Beyond the Sovereign State' (1993) 56 (1) *The Modern Law Review* 1–18.

MADURO, MP, 'The Constitutional treaty and the Nature of European Constitutionalism: The Tension between Intergovernamentalism and Constitutionalism in the European Union' in Curtin, D, Kellermann, AE, and Blockmans, S, (eds), *The EU Constitution: The Best Way Forward?* (The Hague, Asser Press, 2005) 81–104.

MAHER, I, 'Competition Law in the International Domain: Networks as a New Form of Governance' (2002) 29 (1) *Journal of Law and Society* 112–36.

MAJONE, G, 'Temporal Consistency and Policy Credibility: Why Democracies Need Non-Majoritarian Institutions' 1996 *RSC Working Paper*, European University Institute 57.

——, 'The Regulatory State and its Legitimacy Problems' 1998 *IfHS Working Paper 56*.

——, 'Delegation of Regulatory Powers in a Mixed Polity' (2002) 8 (3) *European Law Journal*, 319–39.

MARX, K and ENGELS, F, 'Ludvig Feuerbach und der Ausgang der Klassischen Deutschen Philosophie' in *Marx & Engels. Werke, Band 21* (Berlin, Dietz Verlag, [1888] 1975) 262–307.

MAYNTZ, R, 'Governance als fortenwickelte Steuerungstheorie?' in Schuppert, GF (Hrsg.), *Governance-Forschung. Vergewisserung über Stand und Entwicklungslinien* (Baden-Baden, Nomos Verlag, 2005) 11–20.

MEARSHEIMER, JJ, 'Back to the Future: Instability in Europe After the Cold War' (1990) 15 (4) *International Security* 5–56.

MILES, D, 'Integration is not necessarily the right concept to guide integration', *Financial Times*, 16 December 2005.

MOLYNECX, CG, 'IV. Chemicals' in *The Yearbook of European Environmental Law*, 6 (Oxford, Oxford University Press, 2006) 287–317.

MOVRACSIK, A, 'Negotiating the Single European Act: national interests and conventional statecraft in the European Community' (winter 1991) *International Organization* 19–56.

NEYER, J and ZÜRN, M, 'Conclusions. The Conditions of Compliance' in Zürn, M and Joerges C (eds), *Governance and Law in Postnational Constellations. Compliance in Europe and Beyond* (Cambridge, Cambridge University Press, 2005) 183–271.

NOAKSON, N and JACOBSSON, K, 'The Production of Ideas and Expert Knowledge in OECD. The OECD Jobs Strategy in contrast with the EU employment Strategy' (2003) 7 *SCORE Rapportserie.*

O'REILLY, D and SWEET, AS, 'The liberalization and reregulation of air transport' (1998) 5 (3) *Journal of European Public Policy* 447–66.

OKUBO, Y, de Miranda, A and Senker, P, *European Scientific Co-operation and its significance for new EU Member States*, Paper prepared for the 5th Triple Helix Conference, Turin, Italy, 18–21 May 2005.

PANEZI, M, 'Sources of Law in Transition. Re-visiting General Principles of International Law' (2007) *Ancilla Iuris* 66–79.

PAPON, P, 'L'Europe de la recherche: une réponse aux defis de l'avenir (2006) 12 (2) *Revue d'Histoire de l'Integration Européenne* 11–26.

PERNICE, I, 'Maastricht, Staat und Demokratie' (1993) 26 *Die Verwaltung* 449–88.

RHODES, RAW, 'The New Governance: Governing without Government' (1996) 44 (4) *Political Studies* 652–67.

RIKLIN, A, 'Was Montesquieu noch nicht wissen konnte. Überlegungen zur Revision der Gewaltenteilungslehre' (2006) *Ancilla Iuris* 20–28.

ROSENAU, JN, 'Governance, order, and change in world politics' in Rosenau, JN and Czempiel, EO (eds), *Governance without Government: Order and Change in World Politics* (Cambridge, Cambridge University Press, 1992) 1–29.

SABEL, CF and ZEITLIN, J, 'Learning from Difference: The New Architecture of Experimentalist Governance in the European Union' 2006 *La Follette School Working Paper* 18.

SAND, I-J, 'Understanding the European Union/European Economic Area as Systems of Functionally Different Processes' in Fitzpatrick, P and Bergeron, JH, *Europe's Other: European Law Between Modernity and Postmodernity* (Aldershot, Ashgate Publishing, 1998) 93–110.

SANTER, J, *L'avenir de l'Europe.. Quel rôle pour la Commission? Eloge de la méthode communautaire*, European University Institute, Jean Monnet Lecture, 20 October 1995.

SCHÄFER, A, 'Beyond the Community Method: Why the Open Method of Coordination was introduced to EU Policy-making' (2004) 8 (13) *European Integration online Papers* (EIoP).

——, 'A New Form of Governance? Comparing the Open Method of Coordination to Multilateral Surveillance by the IMF and the OECD' 2005 *MPIFG Working Papers* 4.

SCHÄFER, G, 'Linking Member States and European Administrations – The Role of Committees and Comitology' in Andenas M and Türk A (eds), *Delegated Legislation and the Role of Committees in the EC* (The Hague, Kluwer, 2000) 3–24.

SCHMALZ-BRUNS, R, 'Grenzerfahrungen und Grenzüberschreitungen: Demokratie in integrierten Europa?' in Kohler-Koch, B (Hrsg.), *Regieren in entgrenzten Räumen* (Opladen, Westdeutscher Verlag, 1998) 369–80.

——, 'Deliberativer Supranationalismus' (1999) 6 (2) *Zeitschrift für Internationale Beziehungen* 185–244.

SCHMITTER, PC, 'Neo-Neofunctionalism' in Wiener, A and Diez, T (eds), *European Integration Theory* (Oxford, Oxford University Press, 2004) 45–74.

SCHUPPERT, GF (Hrsg.), *Governance-Forschung. Vergewisserung über Stand und Entwicklungslinien* (Baden-Baden, Nomos Verlag, 2005).

SCOTT, C, 'Agencies for European Regulatory Governance: A Regimes Approach' in Geradin, D, Muñoz, R and Petit, N (eds), *Regulation Through Agencies in the EU: A New Paradigm of European Governance* (Cheltenham, Edward Elgar, 2005) 67–87.

SCOTT J and TRUBEK, DM, 'Mind the Gap: Law and New Approaches to Governance in the European Union' (2002) 8 (1) *European Law Journal* 1–18.

SIMMEL, G, 'Über sociale Differenzierung. Sociologische und psychologische Untersuchungen' in Simmel, G, *Aufsätze 1887–1890* (Frankfurt am Main, Suhrkamp Verlag, [1890] 1989) 109–296.

SIMON, HA, 'Notes on the Observation and Measurement of Political Power' (1953) 15 *Journal of Politics* 500–16.

SMISMANS, S, 'Institutional Balance as Interest Representation: Some Reflections on Lenaerts and Verhoeven' in Joerges, C and Dehousse, R (eds), *Governance in Europe's Integrated Market* (Oxford, Oxford University Press, 2002) 89–109.

——, 'New Modes of Governance and the Participatory Myth' 2006 *European Governance Papers (EUROGOV)* 1.

STEIN, E, 'Lawyers, Judges, and the Making of a Transnational Constitution' (1981) 75 *American Journal of International Law* 1–27.

STEIN, JA, 'Science, Technology and European foreign policy: European integration, global interaction' (2002) 29 (6) *Science and Public Policy* 463–75.

STICHWEH, R, 'Dimensionen des Weltstaats im System der Weltpolitik' in Albert, M and Stichweh, R (Hrsg.), *Weltstaat und Weltstaatlichkeit. Beobachtungen globaler politischer Strukturbildung* (Wiesbaden, VS Verlag, 2007) 25–36.

——, 'Structure Formation in World Society. The Eigenstructures of World Society and the Regional Cultures of the World' (2006) MS, available at www.unilu.ch/deu/prof._dr._rudolf_stichweh publikationen_38043.aspx.

STOLLEIS, M, 'Das "europäische Haus" und seine Verfassung' (1995) 78 *Kritische Vierteljahresschrift für Gesetzgebung und Rechtswissenschaft* 275–97.

SWEET, AS and SANDHOLTZ, W, 'Integration, Supranational Governance, and the Institutionalization of the European Polity' in Sweet, AS and Sandholtz, W (eds), *European Integration and Supranational Governance* (Oxford, Oxford University Press, 1998) 1–26.

TEUBNER, G, *Polykorporatismus: Der Staat als 'Netzwerk' öffentlicher und privater Kollektivakteure* in Brunkhorst, H and Niesen, P (Hrsg.), *Das Recht der Republik* (Frankfurt am Main, Suhrkamp Verlag, 1999) 346–72.

——, 'Das Recht hybrider Netzwerke' (2001) 165 *Zeitschrift für das gesamte Handelsrecht und Wirtschaftsrecht* 550–75.

——, 'Societal Constitutionalism: Alternatives to State-Centred Constitutional Theory?' in Joerges, C, Sand, I-J and Teubner, G (eds), *Transnational Governance and Constitutionalism* (Oxford, Hart Publishing, 2004) 3–28.

TRANHOLM-MIKKELSEN, J, 'Neo-functionalism: Obstinate or Obsolete? A Reappraisal in the Light of the New Dynamism of the EC' (1991) 20 (1) *Millennium Journal of International Studies* 1–22.

TREIB, O, Bähr, H and Falkner, G, 'Modes of Governance: A Note Towards Conceptual Clarification' 2005 *European Governance Papers (EUROGOV)* 2.

TRUBEK, DM, COTTRELL, P and NANCE, M '"Soft Law", "Hard Law" and EU Integration' in de Burca, G and Scott, J (eds), *New Governance and Constitutionalism* (Oxford, Hart Publishing, 2005) 65–94.

—— and Trubek, LG, 'The Open Method of Co-ordination and the Debate over "Hard" and "Soft" Law' in Zeitlin, J and Pochet, P (eds), *The Open Method of Co-ordination in Action. The European Employment and Social Inclusion Strategies* (Brussels, Peter Lang, 2005) 83–103.

VANDERSTRAETEN, R, 'Parsons, Luhmann and the Theorem of Double Contingency' (2002) 2 (1) *Journal of Classical Sociology* 77–92.

VOS, E, 'The Rise of Committees' (1997) 3 (3) *European Law Journal* 210–22.

——, 'EU Committees: the Evolution of Unforeseen Institutional Actors in European Product Regulation' in Joerges, C and Vos, E (eds), *EU Committees: Social Regulation, Law and Politics* (Oxford, Hart Publishing, 1999) 19–47.

——, 'The Role of Comitology in European Governance' in Curtain, DM and Wessel, RA (eds), *Good Governance and the European Union. Reflections on Concepts,Iinstitutions and Substance* (Antwerp, Intersentia, 2005) 107–24.

WALKER, N, 'Post-Constituent Constitutionalism' in Loughlin, M and Walker, N (eds), *The Paradox of Constitutionalism* (Oxford, Oxford University Press, 2007) 247–68.

WEBER, M, 'Bureaucracy' in Gerth, H and Mills, CV (eds), *From Max Weber* (Oxford, Oxford University Press, 1946) 196–244.

WEILER, JHH, 'The Community system: The dual character of supranationalism' (1981) *1st Yearbook of European Law* 267–306.

——, 'The Court of Justice on Trial' (1987) 24 *Common Market Law Review*, 555–89.

——, 'The Transformation of Europe' (1991) 100 *Yale Law Journal* 2402–83.

——, 'European Democracy and its Critique' in Hayward, J (ed), *The Crisis of Representation in Europe* (London, Frank Cass, 1995) 4–49.

——, 'Does Europe Need a Constitution? Reflections on Demos, Telos and the German Maastricht Decision' (1995) 1 *European Law Journal* 219–58.

——, 'In der Unterwelt der Ausschüsse', Interview in *Die Zeit*, 22 October 1998.

——, 'Epilogue: "Comitology" as Revolution – Infranationalism, Constitutionalism and Democracy' in Joerges, C and Vos, E (eds), *EU Committees: Social Regulation, Law and Politics* (Oxford, Hart Publishing, 1999) 339–50.

WIND, M, 'The European Union as a polycentric polity: returning to a neo-medieval Europe?' in Weiler, JHH and Wind, M (eds), *European Constitutionalism Beyond the State* (Cambridge, Cambridge University Press, 2003) 103–31.

WÜRTENBERGER, T, 'Legitimität, Legalität' in Brunner, O, Conze, W and Koselleck, R (Hrsg.), *Geschichtliche Grundbegrieffe, Band 3* (Stuttgart, Klett-Cotta, 1983) 677–740.

YATAGANAS, XA, 'Delegation of Regulatory Authority in the European Union. The Relevance of the American Model of Independent Agencies' 2001 *Jean Monnet Working Papers* 3.

——, 'The Treaty of Nice. The Sharing Power and Institutional Balance in the European Union – A Continental Perspective' 2001 *Jean Monnet Working Papers* 1.

ZEITLIN, J, 'Social Europe and Experimentalist Governance: Towards a New Constitutional Compromise?' 2005 *European Governance Papers (EUROGOV)* 4.

ZILTENER, P, 'Gibt es einen regionalen Integrationsprozess in Ostasien?' 2003 *MPIFG Discussion Papers* 2.

ZÜRN, M, 'Politik in der postnationalen Konstellation. Über das Elend des methodologischen Nationalismus' in Landfried, C (Hrsg.), *Politik in einer entgrenzten Welt. Beiträge zum 21. Kongreß der Deutschen Vereinigung für Politische Wissenschaft* (Köln, Verlag Wissenschaft und Politik, 2001) 181–04.

—— and Liebfried, S, 'Reconfiguring the national constellation' in Zürn, M and Liebfried, S (eds), *Transformations of the State?* (Cambridge, Cambridge University Press, 2005) 1–36.

Annex: EU Agencies

AGENCIES ESTABLISHED UNDER THE FIRST PILLAR

1. European Centre for the Development of Vocational Training (Cedefop), established by Council Regulation (EEC) 337/75 of 10 February 1975, located in Thessaloniki.
2. European Foundation for the Improvement of Living and Working Conditions (Eurofound), established by Council Regulation (EEC) 1365/75 of 26 May 1975, located in Dublin.
3. European Environment Agency (EEA), established by Council Regulation (EEC) 1210/90 of 7 May 1990, located in Copenhagen.
4. European Training Foundation (ETF), established by Council Regulation (EEC) 1360/90 of 7 May 1990, located in Turin.
5. European Monitoring Centre for Drugs and Drugs Addition (EMCDDA), established by Council Regulation (EEC) 302/93 of 8 February 1993, located in Lisbon.
6. European Medicines Agency (EMEA), established by Council Regulation (EEC) No 2309/93 of 22 July 1993, located in London.
7. Office for the Harmonisation of the Internal Market (OHIM), established by Council Regulation (EC) 40/94 of 20 December 1993, located in Alicante.
8. European Agency for Safety and Health at Work (EASHW), established by Council Regulation (EC) 2062/94 of 18 July 1994, located in Bilbao.
9. Community Plant Variety Office (CPVO), established by Council Regulation (EC) 2100/94 of 27 July 1994, located in Angers.
10. Translation Centre for the Bodies of the European Union (CdT), established by Council Regulation (EC) 2965/94 of 28 November 1994, located in Luxembourg.
11. European Agency for Reconstruction (EAR), established by Council Regulation (EC) 2666/2000 of December 2000, located in Thessaloniki (closed down as of 31 December 2008).
12. European Food Safety Authority (EFSA), established by Council Regulation (EC) 178/2002 of 28 January 2002, located in Parma.
13. European Maritime Safety Agency (EMSA), established by Council Regulation (EC) 1406/2002 of 27 June 2002, located in Lisbon.
14. European Aviation Safety Agency (EASA), established by Council Regulation (EC) 1592/2002 of the European Parliament and of the Council of 15 July 2002, located in Cologne.

15. Executive Agency for Competitiveness and Innovation (EACI), established by Commission Decision 2004/20/EC of 23 December 2003, located in Brussels.
16. European Network and Information Security Agency (ENISA): established by Regulation (EC) 460/2004 of the European Parliament and of the Council of 10 March 2004, located in Heraklion, Crete.
17. European Centre for Disease Prevention and Control (ECDC), established by Regulation (EC) 851/2004 of the European Parliament and of the Council of 21 April 2004, located in Stockholm.
18. European Railway Agency (ERA), established by Regulation (EC) 881/2004 of the European Parliament and of the Council of 29 April 2004, located in Valenciennes (Lille).
19. The European GNSS Supervisory Authority (GSA), established by Council Regulation (EC) No 1321/2004 of 12 July 2004, provisionally located in Brussels.
20. European Agency for the Management of Operational Coordination at the External Borders of the Member States of the EU (FRONTEX), established by Council Regulation (EC) 2007/2004 of 26 October 2004, located in Warsaw.
21. Executive Agency for the Public Health Programme (PHEA), established by Commission Decision 2004/858/EC of 15 December 2004, located in Luxembourg.
22. Education, Audiovisual and Culture Executive Agency (EACEA):, established by Decision 2005/56/EC of 14 January 2005, located in Brussels.
23. Community Fisheries Control Agency, established by Council Regulation (EC) 768/2005 of 26 April 2005, located in Vigo.
24. The Trans-European Transport Network Executive Agency (TEN-TEA), established by Commission's Decision 2006/5034 of 26 October 2006, located in Brussels.
25. European Chemicals Agency (ECHA), established by Regulation (EC) 1907/2006 of 18 December 2006, located in Helsinki.
26. European Fundamental Rights Agency (EFRA), established by Council regulation (EC) 168/2007 of 15 February 2007, located in Vienna.
27. European Joint Undertaking for ITER and the Development of Fusion Energy (Fusion for Energy), established by Council Decision 198/Euratom of 27 March 2007, located in Barcelona.
28. Research Executive Agency (REA), established by Commission Decision 2007/6262 on 14 December 2007, located in Brussels.
29. European Research Council Executive Agency (ERC), established by Commission Decision 2008/37 of 14 December 2007, located in Brussels.
30. Euratom Supply Agency (ESA), established by Council Decision 2008/114(EC) of 12 February 2008, located in Luxembourg.

AGENCIES ESTABLISHED UNDER THE SECOND PILLAR

31. European Union Satellite Centre (EUSC): Established by Council Joint Action 2001/555/CFSP of 20 July 2001, located in Torrejón (Madrid).
32. European Union Institute for Security Studies (EUISS): Established by Council Joint Action 2001/554/CFSP of 20 July 2001, located in Paris.
33. European Defence Agency (EDA): Established by Council Joint Action 2004/551/CFSP of 12 July 2004, located in Brussels.

AGENCIES ESTABLISHED UNDER THE THIRD PILLAR

34. European Police Office (EUROPOL) Established by the 1992 EUROPOL convention, located in The Hague.
35. European Union's Judicial Cooperation Unit (EUROJUST): Established by Council Decision 2000/820/JHA of 28 February 2000, located in The Hague.
36. European Police College (CEPOL): Established by Council Decision 2000/820/JHA of 22 December 2000, located in Bramshill, Hampshire.

Index